GOD AND JUGGERNAUT

Modern Intellectual and Political History of the Middle East
Mehrzad Boroujerdi, *Series Editor*

GOD AND JUGGERNAUT

Iran's Intellectual Encounter with Modernity

FARZIN VAHDAT

SYRACUSE UNIVERSITY PRESS

Mohamad El-Hindi Books on Arab Culture and Islamic Civilization are
published with the assistance of a grant from Ahmad El-Hindi.

Library of Congress Cataloging-in-Publication Data

Vahdat, Farzin.
God and juggernaut : Iran's intellectual encounter with modernity /
Farzin Vahdat.—1st ed.
p. cm.—(Modern intellectual and political history of the
Middle East)
Includes bibliographical references and index.
ISBN 0-8156-2922-2—ISBN 0-8156-2947-8 (pbk.)
Iran—Intellectual life. 2. Iran—Historiography. 3.
Nationalism—Iran. 4. Historiography—Iran. 5. Religion and state. 6.
Islam and politics—Iran. I. Title. II. Series.
DS316.4 V34 2002
306'.0955—dc21
2002001379

To Seungsook and Mahindokht

FARZIN VAHDAT is a faculty lecturer at Tufts University. His articles have appeared in *Critique, Journal of Iranian Research and Analysis,* and *Scandinavian Journal of Middle Eastern Studies.*

Contents

Acknowledgments

The genesis of this book is in my doctoral dissertation, completed in the Department of Sociology at Brandeis University. My special thanks go to my mentors, Ali Banuazizi, Gordon Fellman, Gila Hayim, George Ross, the late Morris Schwartz, and Maurice Stein. In the evolution of this work, I have benefitted from the encouragement, support and comments of many friends: Ahmad Ashraf, Houchang Chehabi, Ramin Jahanbegloo, Hock Guan Lee, Maziyar Lotfalian, Valentine Moghadam, Nader Rofougaran, Majid Tehranian, and Cumrun Vafa.

I am particularly indebted to Eric Hooglund for his unwavering support for this project. Ali Gheissari's comments and insightful suggestions were crucial for the final shape of the book, and for that I am grateful. As the series editor of Modern Intellectual and Political History of the Middle East at Syracuse University Press, Mehrzad Boroujerdi read different versions of the manuscript, and his comments have immensely benefitted my work; I greatly appreciate all his input. I am also very thankful to the staff at Syracuse University Press for their careful and coordinated efforts in the publishing of the book. I am most grateful to Mary Selden Evans, executive editor at Syracuse University Press, for her cheerful support during the publication process.

I am especially thankful to my wife, Seungsook Moon, for her loving support and insightful discussions, which have helped the shaping of my thought. This book would not have come into existence without her love and support.

Farzin Vahdat

Waltham, Massachusetts
March 2002

Introduction

Nothing so bedevils the peoples of the Islamic world at the beginning of the twenty-first century as the specter of modernity. Indeed, it has occupied a central place in the cultural and sociopolitical agendas of intellectuals, social movements, and state actors in the Islamic world and the Middle East since the nineteenth century. It would hardly be an exaggeration to claim that the question of modernity—its appropriation, its rejection, or its transformation along more acceptable lines—currently constitutes the central issue in many Islamic societies at both the theoretical and the practical level. The cataclysmic revolution of Western modernity has left virtually no part of the globe unaffected. Brutal colonization and territorial expansion, economic exploitation, and cultural objectification, accompanied by the introduction of new ideas, norms, and institutions, constitute the mechanisms by which the modern West has transformed the history of all societies on the face of the earth. Countries have responded to the reshaping of their destinies in the form of bewilderment, denial, emulation, infatuation, confrontation, resentment, or a mixture of these. Iran is no exception: as its destiny has collided with that of Western modernity over the past 150 years or so, such responses have constituted major elements of its history, with certain elements in ascendance over the others at different times.

The Islamic Revolution of 1979 constituted a watershed with regard to the issue of modernity in the Middle East and Islamic societies in general, and Iran in particular. How could a society to all appearances rapidly modernizing suddenly become a theocratic state almost overnight?[1] Iran's presumed revolt against modernity after 1979 is often thought to represent the culmination of a

---

1. It was the belief of the Pahlavi elite and many outside observers that Iran was being rapidly transformed into a modern society in all respects. The Pahlavi elite's desire for modernization was shared by most of the opposition, including the Marxist-oriented Tudeh Party, which sought Soviet-style modernization. See Najmabadi 1987.

backlash to the process of modernizing undertaken since the coup d'état that overthrew Mossadeq and restored the Pahlavi Dynasty in 1953. Accordingly, many analyses of Iran since 1979 can be characterized as laments over Iran's failure to come to terms with the forces of modernity and the institutions of democracy. The thwarting of the democratic aspirations of the Constitutional Revolution of the early twentieth century, the defeat of the liberal and anti-colonial nationalism of the Mossadeq era in the middle of the century, and the takeover of the potentially emancipatory revolution of 1979 by Islamic forces are often viewed as the signs of Iranians' failure to reconcile themselves with the realities of the modern world.

There is no doubt that these were indeed great impediments to the development of modernity in Iran. But nowhere has the development of modernity taken a straight path. The main thesis of the present study suggests that Iran's century-and-a-half experience with modernity should be understood in terms of a dialectical process involving aspects of modernity conducive to emancipation, on the one hand, and those more conducive to domination, on the other. In this dialectical process, different elements of modernity often vied with each other, leading to different phases in the development of the new civilization in Iran. Furthermore, at different times different aspects of modernity were developed and elaborated upon by different social groups. Thus, for example, the early reformist intellectuals of the late nineteenth century, at least in their theoretical approaches, placed more or less equal emphasis on the democratic and positivistic aspects of modernity, whereas, beginning with the Pahlavi era, the emphasis was shifted more to the positivist and instrumental sides of modern civilization, eclipsing the emancipatory moments of modernity. In like manner, the Marxist Left came to place great emphasis on expanding and deepening the potential for the liberation and empowerment of Iranians in the twentieth century, although such liberation was to be experienced not by individuals, the greatest beneficiaries of modernity, but the collectivity, thus severely attenuating its liberatory potential. The lopsided augmentation of selective aspects of modernity by various social groups in Iran, such as the emphasis on instrumental rationality and collectivity by Pahlavi technocrats, Communists, and Socialists, has worked to impede the overall development of a viable modernity there. Yet the experiences of these different social groups should not be dismissed: they constitute a form of cultural capital for the establishment of more balanced modern institutions in Iran.

The Islamic revolutionary movement of the sixties and seventies should be seen as a dialectical attempt to seriously challenge the discourse of modernity. As noted in the final two chapters of this study, in its own discourse this movement was very much affected by the discourse and the phenomenon it set out to challenge. The Islamic discourse can thus be seen as an internal dialogue, chiefly at the theoretical and philosophical level, with regard to cultural aspects of modernity. In its own peculiarly dialectical manner, this discourse has not completely abandoned the principles of modernity. Indeed, the contradictions it has engendered can be viewed as driving the dynamic search for modernity since the establishment of the Islamic Republic in 1979.

To analyze the dialectical process of Iran's intellectual and cultural encounter with modernity, this study focuses on the variegated sociopolitical discourses that have emerged there since the second half of the nineteenth century and on their interrelationship with the discourse and conditions of modernity. Its main task is thus twofold: first, to examine the concept and phenomenon of modernity in its Western and global context; and second, to examine Iran's intellectual and cultural encounter with modernity in the period between mid-nineteenth century until now, focusing on the major sociopolitical discourses and themes that have helped shape Iranian consciousness and institutions in this period.

German critical thought, starting with Kant and Hegel, yields a particularly appropriate theoretical framework for the analysis of the concepts and conditions of modernity. The emergence of modernity in Germany in the early nineteenth century was belated compared to its emergence in England and France. As a result, in the thoughts of Kant, Hegel, and their heirs in Critical Theory, we find mature and complex insights into the notions and conditions of modernity, insights afforded by the hindsight.[2] Similar conditions obtain today in those countries, such as Iran, where modernity has also made a belated appearance.

∞

As will be elaborated in chapter 1, for Kant and Hegel, subjectivity and universality constituted the two pillars of modernity. These two concepts, rooted in the tradition of the Enlightenment, received elaborate treatments by the two German philosophers. By "subjectivity," I mean the property characterizing the

2. On the central position that the concept and phenomenon of modernity occupied in German thought generally, and Critical Theory specifically, see, for example, Kellner 1989.

autonomous, self-willing, self-conscious, and self-defining agent.[3] By "universality," I refer to the mutual recognition among the individual subjects of each other's subjectivity. Although, as we will see throughout this study, the meaning of universality varies widely, in its social and historical contexts it refers to the elimination of restrictions based on privileges, status, or other essentialized considerations.[4] In the modern era, subjectivity and universality have had a most peculiar relationship to each other, at once closely connected and complementary, yet also polar opposites. On the one hand, the subject, to be a subject, needs an object—that is, to deny the subjectivity of others. On the other hand, once some of us acquire subjectivity, we all want to have it. This contradiction is probably one of the central paradoxes of modern times, one that has shaped the efforts to objectify "others"—for example, class exploitation, colonialism, sexual and racial oppression—while at the same time also shaping the impulse toward liberation and struggles against objectification and domination.

Although I have called subjectivity and universality the "pillars" of modernity, in its conceptual and phenomenal dimensions, modernity cannot be confined to these two fundamental principles, which have given rise to elaborate ramifications and consequences. In the political sphere, the most visible consequences of universalized subjectivity have been the birth of civil society, the emergence of the individual, and the emergence of political and civic rights and freedoms. In the cultural sphere, the most prominent and probably most important effect of the emergence of self-defining, autonomous subjects has been to transform the primary relationships of domination and subordination, prototypically, the relationship between the transcendental God of monotheism and human worshippers. The weakening of this relationship has in turn weakened all other types of primary relationships: between priest and parishioner, between sovereign and vassal, and most notably between parent and child.

In a similar vein, as Jürgen Habermas argues, modern subjectivity has separated the three spheres of the everyday experience of the world we live in (what Habermas calls the "lifeworld") from their religious-metaphysical grounding:

3. A cursory look at recent titles shows how central the notion of subjectivity is to any discussion of modernity.

4. It is the principle of universality, in its sociological aspect, that leads to the formation of the "general will" in modernity—what Habermas has called "communicative ethics." See "Habermas: Language Mediating Subjectivity and Universality" in the appendix.

the objective, the social, and the subjective.[5] The "objective" sphere relates to cognitive and scientific propositional truths; the "social" sphere, to normative, moral, and legal truths; and the "subjective" sphere, to aesthetic and "expressive" truths (Habermas 1984, 71–72). In the premodern era, these component spheres of the lifeworld were mediated through the sacred and were part and parcel of the religious establishment. It is only as a result of modernity that they are separated out and the sacred becomes "linguistified." The result is that validity claims within each sphere are now exposed to criticism and open to revision (Habermas 1984, 52).[6]

Yet modernity, especially modern subjectivity, has given rise to certain types of discontent that have limited and marred its emancipatory potential, chief among which are (1) discontent the subject imposes on the "other"; and (2) discontent in which the subject suffers more directly. To the first type belong the problems of colonialism, the exploitation of the working class, the oppression of women, minorities, and so on. The subject of modernity—namely, the male, white, middle- or upper-class Euro-American—in order to become the subject, has objectified the "subaltern" inhabitants of the world, women, Third World peoples, the indigenous proletariat, immigrants, and minorities. This objectification has had enormous consequences for the majority of the inhabitants of the world; indeed, it has shaped world history and will continue to do so for a long time to come.[7] The second type of discontent brought about by modernity pertains more to the "self" of the modern subject and can be traced back to what has been called "diremption" or separation from nature. The modern subject, to achieve its subjectivity, attempted to impress its purpose on nature and thus caused a separation between reason and nature, a problem to which Hegel and his Romantic predecessors paid a great deal of attention. The

---

5. For a brief discussion of Habermas's use of "lifeworld," see "Habermas: Language Mediating Subjectivity and Universality" in the appendix.

6. Notwithstanding the merits of such a critique, the enormous contributions that monotheism has made to the emergence of modernity in the West should not be neglected. As we will see in this study, the structure of monotheistic metaphysics in Islam is dialectically linked to the emergence of modernity in Iran; indeed, it would be hard to imagine the rise of modernity in that country without such structure. See especially chapters 4 and 5.

7. At the same time, the process of objectification has shown itself to be subject to those same "subalterns," whose struggle for the universalization of subjectivity has engendered women's, national independence, civil rights, and international human rights movements, as well as movements for social and economic justice.

consequences of this separation can be divided into two subtypes of discontent. The first has its roots in the development of what Habermas has called the "cognitive" sphere and the related extension of instrumental rationality. The second has to do more directly with the loss of the real or imagined harmony of the premodern world, embodied in a notion of an eternal order, namely, the loss of the "firm grounding" of the traditional society and its putative "contentment." In considering the phenomenon of modernity in its entirety, this study will take its various aspects into account.

The framework outlined above is thus grounded in theoretical formulations that go well beyond those of Kant and Hegel. It also encompasses the philosophical writings of Marx, Weber, and Freud, the works of the Frankfurt school and of Habermas, and the debate on modernity and postmodernity—or what constitutes Critical Theory.[8] I use "Critical Theory" to describe this cluster of heterogeneous theoretical constructs, which are, I maintain, embedded within a larger homogeneity. Although such an approach must necessarily be eclectic, its eclecticism need not therefore be incoherent.

Against such a theoretical understanding of modernity, I will evaluate the key intellectual elements of the Iranian encounter with modernity over the past century and a half. Iran's early intellectual encounter with modernity in mid-nineteenth century, like that of many other Third World countries, began as a response to the imperialist onslaught waged primarily by tsarist Russia and Britain. In their attempts to counter the onslaught, the intellectuals and reformers appropriated two aspects of modernity available to them: the "positivist" aspect, emphasizing such categories as technology and efficient bureaucracy found in Western modernity; and the cultural aspect of modernity, focusing on the more democratic facets of modern civilization. This dualist approach to modernity has characterized much of Iran's experience with modernity even though the democratic aspect has been eclipsed by the positivist for most of this relatively short history. Nonetheless, the democratic aspect of modernity in Iran, reflected in attempts to build modern institutions, specifically those of the Constitutional Revolution of 1906, has never been eradicated from Iran's cultural soil. As I will show in chapters four and five, even the Islamic revolutionary discourse contains elements of this aspect of modernity and, as such, cannot be dismissed as simply negating modern thought.

8. For a good discussion of the contributions of Marx, Weber, Freud, the Frankfurt School, and Habermas to Critical Theory, see, for example, Held 1980.

To analyze nineteenth—and twentieth-century Iranian intellectual works and their relation to modernity, I have used primary sources in Persian and English and, when primary sources were not available, secondary sources that closely represent the original works. Some of the works by prominent authors have for various reasons, chief among them political, never been published in Iran; I have therefore had to make use of other scholarly works where these authors are extensively quoted and represented.

As has been apparent from the outset, the theoretical component of this study is of central significance. For this reason, almost all of chapter 1 is devoted to a discussion of modernity in the works of Kant and Hegel. The introductory chapter is intended to provide a clear theoretical framework for the analysis of modernity and its philosophical tenets, the Iranian encounter with modernity being discussed in subsequent chapters. Analyses of the responses to modernity since Hegel by thinkers such as Marx, Weber, Adorno, Foucault, and especially Habermas, whose work constitutes the core of contemporary Critical Theory, are presented in the theoretical appendix to this volume.

Part one (chapters 2 and 3) examines the early Iranian intellectual appropriation of modernity and traces subsequent developments based on this appropriation. Chapter 2 focuses on the intellectuals of the mid-nineteenth century and the analyzes their crucial role in laying the foundations of the discourse on modernity in Iran. Chapter 3 discusses twentieth-century developments in that discourse, focusing on major intellectual trends and themes and their relations with and appropriations of different aspects of modernity.

Part two (chapters 4 and 5) examines Iran's intellectual encounter with modernity in the aftermath of the Islamic Revolution. Chapter 4 examines the Islamic revolutionary discourse of the sixties and seventies and its relations to the ideas of modernity, closely analyzing the thought of Ayatollah Khomeini, Ali Shariati, and Ayatollah Motahhari, the so-called architects of the Islamic Revolution. Chapter 5 analyzes developments in postrevolutionary Islamic sociopolitical thought and their ramifications. Because of the close relationship between thought and reality, this study will constantly shift its attention between the ontological foundations of the discourses involved and their sociopolitical implications. To communicate with a larger audience interested in the topic of the Middle East and modernity, I have tried to keep jargon to a minimum without, I hope, compromising essential concepts. The intellectuals whose works and discourses I have chosen to analyze fall mostly within the mainstream as understood by the historians of Iran; although some may not be well known, at least not outside Iran, all have served to pave the way for the emergence of certain important themes at different junctures in the 150-year period under consideration.[9]

Most studies of the Middle East confine themselves to traditional approaches, whether "orientalist," developmental, Marxist, structural, or some variation of these. Despite the recent appearance of works taking a theoretical or cultural approach, this area is still largely unexplored. My hope is that this work, grounded as it is in critical sociology, will make a valuable contribution to theoretical studies of the Middle East. Although Islam and the Middle East have been mostly analyzed in juxtaposition and opposition to the modernity of the West, this modernity has always been posited in a linear and unidimensional fashion. On the other hand, because it analyzes and evaluates modernity as a complex, multidimensional phenomenon, Critical Theory can yield rich insights with important implications and applications for the study of the Middle East. Thus it is also my hope to open the way for applying Critical Theory to current conditions in Third World countries generally and in the Middle East and Iran specifically. Because Critical Theory developed in response to similar struggles, challenges, and processes in the West, it has valuable lessons and insights for these countries, which have been plunged into the modern situation and must somehow contend with it. One of these insights, stressed by more recent theorists within Critical Theory, is to point out how closely cultural development, economic development, and political democracy are interrelated. Indeed, as this study hopes to make clear, in the context of Iran and the Middle East, the three are inseparable.

---

9. Thus, even though the later works of Hussein Kazemzadeh Iranshahr may not be well known, they paved the way for the emergence of crucial themes inherited and elaborated on by the very influential and ever-controversial thinker Ahmad Kasravi.

GOD AND JUGGERNAUT

1

The Nature of Modernity

The purpose of this chapter is to fashion a theoretical framework for analyzing the Iranian intellectual experience and experiment with modernity, which will be thoroughly addressed in subsequent chapters.

Two Pillars of Modernity: Subjectivity and Universality

One of the shortcomings of the classical sociological accounts of modernity, with the exception of Weber's and, to a lesser extent, Marx's, is their lack of a historical contextuality. The theoretical constructs, from Ferdinand Tönnies's gemeinschaft-gesellschaft dichotomy to Talcot Parsons's pattern variables and the modernization school, neglect the medieval embedding of the emergence of modernity in European history, ignoring the very conditions that gave rise to modernity in the first place (see Tönnies 1963; Parsons 1963).

In his essay "What Is Enlightenment?" Kant clearly expressed what those conditions were. At the core of premodern society and culture, he noted, was "immaturity . . . the incapacity to use one's intelligence without the guidance of another" (Kant 1949, 132). The opposite of this condition, on which modernity is predicated, is referred to in the literature since Kant as "subjectivity." Hegel viewed the modern world chiefly in terms of subjectivity: "The principle of the modern world is freedom of subjectivity, the principle that all the essential factors present in the intellectual whole are now coming into their right in the course of their development" (Habermas 1987a, 16). In this passage and elsewhere (e.g., Hegel 1967, para.124), Hegel seems to be emphasizing not only human autonomy but also its beneficiary, the individual. Thus, as the first pillar of modernity, *subjectivity* can be defined as "the property characterizing the autonomous, self-willing, self-defining, and self-conscious individual agent." Although Hegel himself seems to have used "subjectivity" and "freedom" interchangeably, there is a difference between the two. Whereas "freedom" usu-

1

ally refers to a lack of restraint, "subjectivity" refers to more, to positive action on the world.[1]

As the second pillar of modernity, and a somewhat more elusive category to analyze, *universality* can be defined as "the mutual recognition among the plurality of subjects of each other's subjectivity." Expressed differently and in its historical context, "universality" refers to elimination of restrictions based on privilege, status, or other substantive considerations. In another, restricted sense, universality can be considered as the bourgeois principle of formal equality before the law.

Hegel (1967, 110) saw subjectivity and universality as epitomized in the notion of civil society, namely, "an association of members as self-sufficient individuals in a universality which because of their self-sufficiency is only formal."[2]

Descartes: The Beginnings of Modern Subjectivity

It was Descartes who most successfully gave human subjectivity its concrete and practical aim—the mathematical-scientific apparatus. Descartes saw human subjectivity modeled after God's subjectivity as the goal of activity:

> If I examine the faculties of memory or imagination, or any others, I discover that in my case each one of these faculties is weak and limited, while in the case of God it is immeasurable. It is only the will, or freedom of choice, which I experience within me to be so great that the idea of any greater faculty is be-

1. As Goethe's Faust would have said, in modernity, "man asserts himself against nature's tyrannical arrogance." See Berman 1988, 61.

2. Although the earliest concrete embodiment of the integration of subjectivity and universality can be found in natural law and the positive legal edifice later built upon it, it is wrong to assume that these two pillars of modern society came into existence ex nihilo, without any roots in the premodern society. In the Judeo-Christian and Islamic traditions, "man" is created in the image of a true sovereign subject, God, in whose image and vicariously humans aspired to subjectivity. In the same vein, universality has deep roots in the premodern cosmology. World religions such as Christianity and Islam transformed the basis of social relations from that of blood—tribe in particular—to that of faith, which was universal, although this premodern universality was mediated by feudal forces, chief among which were religious hierarchies. "The growth of a world empire in China," asserted Weber (1964, 23), "the extension of the power of the Brahmin caste throughout all the varied political formations in India, and the development of the Persian and Roman empires favored the rise of both universalism and monotheism, though not always in the same measure and with quite different degrees of success."

yond my grasp; so much so that it is above all in the virtue of the will that I understand myself to bear in the same way the image and likeness of God. (Cascardi 1992, 40)

Mathematics crowned all other areas of inquiry and enabled the subject to master the world: "We can see how much [mathematics] excels in utility and simplicity the sciences subordinate to it by the fact that it can deal with all objects of which they have cognizance and many more besides" (Descartes 1927, 55).

What Descartes achieved was nothing less than the shattering of the authority of tradition and the religious-metaphysical worldview. But this shattering resulted in the loss of the transcendental position, provided principally by religion, through which a coherent understanding of the world was possible. Descartes attempted to substitute for the loss another "transcendental" platform, embodied in the modern mathematical-scientific approach, from whose point of view different positions could be coherently assessed (Cascardi 1992, 58). Thus in his work one can identify both sides of subjectivity—the subject emancipating itself and the subject objectifying the "other," in this instance, nature. Whereas Descartes pushed the notion of subjectivity as human will toward objectification of nature and utilitarianism, Kant pushed it toward universality, as we will see below.

Kant: Philosopher of Modernity par Excellence

Ontology and epistemology are, for Kant, closely related, both being mediated by the concept of reason. Through reason, the human is prior to all forms of knowledge and existence or essence, and is the pivot around which everything revolves. Kant was probably one of the first philosophers to explicitly make the human the foundation of knowledge and being. It was through his three critiques that the fundamental principles of science, morality, and aesthetics (principles such as the form of space and time), came to be viewed as products of human thought alone (Guyer 1992, 11).

Kant's synthesis of ontology and epistemology is expressed in his conception of the transcendental a priori of knowledge, which rejects any "external" criterion of knowledge, be it our own sensory apparatus (empirical data) or given traditions, and which holds certain a priori "intuitions" as the basis of human knowledge and, by extension, precepts for our mode of existence.

Hitherto it has been assumed that all our knowledge must conform to objects. But all attempts to extend our knowledge of objects by establishing something in regard to them a priori, by means of concept, have, on this assumption ended in failure. We must therefore make trial whether we may not have more success in the tasks of metaphysics, if we suppose that objects must conform to our knowledge. (Cahoone 1987, 50)

The primacy of the subject in this epistemological-ontological formula in turn translates into the radical notion of the autonomy of the individual acting in the moral-practical sphere. As Kant (1960, 40) put it in *Religion Within the Limits of Reason Alone:* "Man himself must make or have made himself whatever, in a moral sense, whether good or evil, he is or is to become. Either condition must be an effect of his own free choice; for otherwise he could not be held responsible for it and could not therefore be morally neither good nor evil."

It is central to Kant's theory of ethics that normal adults are fully capable of self-government and self-determination in matters of morality (Schneewind 1992, 309). Kant himself recognized the influence of Rousseau in this issue of the moral autonomy of humans.[3] The Rousseauian "Revolution" in Kant, as Lewis White Beck (1988, 21) has designated it, elevates the human above mere executor of moral law to legislator of this law as well, making him sovereign with regard to its ends.

Thus in Kant's ethics, rationality is based on a radical notion of human volition. As Charles Taylor (1979, 4–5) has put it, in Kant's view, "moral life is equivalent to freedom, in this radical sense of self-determination by the moral will. This is called autonomy. Any deviation from it, any determination of the will by some external consideration, some inclination even of the most joyful benevolence; some authority, even as high as God himself, is condemned as

3. J. B. Schneewind and Lewis White Beck, among other Kant scholars, have observed the crucial influence of Rousseau's notion of freedom on Kant's concept of moral autonomy, a concept central to his philosophical system. In quoting Rousseau's observation that "the impulse of appetite alone is slavery, and obedience to the law one has prescribed for oneself is freedom," Schneewind notes that Kant adopted Rousseau's belief in our ability, through laws of our own making, to lay the foundations of a just and free society and made it the cornerstone of his moral-practical philosophy (Schneewind 1992, 314). Beck goes further, arguing that "the influence of Rousseau on Kant is comparable to that of Copernicus. We may, indeed, speak of a Revolution" (Beck 1988, 15).

heteronomy." For Kant, reason or rationality is the embodiment of the autonomous volition of the subject; in Taylor's words (1979, 5): "The numinous
which inspired awe was not God as much as the moral law itself, the self-given
command of reason."

However, a problem immediately arises with Kant's formulation of the rational as the moral act based solely on the radical autonomy of the free subject.
Something is needed to counter the moral chaos flowing from such a radical notion of subjectivity, with its potentially solipsistic implications. Kant proposed
to cure this problem by combining the notion of subjectivity with the principle
of universality, again invoking the transcendental a priori as the ontological-
epistemological basis for such a combination (Taylor 1979, 75).

By "transcendental," Kant meant anything that is the ground for a priori
knowledge, the most basic and elemental intuition, which is not grounded in
any empirical, experiential, or otherwise produced data. Kant (1970, 134–35)
believed that the very conditions of our existence force us to recognize the
combination of subjectivity as freedom and its universality, or what I will refer
to as "universalizability," a combination embedded in the concept of right: "The
concept of right should be seen as consisting immediately of the possibility of
universal reciprocal coercion being combined with the freedom of everyone,
. . . Reason has taken care that the understanding is as fully equipped as possible
with a priori intuitions for the concept of right." For Kant, the combination of
subjective freedom and its universalizability were in reality inseparable and embedded in our intuitive knowledge stemming from our conditions of being. He
expressed this using the example of the universal prohibition on lying (Kant
1930, 13). After laying the epistemological foundations for the combination of
the principles of subjectivity and universality as a transcendental a priori, Kant
introduced the concept of the "categorical imperative" as the manifestation of
the combination at the deontological level. I contend that, through this categorical imperative, Kant attempted to achieve a "general" combination of the
principles of subjectivity and universality. On the one hand, he described the
categorical imperative in terms of free will associated with subjective autonomy, regardless of any given telos or consequence (Kant 1930, 5). On the other
hand, he defined the categorical imperative by the criterion of universalizability: "In all moral judgments the idea which we frame is this, 'What is the character of action taken by itself?' If the intent of the action can without
self-contradiction be universalized, it is morally possible; if it cannot be so uni-

versalized without contradicting itself, it is morally impossible" (Kant 1930, 44).[4]

Kant's attempt at combining subjectivity and universality found social and political embodiment in his conception of right. Because he defines right as "the totality of conditions, under which the will [*Willkür*] of one person can be unified with the will of another under a universal law of freedom" (Kersting 1992, 344), right, for Kant, consists of the conditions under which freedom of every subject can coexist with the freedom of *all other* subjects. His conception of right entails certain very important legal and ethical implications and corollaries. For one, it implies the ethical exhortation and legal requirement that each person be treated as an autonomous subject and as an end: "Act always so that you treat humanity whether in your person or in that of another always as an end, but never as a means only" (Reiss 1970, 18).[5] For another, it entails that the freedom of each individual be restricted so that it can be harmonized with the freedom of everyone else. This in turn entails a concept of public right, embedded in a general and external law guaranteeing freedom, which makes this constant harmony possible (Kant 1970, 73). Indeed, modern law arises as a corollary to this conception of right. As J. B. Schneewind (1970, 134–35) has observed, "the domain of law which extends to civil law, arises from maxims that are vetoed because they cannot even be thought coherently when universalized. The rejection of such maxims turns out to provide a counterpart to the recognition of the strict rights of others."[6]

In this regard, Kant addressed the necessity of a civil constitution in which a contractual view of law could be embedded. Because the relation of equal and free subjects involved restrictions of freedom and thereby coercion, to make universalized subjectivity possible, a civil constitution, "a relationship among free men who are subject to coercive law while they retain their freedom within the general union with their fellows," became necessary (Kant 1970, 73).

4. Kant's categorical imperative can be phrased as follows: "So act that the maxim of your will could always hold at the same time as a principle establishing universal law" (Mothersilk 1967, 443). Thus any act is permissible (freedom of subjectivity) on the condition, and only on the condition, that it can become universalized.

5. Kant's exhortation and requirement represents one of the few occasions where the domains of morality and law actually converge in modernity.

6. The moral sphere, on the other hand, involves actions that could be universalized but that are not compelled by any force. For a good discussion of the Kantian distinction between the "domain of law" and the "domain of virtue," see Schneewind 1992.

A constitution allowing the *greatest possible human freedom* in accordance with laws which ensure that freedom of each can co-exist with the freedom of all others (not one designed to provide the greatest possible happiness, as this will in any case follow automatically) is at all events a necessary idea which must be made the basis not only of the first outline of a political constitution but of all laws as well. (Kant 1970, 191; emphasis original)

According to Kant (1970, 163), the ideal and "only rightful" constitution was that of a republic. Moreover, he considered a public sphere, based on the critical judgment of all social actors, to be a crucial counterpart to a republican constitution: an independent space outside the direct influence and power of the state where there was rational dialogue among actors and where they could take part in a political society (Rundell 1987, 5, 28). The republican constitution and the public sphere, as components of the civil society, were mechanisms whereby the civil society maintained its independence from the state. Political participation is thus a crucial element in Kant's political theory. The critical subjects can only realize their autonomy through active participation in a civil state (Rundell 1987, 25). Although Kant imposed certain, by today's standards debilitating, restrictions on the notion of democratic political participation (noted below), "despite his suspicions toward democracy, Kant generate[d] a model of a democratic social form that is guided by the notions of universal participation and critical judgment" (Rundell 1987, 30).[7]

Kant considered the separation of powers to be as necessary as citizenship rights for the realization of subjects' autonomy (Kant 1970, 138). Often taken for granted in liberal democracies, where it has a relatively long history, this organizational principle is both based on and connected to the two pillars of modernity, subjectivity and universality. As such, it is of utmost importance. In this regard, the power to legislate has a particularly important function for Kant: it can belong only to the united will of the people. Because all rights are supposed to emanate from this power, the laws it gives must be "absolutely incapable of doing anyone an injustice." Thus only the combined and unanimous will of everyone, whereby each decides the same for the collective and the col-

---

7. The notions of universal participation and critical judgment that arise in modernity are fundamental in any political structure claiming to be a form of democracy. In the chapters to follow, I will discuss their relevance to the thought of Khomeini and Shariati.

lective decides the same for each— "the general and united will of the people"— should be allowed to legislate (Kant 1970, 139).

Kant calls the members of such a civil society "citizens," whom he endows with three inalienable rights: (1) the right to obey no law to which they have not given consent; (2) the right to equality; and (3) the right to civil independence, whereby citizens owe their existence and sustenance to no one except their own rights and powers as members of their commonwealth (Kant 1970, 139). Finally, to guarantee these citizenship rights and freedoms, Kant advances the right to freedom of expression ("freedom of the pen") as part and parcel of a public discourse (Kant 1970, 85).

Kant's contribution to the democratic tradition of a civil society was enormous. Nevertheless, he restricted citizenship in two improtant respects: first, he categorically excluded women from citizenship; second, he required that a citizen "must be his own master (*sui juris*) and must have some property (which can include any skill, fine art or science) to support himself" (Kant 1970, 78). Thus Kant excluded whole categories of people, such as women, laborers, shop assistants, and domestic servants, from citizenship rights (Kant 1970, 78). These categories represent vast numbers of people, who even in the industrialized countries of today's world constitute the overwhelming majority of the population.[8]

In contrast to his narrow view of "domestic" citizenship, Kant's view of international relations is quite broad and open; his visions for moral, intellectual, and political development are not confined to any particular nation or region.

---

8. Kant excluded women and those not their own masters and not having property from citizenship rights based on his understanding of the principles of freedom, equality, and independence, which he held to be indispensable for the operation of a civil society. Whereas the first two principles, freedom and equality, are given a priori, the third principle, independence, is not given but acquired, thus undermining all claims to universality. On the theoretical level, however, as a criterion, the principle of independence may be interpreted as a warning and an allusion to the fact that in a society whose members lack literacy, technical skills, and education—the basis for genuine independence—the principles of freedom and equality cannot take root. This interpretation gives credence to the argument that social and economic developments are necessary counterparts and complementary to cultural and political developments. Moreover, Kant's independence criterion might also be interpreted to mean that citizenship (freedom of subjectivity universalized) is a right to be acquired and not something that can be granted from above. Those social experiments, especially in postrevolutionary situations, where an elite attempts to force equality on the populace paternalistically, from above, have usually failed and have hindered universalized subjectivity.

In the essay "Idea for a Universal History with a Cosmopolitan Purpose," he develops a utopian scheme for egalitarian international relations:

> The same unsociability which forced men to [form a commonwealth] gives rise in turn to a situation whereby each commonwealth in its external relation . . . is in a position of unrestricted freedom. Each must accordingly expect from any other precisely the same evils which formerly oppressed individual men and forced them into a law-governed civil state. Wars, tense and unremitting military preparations . . . are the means by which nature drives nations [toward] abandoning a lawless state or savagery and entering a federation of peoples in which every state, even the smallest, could expect to derive its security and rights not from its own power or its own legal judgment, but solely from this great federation. (Kant 1970, 47)

Here again, Kant demonstrates his consistency and the coherence of his ethical-political system. The same motivations that drive the subjects within a social formation toward intersubjectivity should drive nations toward equitable international relations.[9]

A corollary of this formulation by Kant is found in his anticolonial and anti-imperialist position. He condemned the Europeans for considering American, African and other non-European countries "ownerless territories" and subjugating them by conquest and colonization (Kant 1970, 106–7). In an era when the ugly side of subjectivity domination—prevailed in the relationship of Europeans with non-Europeans, such an anticolonial position, which is consistent with the rest of Kant's thought, is commendable.

The formulations by Kant outlined in this section, extending from ontology and epistemology to an ethical system and a political theory, constitute the highest achievements of Enlightenment philosophy and make Kant the philosopher of modernity par excellence, although they have also been the target of criticism from different quarters. The most salient feature of Kant's system might be described as its "nonteleological" and "nonconsequential" character. In Kant's ethics, value is not to be found in any a priori desired end, nor is any specific action, such as telling the truth, considered to be intrinsically right or valuable (Beck 1988, 15).

---

9. To what extent these ideals are realized in the "real world" is beyond the scope of this discussion. Suffice it to say that a desire for these ideals exist in many of us, which, in itself, is important, though by no means sufficient.

The object or aim of the will can be of any kind what so ever (even including happiness). But in this case, we completely abstract from whatever particular end is adopted. Thus so far as the principle of morality is concerned, the doctrine of the highest good as the ultimate end of a will which is determined by this doctrine and which conforms to its laws can be by-passed and set aside as incidental. (Kant 1970, 66)

In this way, Kant rejects all ethical systems not based on human will, whether they originate in our senses and instincts or in "outer grounds," that is, custom and received law (Kant 1930, 12). He also dismisses any ethics derived from religion. Such positions make Kant's philosophical system vulnerable to charges of formalism, abstractness, and vacuity.

Because Kant's combination of subjectivity and universality is based solely on the radical notion of subjective autonomy, it has been attacked for its alleged formalism. One should not dismiss these allegations as irrelevant and baseless, however. As we will see, they constitute the core of the discontent of modernity. Kant himself was probably aware of the problems of the ethical and cultural structure of the emerging modern world. Thus he recognized the need for religion to give "weight" to morality: "Without religion, obligation is motiveless. Religion supplies the condition under which the binding force of the laws can be thought" (Kant 1930, 82). He even identified the problem of vacuity specifically and directly: "Moral laws can be right without a third being, but in the absence of such a being to make their performance necessary they would be empty" (Kant 1930, 40). Although these qualifications on the part of Kant are completely external to his system, which is based on the transcendental a priori, they point out the ethical and cultural problems of modernity, to which many thinkers, foremost among them Hegel, responded. It is with this backdrop in mind that I turn to Hegel's attempt at a substantive synthesis of subjectivity and universality.

Hegel: The Grand Synthesis

The critique of Kant's type of combination of subjectivity and universality is a prominent feature of Hegel's philosophy. Hegel (1991, 58) criticizes Kant for "reducing" the concept of the right to "the limitation of my freedom or arbitrary will in such a way that it may coexist with the arbitrary will of everyone else in accordance with a universal law." In Hegel's view, the problem with this definition of right is that, first, it is negative, which is to say, it is based on a limitation of freedom, and, second, it is formal (Hegel 1991, 58). By "formal," Hegel means that the will involved in the Kant's formulation is merely human and ephemeral will, not what Hegel considered to be the true will— the will of the infinite spirit (explored below in greater detail; see discussion of Hegel's ontology).

The same criticism, in Hegel's view (1967, 90; emphasis original), applies to Kant's concept of categorical imperative: "Kant's further formulation, the possibility of visualizing an action as a *universal* maxim does not lead to the more concrete visualization of a situation, but in itself contains no principle beyond abstract identity and the 'absence of contradiction' already mentioned." Because both subjectivity and universality lack "substance," the same problem of vacuity obtains in the civil society, the embodiment of the Kantian combination:

> In civil society the Idea is lost in particularity and has fallen asunder with the separation of inward and outward. In the administration of justice, however, civil society returns to its concept, to the unity of the implicit universal with subjective particular, although here the latter is only that present in single cases and the universality in question is that of abstract right. (Hegel 1967, 145)

In critiquing the vacuity of the Kantian view of modern civil society, Hegel considered the withdrawal of the essence of religion from the civil society as another aspect of its abstractness. To be certain, Hegel's own view of religion was far from orthodox, and he advocated the separation of Church and State. But he believed that divorcing political institutions from the "realm of inwardness" and from the "innermost shrine of conscience," as well as from the sanctuary of religion, had caused these institutions to be indeterminate and abstract and to "lack any real center" (Hegel 1975, 104).

To better understand Hegel's problematic, we need to turn to a discussion of the intellectual and political milieu of Hegel and his immediate predecessors.[10] In late-eighteenth-century Germany, there were two reactions to the mainstream of Enlightenment thought. One was the Romantic throwback loosely associated with the Sturm und Drang movement, and the other was the

---

10. For my understanding of Hegel's work generally and his project for modernity specifically, I am much indebted to Charles Taylor's works (1975, 1979) on Hegel, which I recommend to my readers, and on which I have extensively drawn. Other important sources for understanding of Hegel are Kojeve 1980, Jean Hyppolite 1974, and Dallmayr 1993.

system of thought built around the idea of a radical freedom, in which Kant figured most prominently (Taylor 1979, 1–3).[11] The main thrust of the Romantic critique of the Enlightenment revolved around Kant's view of the human as the "subject of egoistic desires, for which nature and society provided merely the means to fulfillment" (Taylor 1979, 1). The Romantics thus charged the Enlightenment philosophy with being utilitarian in its ethics, atomistic in its social philosophy, analytical in its view of man, and mechanistic in its attitude toward interpersonal relations (Taylor 1979, 1). To counter such a philosophy, the Romantics, of which Herder was the most prominent, proposed a view of man that Charles Taylor (1979, 1–2), following Isaiah Berlin, has described as "expressive unity." According to this view, human life was to be seen as a Gestalt, like a work of art, where there was an organic relation between all the constituent parts and aspects (Taylor 1979, 1–2). The greatest problem of the mainstream Enlightenment view of man, from the Romantic perspective, was its "analytical" approach, which broke down everything into smaller parts and separated the parts from the whole. Reason and sensibility, soul and body, reason and feeling were torn asunder in this modern view of man. The separation and breakdown also applied to the relationship between the individual and society and between society and nature (Taylor 1979, 1–2).

Whereas Kant, proceeding from his idea of radical freedom, was opposed to the objectification of humans from any source, within or without, the Romantics found his radical view of freedom possible only at the cost of a "diremption with nature" and a division within the human between reason and sensibility that was even deeper than the one caused by the utilitarian and materialist philosophy of the Enlightenment (Taylor 1979, 6).

Partly because of the French Revolution, with its promise of subjective radical freedom, and partly because of the Terror, which was perceived as a political echo of the separation from nature and the larger order, including the premodern social order, the ideas of "radical autonomy" and "expressive unity" held a strong appeal for German intellectuals of the early nineteenth century, who aspired to unite them (Taylor 1979, 6).

Hegel, undoubtedly the most prominent among their heirs, sought nothing less than a synthesis between subjectivity and universality—a unification in

---

11. Sturm und Drang, literally meaning "storm and stress," was a late-eighteenth-century German movement closely associated with the Romantics and opposing the rationalism of the French Enlightenment.

which the formality of Kant's combination was to be overcome. For Hegel, the second term of the synthesis, "universality," included concepts such as inner and outer nature in addition to the social collectivity; "synthesis" meant that freedom of subjectivity and universality in its expanded sense would be "reconciled" in a new unification, with neither term losing any of its character and with neither overpowering the other.[12] Because the two terms are, at least in some respects, opposites, such a task seems impossible. But Hegel thought otherwise, and his ontology, which may look peculiar to many of us now, was designed to accomplish it.

Hegel appreciated the freedom of subjectivity. He maintained that, whereas property was of "external nature" and therefore alienable, freedom was constitutive of the self and, as such, inalienable (Hegel 1991, 95); he considered the forfeiture of freedom of subjectivity as "alienation of personality," which was exemplified in slavery, serfdom, disqualification from owning property, and restrictions of freedom of ownership (Hegel 1991, 95). Furthermore, what he called "return to self" (or the reversal of alienation) involved the restoration of freedom to subjects with regard to their "capacity for rights," ethical life, and religious beliefs (Hegel 1991, 95).

The freedom of subjectivity, in Hegel's view (1975, 54), was one of the goals of history: "World history is the progress of the consciousness of freedom . . . a progress whose necessity it is our business to comprehend." For Hegel (1975, 52), "freedom" meant human freedom; its realization was very concrete: "The ultimate phase of [spirit's] consciousness, on which everything depends is the recognition that man is free."

The important position that the concept and phenomenon of freedom occupied in Hegel's formulations can be understood when we realize that he defined reason in terms of freedom. As he put it, reason "is directly conceived with the consciousness of the concept of freedom, and the way in which it expresses itself in individuals" (Hegel 1975, 143). The relationship between thought and freedom holds a significant place in Hegel's philosophy. It is probably no exaggeration to say that, for Hegel, "intelligence" constitutes the very basis of freedom, that only an intelligent being can be free, and that an intelligent being is

---

12. The relation between the subject and the three spheres of outer nature, inner nature, and social collectivity is central to the works of many thinkers following Hegel, including critical theorists. It also strongly bears on Habermas's three value spheres of cognitive-instrumental, moral-practical, and aesthetic-expressive.

necessarily free: "Since man alone—as distinct from animals—is a thinking being, he alone possesses freedom, and he possesses it solely by virtue of his ability to think" (Hegel 1975, 144). In a passage reminiscent of Descartes—although Hegel's project was very different from that of Descartes and indeed would bridge the Cartesian dualism—Hegel (1975, 104) refers to the grounding of the subject as "knower" and "willer" in a view of the subject as a "thinker": "If we consider subjectivity itself, we find that subjective knowledge and volition are the same thing as thought." Hegel himself arrived at the logical conclusion of grounding freedom in intelligence by declaring the mind to be the very basis of right (Hegel 1967, 20).

In an argument that seems directed both at Kant and at the Romantics, Hegel upholds the importance of thought in his synthesis:

> The good is in principle the essence of the will in its substantiality and universality, i.e., of the will in its truth and therefore it exists simply and solely in thinking and by means of thinking. Hence assertions such as "man cannot know the truth but has to do only with phenomena" or "thinking injures the good will" are dogmas depriving mind not only of intellectual but also of all ethical worth and dignity. (Hegel 1967, 132)

Indeed, the central role Hegel assigned to thought directly bears on the Romantics' solution to the diremption caused by the modernity of the Enlightenment. This solution was to be achieved through a unification with the cosmic order, but at the price of sacrificing the freedom of subjectivity, which was based on reason. Because Hegel's project was all about the "preservation" of subjectivity while reconciling it with the "lost" cosmic order, his emphasis on thought as the foundation of subjectivity was vital (Taylor 1979, 48).

Even though Hegel believed that the freedom of subjectivity was grounded in thought, he posited that the manifestation of that freedom was in the will. In his parlance, what was necessary to bring freedom, which existed only in itself as mere potentiality, into existence and actuality was the will, defined here as "the activity of mankind in the world at large" (Hegel 1975, 69–70). However, this "human will" was based on a higher level of abstraction: "The abstract concept of the Idea of the will is in general *the free will which wills the free will*" (Hegel 1991, 57; emphasis original). In connection with the issue of right, Hegel argued that will properly belongs to the (cosmic) *Geist*, not that of the individual;

he accused Kant and Rousseau of "reducing" the essence of will to that of the human individual:

> The definition of right in question embodies the view, especially prevalent since Rousseau, according to which the substantial basis and primary factor is supposed to be not the will as rational will which has being in and for itself or the spirit as *true* spirit, but will and spirit as the *particular individual*, as the will of the single person [*des Einzelnen*] in his distinctive arbitrariness. (Hegel 1991, 58; emphases original)

To better understand what Hegel meant by *Geist*, or cosmic spirit, we need to examine some aspects of his ontology. Believing that subjectivity as radical autonomy afforded by reason and universality as being part of nature were not mutually exclusive and that a synthesis between them was therefore possible, Hegel maintained that the two constituted a dialectical rather than a Cartesian duality, that they stood in simultaneous opposition and unity, as did thought and life, reason (freedom) and nature. In other words, to exist at all as a conscious being, the subject had to be embodied in life; but to realize the perfection of consciousness, it had to fight and overcome the natural bent of life as a limit (Taylor 1979, 21). This dialectic constituted the "motor" of history, first separating us from the cosmic order and nature and later reuniting us with them. To achieve this grand unification between subjectivity and universality, Hegel conceived of nature as having some kind of foundation in spirit, reasoning that, if the most important aspect of our existence, our morality as radical freedom, was to be in harmony with our natural being, then nature itself had to have a spiritual tendency (Taylor 1979, 9). Hegel found this spiritual tendency in the concept of *Geist*, which, as the cosmic spirit—what Spinoza called the "Substance" or what the proponents of the Sturm und Drang perceived as the divine life, which flowed in everything—underlay all reality (Taylor 1979, 23). The essence of this spirit was freedom or rationality; indeed, Hegel used "spirit" and "mind" interchangeably. Furthermore, this spirit "posited" the world and thus embodied it. In Hegel's schema, we, as humans, are the vehicles of this cosmic spirit in its physical embodiment as it comes to self-consciousness. With the aid of the concept of *Geist*, Hegel attempted to resolve the dilemma that none of his contemporaries could. As Taylor (1975, 17) explains:

Hegel solves the problem of uniting the finite to infinite spirit without loss of freedom through his notion of reason. . . . [His] contemporaries . . . either . . . held to vision of an unboundedly free creative subject, but at the cost of exile in a God-forsaken world; or they sought unity with the divine beyond, but at the cost of abandoning their autonomy to a larger order beyond their comprehension. For Hegel, too, the finite subject must be part of a larger order. But because this is an order deployed by an unconditional rational necessity, it is at no point foreign to ourselves as rational subjects. Nothing in it must be accepted as brute "positive" fact. The rational agent loses none of his freedom in coming to accept his vocation as vehicle of cosmic necessity.

Thus Hegel considers his synthesis to be substantive and not merely formal: the freedom involved here is not that of the mere human individual but rather belongs to the more substantial *Geist* or cosmic spirit.

Although, to be certain, Hegel's concept of *Geist* seems phantasmagorical and chimerical to today's sensibility, its purpose was to reconcile the principle of subjectivity (and the individual subject) with at least three spheres within the concept of the universal. These three spheres were what we would now call "inner nature," "outer nature," and "community." Humans in their original state were enmeshed in nature, whether in their own instincts or that of the external nature. They had to oppose nature as free agents to realize their freedom. But, in Hegel's ontology, as the vehicles of the *Geist*, we no longer have to stay in a state of alienation from inner or outer nature. Yet at the same time, we can preserve our freedom and rationality and not go back to the original state of being enmeshed in nature because the *Geist* itself is made of freedom and rationality (Taylor 1979, 50–51).[13]

Although Hegel's reconciling subject with inner and outer nature is of ut-

13. In our age, one might think that subject and inner nature have been reconciled through psychoanalysis, sparing us the fantastic aspects of the notion of *Geist*, while allowing us to retain its theoretical substance in Freudian theory. Furthermore, certain aspects of the sexual revolution of the sixties and the movement built around the human body, such as control and choice over one's body, may be said to represent a genuine reconciliation between freedom and inner nature, especially because both freedom as choice and our bodies as the embodiment of our inner nature are equally preserved. In a similar vein, strands of the contemporary environmental movement that preserve the principle of human subjectivity while trying to reconcile it with a broader order may be seen as attempts to reunify subject and outer nature without resorting to the concept of "cosmic spirit."

most importance and relevance to us in the first decade of the twenty-first century, it is his reconciling the individual subject with the universal of the social collectivity—the third moment of his overall reconciliation of subjectivity with universality and a theme central to his *Philosophy of Right*—that I wish to elaborate on next.

In *Lectures on the Philosophy of History*, Hegel explicitly identifies the social collective as a universal (Hegel 1975, 60). The general synthesis between the finite and the infinite in the special case of the individual and the social collectivity here takes the shape of universalized subjectivity. In this famous passage, Hegel historicizes the evolution of universalized subjectivity: "The Orientals . . . knew only that *One* is free . . . the Greek and Roman world . . . knew that *Some* are free, and finally, [we know] that *All* men as such are free, and that man is by *nature* free" (1975, 54–55; emphases original). Hegel's sociology has its roots in his ontology of the *Geist*, whose

> substance . . . is freedom. From this, we can infer that its end in the historical process is the freedom of subject to follow its own conscience and morality and to pursue and implement its own universal ends; it also implies that the subject has infinite value and that it must become conscious of its supremacy. The end of the world spirit is realized in substance through the freedom of each individual. (Hegel 1975, 55)

The combination of subjectivity and universality in the reality of the civil society is, however, only formal and vacuous and not a genuine, substantive synthesis. Indeed, Hegel himself finds the relationship between the individual and the collectivity in the civil society to be a universalized subjectivity that is only formal, alluding to it as a "form of universality" in the following passage:

> The concrete person who, as a particular person, as a totality of needs and a mixture of natural necessity and arbitrariness, is his own end, *is one principle* of civil society. But this particular person stands essentially in relation [*Beziehung*] to other similar particulars, and their relation is such that each asserts itself and gains satisfaction through the others, and this at the same time through the exclusive mediation of the form of universality, which is the *second principle*. (Hegel 1991, 220; emphases original)

To be sure, Hegel (1991, 285) believes that particular interests of the individual subject "should certainly not be set aside, let alone suppressed; on the contrary they should be harmonized with universal, so that both they themselves and the universal are preserved." Nevertheless, the kind of combination of these two principles as found in the civil society is severely inadequate because in it the principle of universality is based on an abstract notion of right (Hegel 1967, 145).

Hegel (1991, 118) attributed the abstraction, and therefore also vacuity, of the universal in the civil society to the nature of contract, its modus operandi, "where the universal is . . . reduced by the particular will to a mere semblance, and . . . contract [itself] is reduced . . . to a purely external community of wills."[14] Hegel believed that mere contract was vacuous and could be no basis for a society, whether it was a contract of all with all or a contract between all and sovereign or government (Hegel 1991, 105). Indeed, he went so far as to hold the vacuous contractual nature of universality in civil society responsible for the Terror in the French Revolution (Hegel 1967, 157). Hegel's solution to the problem of the vacuity of the combination of subjectivity and universality based on contract in civil society was the concept of *Sittlichkeit* or what has been translated as "ethical life."

This "ethical life" constituted for Hegel the substantive synthesis of the freedom of individual subjectivity and the social universal. It is in this synthesis that Hegel attempts to preserve both the "right" of the individual subjectivity and that of the collective universal, which, as we have seen, is based on the ontology of the *Geist*. To be sure, this "identity" of the subjective particularity and collective universality is dialectical, with identity and opposition coming together:

> The right of the subject's particularity, his right to be satisfied, or in other words the right of subjective freedom, is the pivot and center of the difference between antiquity and modern times. . . . Now this principle of particularity is, to be sure, one moment of the antithesis, and in the first place at least it is just as much identical with the universal as distinct from it. (Hegel 1967, 84)[15]

---

14. Hegel (1991, 148) also criticized civil society for weakening the family: "Civil society tears the individual from his family ties, estranges the members of the family from one another, and recognizes them as self-subsistent persons. . . . Thus the individual becomes a son of civil society."

15. In the paragraph where he identifies his concept of "morality," which pitted the individual against social norms, Hegel (1967, 84) says, "Abstract reflection, however, fixes [the principle

Hegel seeks to reunite the individual subject with the larger order, in this case, the social order; the larger order is the very basis of its substantiality, which it lacks in the civil society. As he sees it, "ethical life is the unity of the will in its concept and the will of the individual [*des Einzelnen*], that is of the subject" (Hegel 1991, 64).

The thrust of Hegel's philosophy here is directed at healing the diremption between individual and society in modern society without sacrificing either of them. In premodern society, especially among the ancient Greeks, individuals found identification with public life and the common experience, but this freedom of subjectivity was limited in its scope and confined to a few men (Taylor 1979, 92). In modern society, however, the freedom of individual subject has pitted individual against collective, public life and its institutions, hence the "alienation" of the individual (Taylor 1979, 125). For Hegel, ethical life, as the reconciliation between the individual as the subject and the collectivity, finds its embodiment in the state, by which he means the larger society and its institutions. The initial unity between individual and the collectivity represents the first stage, that of "family," which is followed, in the second stage, by the diremption of individual from society in the civil society.

"But the state," notes Hegel (1991, 64), "emerges only at the third stage, that of ethical life and spirit, at which the momentous unification of self-sufficient individuality with universal substantiality takes place."[16]

Although I have no intention of entering into the continuing and often heated debate over Hegel's concept of state, I believe there is much in his writings to support two points. First, in speaking of "state," Hegel clearly intends us to understand "democratic state." Second, by "state," Hegel means something more than the political institution we now call "the state," which he calls "public authority" (Pelczynski 1984, 11) and which, in his his schema, takes care of the welfare of the needy individuals in the civil society. To be sure, he includes this narrower sense of "state" in its broader sense as the totality of the social col-

---

of particularity] in its distinction from and opposition to the universal and so produces a view of morality as nothing but a bitter, unending struggle against self-satisfaction, as the command 'Do with abhorrence what duty enjoins.' "

16. Hegel (1975, 93; emphasis original) expressed the same view somewhat differently: "This essential being, the unity of subjective will and the universal, is the ethical whole, and its concrete manifestation is the *state*. The state is the reality within which the individual has and enjoys his freedom, but only in so far as he knows, believes in and wills the universal."

lective (Hegel 1975, 96). But even this "state," as community, should not dominate the citizens, nor should its citizens treat it as a means to their ends, as is the case in the civil society (Hegel 1975, 95).

But the state, Hegel warns, should not be confused with civil society. Because the state is not the apparatus for the mere protection of property and personal freedom, as civil society is, membership in it is not optional (Hegel 1967, 156).[17] Even though a structure of command and obedience is necessary for the conduct of affairs of society, however, there should be a constitution that requires a minimum of obedience from the citizens and that permits only a minimum of arbitrariness to those in positions of command. Moreover, the contents of these commands should be determined by the people, by the will of the many or all of the citizens (Hegel 1975, 116–17). To that end, Hegel advocates a parliamentary system to mediate between individual citizens, on the one hand, and monarch, on the other (Hegel 1967, 363). Although, properly speaking, his is more an "Estate" system than what we know today as a parliamentary system, nevertheless, "Estate" is a moment of legislature (Hegel 1967, 195).[18]

In Hegel's "state," the will of the particular individual and the universal are united. This unification in the moral-practical sphere translates into the complementary relations of right and duty: "In the state, as something ethical, as the inner penetration of the substantive and the particular, my obligation to what is substantive is at the same time the embodiment of my particular freedom. This means that in the state duty and right unite in one and the same relation (Hegel 1967, 161).[19]

Yet another aspect of the unity of the particular subjectivity and the universal in Hegel's "state" is his conception of the law, which he sees as the means by which individuals relate to the collectivity—society—without surrendering their individuality to it (Hegel 1975, 100–101). The individual, by obeying the laws of this society, "knows that he owes his freedom to this obedience," thus

17. Characterizing membership in the state as not being optional is another way of expressing the substantial nature of the state. In *Philosophy of Right*, Hegel refers to the substantiality of the state in terms of its claim to the lives and property of the citizens and its right to require their sacrifice (Hegel 1967, 126).

18. Hegel's method for selecting representatives was not through popular elections but through corporative bodies. See Hegel 1967, 202.

19. One of the perilous attitudes of modern society views rights as the sole constituent of social relations and duties as cumbersome limitations on the freedom of the individual.

enjoys a position of independence within the state, while being in harmony with the general will of that society (Hegel 1975, 100).[20]

A potential problem associated with Hegel's concept of the state is the balance between the principles of subjectivity and universality. Although, in some instances, Hegel seems to consider society as essence and its citizens as mere accidents (Inwood, 1984, 40), in others, his synthesis comes alive, and he strikes a careful balance between subjectivity and universality:

> The state does not exist for the sake of the citizens; it might rather be said that the state is their end, and the citizens are its instruments. But this relation of end and means is not at all appropriate in the present context. For the state is not an abstraction which stands in opposition to citizens; on the contrary, they are distinct moments like those of organic life, in which no one member is either means or end. The divine principle in the state is the Idea made manifest on earth. (Hegel 1975, 94–95)

In *Philosophy of Right*, Hegel criticizes Plato for denying the right of the individual, or the principle of subjectivity, in *The Republic* (Hegel 1967, 124). In a similar vein, he charges the "primitive" state with annihilating the will of the individual. "In primitive political conditions, the particular aspects of the will are disregarded, and the universal will is alone essential" (Hegel 1975, 95). Yet Hegel also criticizes the overdevelopment of subjectivity, especially in the United States of his time, where "the private citizen is concerned above all with industry and profit, and particular interest, which look to the universal only in order to obtain private satisfaction, are dominant [and] the universal purpose of the state is

20. That the category of universality is central to Hegel's philosophy should not make us think he was unaware of a major problem that stems from universality and general will, namely, the problem of homogeneity and identification, of especial concern to social theories working with any form of the concept of universality in the age of "mass society." Hegel's solution to this problem lay in the institution of the "Estates," where different social groupings were to provide differentiation in the larger state (community) and to create an organic articulation of these different social groups, which in turn would mediate between these partial groups, on the one hand, and the government, on the other (Hegel 1967, 195–99). To be sure, by twenty-first-century standards, Hegel's solution is far from democratic. Yet the issue of homogeneity and identification in modern society, where, because of universal subjectivity, the differentiation of traditional society tends to disappear (however gradually), remains. (As noted in the appendix, the same problem faces Habermas's formulations, to which Seyla Benhabib [1986] has responded.)

not yet firmly established" (Hegel 1967, 168). Fully aware of the destructive aspects of unchecked subjectivity, he warns against individuals becoming isolated
from one another and from society and against selfishness and vanity becoming
prevalent at the expense of the whole (Hegel 1975, 146).

Thus, even though Hegel pointed out the enormous potentiality of the
human that could be released as a result of the modern revolution of subjectivity, he also pointed out the destructive power of this released and realizing subjectivity, which he wished to curb through a synthesis with the "infinite" as the
universal. And as we have seen, he proposed to achieve this synthesis through a
concept of *Geist* or cosmic spirit, whose essence was freedom and whose vehicles were humans.

However one might view Hegel's concept of the *Geist*, achieving some kind
of accommodation between the principles of subjectivity and universality remains a reasonable goal. As elaborated on by Habermas and discussed in the appendix to this volume, the reconciliation between individual subjectivity and
the three spheres of outer nature, inner nature, and society is a major issue of social theory to this day.

Another issue that Hegel constantly referred to is the role of reflection in
the history of modernity. For Hegel, one of the most important corollaries of
subjectivity was conscious reflection; indeed, the two were inseparable in his
philosophy. Hegel had high praise for a nation that had reached the level of reflection and self-consciousness necessary to view its own culture as an "object."
Such a nation could consciously change its culture, "belief, trust and custom,"
even though such phenomena were ultimately rooted in the *Geist* (Hegel 1975,
146). In a similar vein, Hegel took religion to task for making its assertion un-
criticizable, noting that the "truth" of religion was a "given content" and not
based on "thinking and the use of concept" (Hegel 1967, 168; 1975, 171). In
contrast to religion and the church, the "state," in Hegel's larger sense of the
modern community of the synthesis, was "that which knows."[21]

21. Hegel's position has intriguing implications for the sociology of religion. In harmony
with his philosophy of history, Hegel sees the development of religion—that is, monotheistic religions rooted in the Middle East—as part of the evolution of subjectivity itself. Thus his philosophical system regards the monotheistic religions as a necessary transition to modern
subjectivity. The major difference between subjectivity in the premodern (monotheistic) period
and in the modern period is that it was "implicit" or unconscious in the former and is conscious,
indeed, self-conscious, in the latter. It seems that Hegel (1975, 150; emphases added) had this
phenomenon in mind when he wrote: "What the spirit is now, it has always been *implicitly* and the

The significance this approach holds for the process of secularization, cultural reflection, and accommodation of social change is clear. Indeed, its implications for secularization in many of countries of the Middle East struggling with the forces of social and cultural change are far reaching.

The theoretical insights delineated in this introductory chapter provide us with a conceptual framework for our analysis of Iran's intellectual encounter with modernity since the late nineteenth century. Critical thinking on both the emancipatory and the dominative aspects of modernity by the most influential social thinkers and philosophers of the nineteenth and twentieth centuries has produced a rich and extensive literature. The latest attempt to reconcile the pillars of modernity is to be found in the works of Jürgen Habermas, who has attempted to mediate subjectivity and universality by shifting the ontological foundations of modernity from mere subjectivity to intersubjectivity. In Habermas's theory of communicative action, subjectivity and universality can coexist without cancelling each other out. To keep our focus on the central concerns of this book, however, I have reserved discussion of the continuing discourses on modernity for the appendix, which I commend to the serious reader.

---

difference is merely in the *degree* to which this implicit character has been developed. The spirit of the present world is the concept which the spirit forms of its own nature. It is this which sustains and rules the world, and it is the result of 6,000 years of effort."

PART ONE

Iran's Experiment with Modernity

To be sure, there is little evidence that Iranian intellectuals of the second half of the nineteenth century were directly familiar with the theoretical notions of modernity delineated thus far. As demonstrated below, however, they were quite engaged with the most important ramifications of these concepts, which in turn allowed them to broach the principles of subjectivity and universality and their sociopolitical implications, albeit using terms of their own coinage.

Against the theoretical insights explored in chapter 1, chapter 2 closely examines and evaluates the works of five of the more important intellectual contributors to the sociopolitical discourse in Iran in the last decades of the nineteenth century, focusing on the ontological foundations and sociological ramifications of their contributions. It then considers some of the contending ideas in the discourse of the Constitutional movement at the turn of the century.

Chapter 3 traces the events leading to the unipolarization of the discourse on and the practice of modernity in twentieth-century Iran, where the positivist aspects of modernity took the upper hand at the expense of its more democratic elements. It then discusses the responses of the different "leftist" groups in Iran to this development, focusing on particular elements in their pursuit of a discourse on modernity.

2

The Dawn of Modernity in Iran

Positivist Subjectivity and Universalizable Subjectivity

Modernity struck Iran, as many other countries, in its most traumatizing and therefore most awakening form, militaristic imperialism. The Qajar Dynasty (1794–1925) had inherited a semiunified state from the Safavids (1501–1730), who had united the country in the early sixteenth century, for the first time since the Arabs invaded in the seventh. Now, at the beginning of the nineteenth century, the Qajars found themselves powerless before the onslaught of modernity, which came in the form of military pressure and invasion by imperial Russia from the north and, in the middle of the century, by Britain from the south. The Russian forces, equipped with the modern means of warfare, easily defeated the ill-prepared Iranian army, which relied for the most part on tribal military forces and methods. In the humiliating treaties of Gulestan (1813) and Turkamanchai (1828), Iran lost territory and suzerainty in Transcaucasia as well as navigational rights for its warships in the Caspian Sea (Kazemzadeh 1991, 334).[1]

The first notable measure taken by the Iranian government to counter the hegemony of the modern West was to send Iranian students to Europe and to employ European experts, mostly military advisors. It is interesting to note that four of the five male students sent to England in 1815 by Crown Prince Abbas Mirza (d. 1833), commander of the Iranian army in the war against Russia, were to study military or technical subjects: artillery, engineering, chemistry (Miza Ja'far), and modern gun making (an artisan, Mohammad Ali); the fifth (Mirza Saleh) was to study languages (Farman Farmayan 1966, 121). Similarly, the list

---

1. One can imagine the shock and humiliation felt by the Iranians when a Russian military force of 2,260 warriors defeated an Iranian army of 30,000 in a battle that lasted only two days (Kazemzadeh 1991, 334–38; see also Bina 1954 for the text of the 1813 and 1828 treaties).

of the books later ordered from France by the Qajar premier Haji Mirza Aghasi (d. 1848) reveals the regime's interest in technical, scientific, and military matters (Nateq 1988, 239–43), an interest that reflected Iran's intense concern about military affairs and its desire to resist the military threat posed by Britain and Russia. Indeed, so keen was this interest that one of the first questions Mohammad Shah (d. 1847) asked two French botanists visiting Iran in 1835 had to do with the stability of the French state and the strength of its military (Nateq 1988, 108).

Although in Iran's early encounter with modernity, interest was greatest in the military and technological spheres, there was interest in and curiosity about the sociopolitical sphere as well. Mirza Saleh, who had been sent by Abbas Mirza to study languages in England in 1815, could not hide his enthusiasm for the Magna Carta, "freedom of the people," the House of Commons, and the concept of representative democracy (Adamiyat 1961, 30). He also wrote an account of freedom of speech—probably the earliest of its kind in Iran—as the foundation of the British parliamentary system in the early nineteenth century (Adamiyat 1961, 31). Thus, from the very beginning of Iran's encounter with modernity, we can see a duality: a strong interest in the military and technological aspects of modernity side by side with a weaker appreciation of its sociopolitical aspects—in particular, democratic institutions.

This duality can be observed in the major reforms initiated by Amir Kabir (d. 1851) during his short tenure as premier. Thus Amir's primary motivation in building the polytechnic of Darolfonun, one of his most important reforms, was to bring modern sciences and technology to Iran and to gain access to the military sciences (Adamiyat 1982, 353–54). The central curriculum of the new polytechnic, taught by professors recruited mostly from Austria—to circumvent any possible imperialist manipulation by the Russians, British, and French—consisted of "engineering, infantry, cavalry, artillery, medicine and surgery, mineralogy, and natural science including physics, chemistry and pharmacology," with instruction also offered in history, geography, cartography, traditional Persian medicine, mathematics, Persian, Arabic, French, and Russian (Adamiyat 1982, 363).

However, Amir Kabir also introduced important reforms in the sociopolitical sphere.[2] His judicial reforms included establishing new civil courts, and pro-

---

2. Amir Kabir's "radical" reforms were perceived to pose so severe a threat to the power of the Qajar court elite and the clergy that, after only two years in office as the premier of Iran, he was dismissed by the shah, who later ordered that he be killed. Sometime between his dismissal

tection of religious minorities in particular (Farman Farmayan 1966, 128). He also established the first regular newspaper in Iran with the intention of "enlightening and educating the people of Persia, whether nobles, merchants, peasants, or government officials" (Farman Farmayan 1966, 128).

To be sure, this duality in Iran's appropriation of modernity reflected the very same duality that modernity had exhibited in its European birthplace; we observe a positivist interpretation of subjectivity side by side with what I have designated as "universalizable subjectivity." The duality of progress, for example, is of pivotal importance in both Europe and Iran: in the positivist interpretation, "progress" refers to the development of science and technology and their application to the social sphere, whereas, in universalizable subjectivity, "progress" refers more to the possibility of democratic change and to the transformation of oppressive institutions in which the concept of critique plays a central role. The same duality is expressed in the notion of law. From the positivist perspective, law is viewed primarily as order, regulation, and codification. In contrast, "positive law" manifests the universalizability of freedom and the rights and responsibilities of citizenship and the notion of government by consent and consensus.[3] At the institutional level, this duality is displayed in the creation of an efficient bureaucracy such as the Majlis Tanzimat (Organization Assembly), on the one hand, and in a parliamentary constitution and representative assembly, on the other.

Although both positivist and universalizable approaches appropriated the idea of the nation-state and nationalism from the modern West, the positivist approach placed greater emphasis on a nationalism based on ethnic and historical identity (in this case, the purported Aryan and pre-Islamic identity of Iran), whereas the universalizable approach leaned more toward a nationalism based on popular sovereignty within the confines of a nation-state. It is important to keep in mind that each of the theories we will examine in this chapter embodied both approaches at the same time, though each would emphasize different aspects of the approaches and to different degrees.

Before proceeding further, however, let us consider the conditions underlying the duality of "positivist" and "universalizable subjectivity." Although partly

and death, he was reported to have said he had "contemplated a constitution for Iran" (Adamiyat 1977, 15).

    3. Here, "positive law" should not be confused with a positivist interpretation of law; despite their common etymology, "positive" and "positivist" mean opposite things in this context.

a reflection of the same duality in Europe, the dualistic appropriation of modernity in Iran also reflected the impact of foreign imperialism, on the one hand, and that of domestic despotism, on the other.[4] The encroachment of foreign imperialism could not but result in a heightened interest in the appropriation of positivist aspects of European subjectivity. The inability of domestic despotism to counter European hegemony served to reinforce interest in positivist subjectivity, even as it aroused interest in universalizable subjectivity by making Iranians aware of the nature of that despotism, and by making them seek for ways to distribute the power invested and concentrated in it.

Malkum Khan: Positivist Law and Positive Law

The concept of law (qanun) emerged from a central theme in the sociopolitical discourse of the late nineteenth century among the leading advocates of reform in Qajar Iran. Mirza Malkum Khan (1833–1908) was one of the earliest and most influential theorists to systematically address issues pertaining to modernity in Iran. Born into an Armenian family in Esfahan, he was sent to France to study engineering on a state scholarship. There he developed an interest in political philosophy, especially in Saint Simon's ideas about social engineering and in Comte's "Religion of Humanity." Upon returning to Iran, he ostensibly converted to Islam, securing a teaching job for himself at the recently established polytechnic of Darolfonun. Shortly thereafter, he created a semisecret association modeled on European freemasonry, though not related to it, and engaged in a campaign to persuade the Naser al-Din Shah and the court elite to initiate modern reforms, chiefly based on the Ottoman notion of organization (tanzimat) (Abrahamian 1982, 65–66). Although the shah first received Malkum Khan's proposals for reform favorably, he soon became suspicious of his intentions and exiled him to Turkey. Malkum Khan's ideas for reform would result in his falling in and out of favor with the shah until the last decade of the nineteenth century, when he would lose his ambassadorship to Britain, become a radical critic of the political situation in Iran, and publish his famous and influential newspaper, Qanun (Law), in London.[5]

Malkum Khan's discourse on modernity embodied the duality discussed above. On the one hand, he advocated the wholesale importation of European

4. For a discussion of the centrality of despotism in Iranian history, see Katouzian 1981.
5. For a detailed but hostile account of Malkum Khan's career and life, see Algar 1973.

bureaucracy and its Ottoman model (*tanzimat* or "organization"); on the other, he displayed interest in democratic institutions, at least in rudimentary form, especially in their ontological foundations.[6] He equated progress with the principles of order and organization: "If we want to find the path to progress through our own mental exercises, we will have to wait for three thousand years. The Europeans have discovered the road to progress and the principles of organization, just as they have discovered the principle of the telegraph during the past two or three thousand years, and they have developed certain formulas for these principles" (Malkum Khan 1948a, 13).[7]

Malkum Khan's deep-seated attachment to the principle of organization stems from his ideas about the lack of a strong administrative system in nineteenth-century Iran: "In a nutshell, we do not have an 'executive apparatus' in Iran and as long as we do not set up this principal apparatus, all our words and writings are entirely futile and a source of disgrace." Malkum Khan also seems to have been powerfully impressed by the efficiency of European bureaucracy, especially the state bureaucracy. The Europeans, in his view, had not only developed factories for the production of objects, they had also developed factories for the production of "humans." Just as in the first type of factory, in which from one end enter raw materials and from the other end come the products, there are human factories where into one end are poured ignorant children and from the other come engineers and perfect thinkers. Malkum Khan extends his factory analogy to explain the working of the European legal system and modern banking in terms of "production" of justice and money (Malkum Khan 1948a, 10–11). But the most impressive of this second type of "factory" for Malkum Khan (1948a, 11) was the "state apparatus":

> In Europe, among these human factories, they have one factory which is located at the center of the government and animates all other factories. This great apparatus is called the apparatus of bureaucracy. Anyone who is interested in knowing what miracles human reason is capable of should investigate this apparatus of bureaucracy. The organization, welfare, prosperity, great-

---

6. The concept of *tanzimat* or "organization" first emerged in the Ottoman Empire in the early part of the nineteenth century; reforms initiated there were designated by this term, which is derived from the Arabic word *nazm*, meaning "order."

7. Translations of Persian-language quotations throughout this volume are mine unless otherwise noted.

ness, [indeed,] the entire progress of Europe depends on the proper organization of this apparatus.

Although Malkum Khan spoke often of the urgent need to reform Iran's military in light of its defeat at the hands of Russia in 1813 and 1828, he was quick to point out that such reform could succeed only if the state apparatus were organized (Malkum Khan 1948b, 89, 90). His near-obsessive interest in "organization" (*nazm*), typical of his age and region, stemmed from the reality of the imperialist onslaught:

The government of Iran in facing the encroachment of European hegemony is not any different from the Ottoman government. . . . The point is that the surge in the power of Europe has made the survival of barbarian governments impossible. From now on, all governments of the earth must be organized like European governments or they will be conquered and subjugated by them. (Malkum Khan 1948b, 95)

The precondition for acquiring Western bureaucratic organization was modern science and technology; the misfortune of the previous rulers of Iran was rooted in their ignorance of the new sciences and technologies. Japan had succeeded because its statesmen had been sympathetic to modern science, even though they lacked formal scientific training. Whereas "in Tahmasb Shah's time the organization of affairs rested on 'natural reason,' " Malkum Khan argued, "the contemporary organization of all European governments rests entirely on science" (Adamiyat 1961, 117).

In response to Naser al-Din Shah's intransigent despotism and his inability to counter Western hegemony in the 1880s and 1890s, Malkum Khan's later discourse focused on the role of law.[8] In close agreement with the positivist aspect of his views, as manifested in his emphasis on order and organization, Malkum Khan held an altogether instrumental view of the role of law, seeing it as a means to counter hegemonic forces employed by foreign states against Iran. In an article in his newspaper, *Qanun*, he proposed as a model for the Iran-

8. Malkum Khan's motivations for his critique of Naser al-Din Shah's despotism were not entirely high-minded. He was also vexed with the shah for dismissing him as his ambassador to Britain in the aftermath of the lottery fiasco in December 1889. See Algar 1973.

ian state the Russians' bureaucratic institutionalization of power, which they had achieved to their advantage without limiting the power of the emperor:

> The maximum power imaginable is concentrated in the hands of the Russian emperor. But despite such a dominating power, he is not able to mete out punishment on anyone without the order of the [judicial] bureaucracy. No one has placed any limitations on the emperor's power. The emperor himself owing to his education and enlightened knowledge willingly has made the enactment of laws and observations thereof, the basis of his splendor. The emperor has made himself, more than anyone else, obedient to the law because obeying the law has given him dominance over twenty "lawless" kings. (Malkum Khan 1890, April 20)

Although Malkum Khan's remarks might be interpreted as a ruse to induce the shah to give up some of his power, they also represent a strong argument for establishing a modern bureaucracy in the state apparatus of Iran, and one of the earliest theoretical attempts to replace autocratic with bureaucratic rule there. As we will see in chapter 3, with the advent of the Pahlavi Dynasty, despotism and instrumental-bureaucratic rationality were combined to concentrate state power in the hands of the Pahlavi monarchs. To institutionalize his ideas regarding this conception of law, Malkum Khan proposed the creation of a Majlis Tanzimat (Organizational Assembly). Although he was careful to point out that such an assembly had nothing to do with a parliamentary system or a representative assembly, the court ministers, to discourage the shah from instituting such reforms, attempted to create confusion on that account. Malkum Khan charged the Organizational Assembly with creating laws for the country. Writing in his monograph *Daftar Qanun* (The book of law), he noted that "every injunction that is issued from the legal apparatus [*dastgah qanun*] in accordance with a 'determined agreement' is called law, and it is necessary for this law to be definitely issued by the legal apparatus" (Malkum Khan 1948c, 138). Although the phrase " 'determined agreement' " (*qarar mo'ayan*) stems from the nonrepresentative Majlis Tanzimat, it nevertheless contains the seminal concept of contract and therefore the potentiality of law based on a consensus of citizens. This crucial view is later reflected in a passage from Malkum Khan's letter of May 28, 1903, to Mirza Nasorllah Khan Moshir al-Dowleh:

World history in the course of five thousand years has proved that the "essence" of human reason does not manifest itself except through the interplay of discourse and consensus of opinion. According to an eternal principle, justice, security, progress and prosperity, and the entire benefits of life have never appeared in any part of the world except through the practice of consultation. (Adamiyat 1961, 121)

Such a view is in turn contingent on a conception of basic rights of the individual, a subject Malkum Khan addressed in his 1881 essay *Sirat al-Mustaqim* (The straight path). Asserting that the four basic principles of human rights were security, freedom (*ekhtiyar* or *azadi*), equality, and achieved status, he divided security into the security of the person and that of property. He also elaborated on the concept of freedom by distinguishing such categories as the freedom of the body, speech, pen, thought, business (*kasb*), and association (Adamiyat 1961, 214).

It is important to note that underlying Malkum Khan's conceptualization of freedom is an ontological foundation of human subjectivity: "The nobility of our creation lies in [God's] having created us as subjects [*fa'el mokhtar*] and because of his nobility [he] has made us agents, who through our reason and effort [*ijtihad*] are owners and protectors of our 'rights of humanness' [i.e., human rights]." He goes on to theorize about the "alienation" of this subjectivity and its restoration: "Our great sin and [the cause of] our misfortune is that we have totally lost this nobility and this sacred agency, and for centuries, we have begged others for our rights instead of seeking them in ourselves" (Malkum Khan 1948d, 215).

The word Malkum Khan chose to popularize his concept of subjectivity was *adamiyat*, rooted in the Semitic word *adam*, meaning "human being," and used throughout Islamic culture. According to all world religions and moral philosophies, God had created us as *adam*; as a proof of our being *adam*, God had made every individual human being the inheritor of grand gifts, which collectively might be called the "rights of being *adam*" (Malkum Khan 1948d, 214).[9] As articulated in Malkum Khan's writings, being *adam* had profound implications

---

9. Writing in a mostly religious context, Malkum Khan expressed the concept of subjectivity as "mediated subjectivity." As we will see in chapters 4 and 5, some Islamic approaches to subjectivity have been couched in terms of mediated subjectivity, following Malkum Khan's precedent.

for the concept of justice. The idea of justice in the Middle East was for centuries contingent on the advice that political rulers should exercise restraint in oppressing their subjects. Malkum Khan attempted to reverse the concept of justice by asserting that, to achieve justice, it was incumbent upon the oppressed not to tolerate their oppressors, but to overthrow them (Adamiyat 1961, 213).

While publishing the newspaper *Qanun* in 1890s, Malkum Khan also founded the Jam' Adamiyat (League of Humanity), an organization devoted to the propagation of his views, especially those raising consciousness about the rights of citizens. During his years in exile, Malkum Khan's influence was mostly intellectual; the league was run by his sympathizers in Tehran and other cities.[10] There seems to be little doubt that both Malkum Khan's ideas about *adamiyat* (being human, as he understood the notion of subjectivity) and the League of Humanity were much influenced by Comte's "Religion of Humanity" (Adamiyat 1961, 200). Yet, as further evidence of the duality of Iranian thinkers toward modernity, despite a strong positivist element, the league played a crucial role in promoting the idea of the rights of the individual citizen during the Constitutional Revolution. In a similar vein, although Malkum Khan continually advocated raising consciousness about human rights, his positivist ontology is apparent in the highly mechanical way he proposed to "produce" such conscious humans—by establishing "human-making factories" (*karkhaneh adam sazi*).

Malkum Khan was also concerned with the social universal and with the rights of the public, often invoking familiar Islamic concepts and practices to explain his new ideas. In this way he was able to reach a wide range of Iranians rather than just a small elite.[11] Similarly, even though his conceptualization of the law was encumbered by strong positivist elements, nevertheless, it had universal application. As he put it, "the law, all over the nation of Iran and regarding every individual Iranian subject, is equal" (Malkum Khan 1948a, 26). Another aspect of universality that Malkum Khan addressed was achieved status, which he strongly recommended should be the sole crite-

10. For a detailed account of the League of Humanity and its members, see Fereydun Adamiyat 1961.

11. This issue of Malkum Khan's popularizations is distorted by Hamid Algar to portray Malkum Khan as a hypocrite, using religion merely to advance his own political views and career. See Algar 1973.

rion for recruitment by government services and the military (Malkum Khan 1948b, 75).

In his discourse, Malkum Khan made no attempt to distinguish between the two aspects of modernity I have designated as "positivist" and "universalizable subjectivity"; as time passed, however, he moved closer toward a conception of universalizable subjectivity. His mixture of the two aspects is best captured in a concise formulation of what the law should be: "The law should reflect the emperor's will and guarantee the public interest" (Malkum Khan 1948a, 25). Although this statement represented a step toward limiting the arbitrary will of the shah and achieving popular sovereignty, its ambiguity reflects a similar ambiguity regarding the responsibilities of the shah and popular sovereignty that was later to appear in the Iranian constitution of 1906.

Whereas Malkum Khan focused primarily on the political and legal sphere, epistemology, ontology, and national identity were the chief concerns of Mirza Aqa Khan Kermani, another influential Iranian thinker of the nineteenth century.[12]

Kermani: Epistemology, Ontology, and National Identity

Despite his unsystematic method, Kermani may be considered one of the earliest thinkers in Iran to pay serious attention to philosophical questions and epistemological issues of modernity in the nineteenth century. In his discourse, we can again observe a mixture of positivist and potentially emancipatory types of subjectivity. Although a Persian translation of Descartes's *Discourse on Reason* (the first modern Western philosophical book to appear in Persian) had been published in 1860 (Adamiyat 1978, 73), Kermani was perhaps the first Iranian to ground Iranian thought in modern Western philosophical tenets, and one of the first theorists of modern Iranian nationalism attempting to create a pre-Islamic national identity for Iran.

Abul Hussein Khan, later known as "Mirza Aqa Khan Kermani," was born in 1853 in a small village near the town of Kerman in central Iran. His immediate ancestors on both his mother's and his father's side were distinguished Sufis.

---

12. In his influential treatise *Yek Kalameh* (One word), another thinker and a contemporary of Malkum Khan, Mirza Yusef Khan Mustashar al-Duleh, referred to the law as the key to opening Iran's door to modernity. His arguments closely parallel those of Malkum Khan, albeit with stronger religious overtones. See Mustashar al-Duleh 1985, 55.

His mother's grandfather was a prominent Zoroastrian leader, who would later convert to Islam. Among his other ancestors were famous physicians and judges and long-established aristocrats. One of his heterodox grandfathers had been murdered under a *fatwa* issued by an orthodox mullah (Adamiyat 1978, 14). Kermani's diverse background seems to have had a direct impact on his education and to have deeply influenced his philosophical and political views (see Bayat 1974, 30).

Kermani received a traditional Iranian education including Persian literature, Arabic, Islamic history and "schools of thought," Islamic jurisprudence and Hadith (sayings attributed to the Prophet), mathematics, logic, philosophy, mysticism, and traditional medicine. Among his teachers in philosophy and the sciences (*tabiiyat*) was the renowned Iranian philosopher Haji Sabzevari. Later, Kermani learned French and some English, as well as the pre-Islamic languages of Iran (Adamiyat 1978, 14). When he was about thirty, he had a fierce disagreement with the governor of Kerman and was forced to flee his hometown. He received asylum in Istanbul, where he became familiar with the new ideas and philosophies of the different intellectual and political circles of the Ottoman capital. During this period, he and his close lifetime associate, Sheikh Ahmad Ruhi, married the two daughters of Subh Azal,[13] Kermani's life ended tragically. Extradited to Iran for allegedly plotting the assassination of Naser al-Din Shah, he and Ruhi were put to death in 1896.

Kermani considered philosophy a "sublime and universal science," whose purpose was "to know the truth of objects and beings according to the original and natural order," to eliminate the "chaos [stemming from] the darkness of ignorance," and to achieve "rational order and entrance into the lightness of truth"(Adamiyat 1978, 76).[14] Philosophy was, for him, the primal cause of the "movement of thought" and the "transformation of nations from barbarous primitiveness to the worlds of civilization and urbanity." Indeed, without philosophy, he contended, no real result could be obtained from any other science

---

13. After its bloody repression in the mid-nineteenth century, the Babi movement split in two. One faction was led by Subh Azal, who remained closer to the movement's original doctrines, and the other was led by Azal's half brother, Bahaullah, who founded the Bahai religion.

14. Even though Kermani wrote some twenty books and treatises, few of his works have been published and fewer still remain in print. *Andisheha-ye Mirza Aqa Khan Kermani* (Thoughts of Mirza Aqa Khan Kermani), by Fereydun Adamiyat (1978), seems to be a thorough representation of Kermani's works; I have relied on it for many citations in this section.

(Adamiyat 1978, 76). Fancying himself an archmaterialist, Kermani praised Socrates for "bringing philosophy down from the sky to the earth," but because Socrates posited the subject rather than matter as the center of the enterprise of knowledge, Kermani preferred the Greek "materialist" philosophers such as Pythagoras, Democritus, and Heraclitus (Adamiyat 1978, 77).

Nevertheless, in his own positivist fashion, Kermani acknowledged the centrality of human subjectivity in relation to matter, arguing that, like all beings, this "bipedal animal" followed the laws of matter, but that, because humans intervened in their relations with matter and nature, they deviated from the laws of nature. Indeed, social institutions created by human reason, more often than not, were incompatible with the laws of nature, as humans realized through experience (Adamiyat 1978, 99). Yet Kermani reduced the human body to chemical compounds and considered the workings of the human mind to be a physical function of the central nervous system: "nerves" in the human brain were most of the time in a state of motion, and "thought and reflection appear[ed] as a result of their motion" (Adamiyat 1978, 99).

In accordance with his materialist formulation of subjectivity, Kermani accounted for the perennial nature of despotism in Iran in geographic terms, yet considered individual freedom and freedom of thought as essential (Adamiyat 1978, 173). In his treatise *Inshallah Mashallah* (God being willing), Kermani criticized Iranians for abandoning human volition and resorting to metaphysical explanation for events and the power of providence. Muslims, instead of acting on the world, uttered phrases such as "Inshallah" (God willing). The same fatalistic inaction that had sealed the fate of Byzantine Christians during the siege of Constantinople had defeated Iranians in their confrontations with the Afghan invaders (Adamiyat 1978, 200–202). Indeed, the supreme God had designated a means for achieving every goal and had left the welfare of humankind to the personal efforts of individuals (Adamiyat 1978, 201). In *Rezvan* (Paradise), following the Persian literary tradition of debating a hypothetical opponent, Kermani contrasted human volition and freedom with the idea of providence: "The human essence is always open to progress and unlimited perfection so that the pure God [Haq] has esteemed and privileged it, but its progress or decline is entirely dependent on the will of the self [*nafs*] and his effort" (Adamiyat 1978, 200).

In *Ayeneh Sekandari* (Alexandrian mirror), Kermani also condemned submission to terrestrial powers: "Deterministically, Iranians attribute the adversity or prosperity in the world to the will of the shahs and do not consider themselves as having any role in the changes of the realm. They do not fancy themselves as the origin of any influence in the world." Then, in a footnote, he added that the "reason why the Iranian nation has not progressed in any field is this very false attitude, which derives from the existence of powerlessness or laziness so that Iranians do not consider themselves participants in the rights of the nation" (Kermani 1906, 47).

This view of subjectivity led Kermani to construct a theory of nationalism based on a collectivist interpretation of subjectivity. Using the Arabs and Islam as a foil, he attempted to create a collective nationalist subject: the Iranians, he maintained, had never willingly accepted their Arab and Islamic rulers, who had ruled by bloodshed and oppression. According to this analysis, the politics of oppression was both corrupt and corrupting. It had corrupted the Iranians because a people living under oppression and terror will lose its courage and virtue and succumb to fear, cowardice, deception, hypocrisy, and sycophancy. Thus Arab and Islamic domination of Iran had robbed Iranians of their "ethos of superiority, magnanimity, and nobility" (Adamiyat 1978, 202).

Kermani's portrayal of Arabs is characterized by chauvinist and racist epithets and a pseudo-scientific approach. Describing the Arabs as "ignorant, savage lizard eaters," "bloodthirsty, barefoot camel riders," and "desert-dwelling nomads," he regarded them as the cause of Iran's misery ever since their conquest of Iran in the seventh century (Bayat 1974, 45–47). Thus, in conformity with his positivistic side, he applied nineteenth-century racist phrenology to distinguish the Arabs and Jews as Semites from the Iranians as Aryans by their respective physical features (Bayat 1974, 45–47).

Kermani's solution to this national "alienation" of collective subjectivity at the hands of the Arabs and Islam was a return to the pre-Islamic religion of Iran, Zoroastrianism, and the glories of Iran's pre-Islamic dynasties (Bayat 1974, 48).[15] Yet it is important to note that his reconstruction of ancient Iran as a source of cultural identity was not one-dimensional. Although he praised the state religion of ancient Iran, Zoroastrianism, and the principle of the shah's rights and the people's duty to obey him as one of the pillars of Iran's prosperity, he also paid much attention to Mazdak, the radical prophet of Iran in the late fifth century, for his egalitarian and republican ideas (Bayat 1974, 48).

15. As we will see in chapter 3, after the triumph of positivist modernity in Iran with the advent of the Pahlavi Dynasty, Iranian nationalism drew heavily on the themes of pre-Islamic civilization discussed by Kermani.

Kermani's views on the mode of modernization in Iran were strongly influenced by his positivist epistemology. Very much aware of the positivist school of thought in Europe, he mentioned it by name in his works (Adamiyat 1978, 78). The application of natural science methods and paradigms to social and political discourse, so prevalent in the West at that time, also influenced his writing and thought. Thus he believed not only that the process of thinking stemmed from the physical activity of the central nervous system, but also that both internal perception and external phenomena were determined by mechanical principles: "Geometric equations and arithmetic operations [have become] the guide and the measure of subjective and objective states" (Adamiyat 1978, 100). We can clearly see both positivist and potentially emancipatory elements in Kermani's dynamic ontology of movement, which stood in sharp contrast to the static view of traditional ontology. Originally, human material existence had been unified with that of plants and animals, he posited, but they were separate now. The essence of animal and human existence lay in perception and in movement, which, in his view, was both mechanical and electrical (Adamiyat 1978, 89). Kermani's dynamic ontology of movement would lead him to a dynamic perception of human existence. Drawing on the famous seventeenth-century Iranian philosopher Mulla Sadra, Kermani presented a view of change in terms of "transformation of essence" (*harekat jawhariyyah*) (Adamiyat 1978, 96).[16] But, at the same time, he subjected his dynamic ontology to positivist determinism and social Darwinism (Adamiyat 1978, 96–97). His resultant positivist ontology overemphasizes a "developmentalist" approach to modernization and reduces human subjectivity to Faustian proportions. For example, he considered a society civilized only if "it [could] provide its necessities for life and the means for its livelihood, more or less. Ultimately, the more perfect a civilization, the more developed its means of livelihood would be" (Adamiyat 1978, 106). He took a futuristic and Faustian view of human intervention in nature as human agency, according to which the "ignorant lowly primitive" human had now reached a stage where

16. According to "transformation of essence" (*harekat jawhariyyah*), a concept put forward by the renowned Iranian philosopher Sadr al-Muta'llihin Shirazi (also known also as "Mulla Sadra"; d. 1640), existence is perceived in terms of transformation and change. The concept has influenced religious and social movements such as Shaykhism and Babism, and even now informs the discourse of Abdolkarim Sorush. See Sorush 2000, 11; for an overview of Mulla Sadra's philosophy, see Rahman 1975 and Morris 1981.

he ha[d] made visible the stars . . . created artificial moonlight and inex-
haustible rays [of light,] . . . made ice from fire and from ice [made] electricity, . . .and soon [would] have the audacity to intervene in the planets and
contrive suns and stars from electricity and preserve planets from being destroyed . . . start consorting and fraternizing with their inhabitants . . .
achieve an eternal life . . . and sit on the throne of happiness. (Adamiyat
1978, 92)

Alongside Kermani's strong positivist streak, his discourse also reveals a
well-developed critical streak. Focusing on the state, religion, and philosophy
(*hekmat*), he argued that what was central to the state was force and intimidation
(*tarsandan*). Religion, on the other hand, was primarily concerned with dogma
(*bavarandan*) and belief. Only philosophy, of these three, was concerned with
understanding (*fahmandan*) through reasoning (*estedlal*) or better argument
(Adamiyat 1978, 111–12). Accordingly, he took an independent and critical
stance toward categories of knowledge: "I am proud that after hearing scattered
discourses and consorting with different peoples and reading many books and
works of many persons, without interrogation and close examination, I did not
merely imitate [them, but] walked with my own feet and observed with my own
eyes" (Adamiyat 1978, 80).

Paying homage to the Mu'tazalites, the early critical Islamic theologians,
for their application of the principle of doubt to every belief and for seeking
reason and "incisive argumentation" (Adamiyat 1978, 81), Kermani attempted
to forge a critical conception of positive law.[17] If humans were capable of managing a thousand affairs of their daily life, due to their independent consciousness, and could invent a thousand types of sciences, techniques, and industries,
they surely "would not be helpless [in creating] laws and practical ethics"
(Adamiyat 1978, 120). Because he thought the people must be "participants in
the rights of the nation," Kermani believed lawmaking should be universalized.
In his famous treatise *Haftadu Du Mellat* (Seventy-two peoples), he criticized all
religions and sects known to him for their particularity and their marginalization of the nonfaithful and the heterodox; he criticized and condemned societies based on caste systems. Significantly, he concluded his treatise by

---

17. A group of ninth-century speculative theologians, the Mu'tazalites believed in a contingent conception of human rationality and free will as well as in humans' responsibility for their
actions, while maintaining a notion of God's justice.

reflecting on the comments of an Indian pariah praising the universality of the modern legal system as practiced in Britain (Kermani 1983, 118–21).[18]

The duality in Kermani's quite complicated discourse is captured in his praise of human volition, which he saw embodied in Napoleon, whose despotism he pointedly ignored (Adamiyat 1978, 294–95). Even though most of Kermani's works were not published during his lifetime, his influence on the intellectual discourse and consequent political events in Iran was substantial.

Whereas Kermani addressed ontological and epistemological issues as well as the question of national identity, our next thinker, Akhundzadeh, focused on the domain of culture.

Akhundzadeh: Culture and Cultural Change

In many respects, the work and preoccupations of Akhundzadeh closely parallel those of Kermani, although, perhaps because of their different cultural milieus, the two thinkers emphasized different themes. Just like Kermani, Akhundzadeh wrote from abroad, from the Caucasus, which had been annexed by Russia in the treaty of 1828, when he was still an adolescent. As a result of the subsequent uprising and its suppression, the Caucasus became a fertile intellectual seedbed, where Russian exiles actively pursued revolutionary and cultural discourses.

Mirza Fathali Akhundzadeh (1812–1878) was born in the village of Nukheh near the town of Shaki in the southern Caucasus. When he was still a child, Akhundzadeh's mother separated from his father, and supervision of his education fell to his mother's uncle, a man of letters. At the age of 19, Akhundzadeh began to study logic, theology, and Islamic jurisprudence (*fiqh*) with a mullah of heterodox leanings, who dissuaded him from pursuing a career as a cleric (Adamiyat 1970, 143). After attending a Russian school for one year in 1833, he worked as a translator in Tbilisi, where he frequented diverse and avant-garde intellectual circles and entered into the rich cultural milieu of that city. He became familiar with some of the most prominent contemporary Russian authors, such as Nikolai Gogol and Aleksandr Pushkin (Adamiyat 1979, 19); he was also exposed, through Russian translations, to the French Enlighten-

---

18. Kermani also had many harsh words for Western colonization and exploitation of the East. Indeed, one can sense the glimmerings of discontent toward modernity in his response to Western colonization. See Adamiyat 1978, 288–89.

ment (Sanjabi 1995, 39). Akhundzadeh's intellectual career may be divided into three relatively distinct phases. In the first, he wrote plays and a novel, all promoting a spirit of social critique; in the second, he directed his attention to the question of alphabet reform as a means of effecting dramatic cultural change through mass education; and in the third, disappointed by the idea of alphabet reform, he turned his efforts to a campaign for religious reform as a means of effecting cultural change. It was during this phase that he wrote *The Letters of Kamalodowleh*, which he tried unsuccessfully to publish until his death.[19]

In his first phase, Akhundzadeh thought that the time had passed for the classical Persian literary style, represented in the famous *Gulestan* by Sa'di and the *Zinat al-Majales* (Ornament of assemblies), and that now the most effective vehicle for cultural change would be drama and the novel, which he considered to be part of drama (Adamiyat 1970, 54). Akhundzadeh also advocated the use of satire as a means of critical social analysis in preference to the traditional style; as he would later write:

> *The Letters of Kamalodowleh* is a critique [*kritika*] and not preachment and exhortation. A truth written in the style of preachment, exhortation, and [couched in] patronizing and paternalistic [terms] would never have any effect on human nature, which is used to malefaction. Human nature always loathes reading and hearing preachings and sermons but is eager to read a critique. (Akhundzadeh 1978, 206)

Akhundzadeh's new approach to literature reveals two important aspects of his thinking. First, he was aware of the enormous potential of literature for cultural change. Second and more important, however, he realized that the old style of exhortation and sermonizing was authoritarian and antidemocratic and that satire was a more democratic means of achieving his cultural goals.

This emphasis on culture, it seems, derived from a turning point in the appropriation of modernity by Iranian intellectuals of the late nineteenth century. Akhundzadeh came to believe that the failure of Islamic nations in their efforts to modernize was due to their privileging of technical and practical elements of

19. *Maktubat Kamalodowleh* (The letters of Kamalodowleh) has only been published outside Iran, under the title of *Maktubat* (Letters) by Iranian expatriates after the Islamic Revolution. For a full account of Akhundzadeh's life and intellectual development, see Adamiyat 1970 and Akhundzadeh 1972.

European progress over theoretical aspects of progress in the process of *tanzimat* (Akhundzadeh 1978, 289). He argued that "people must be prepared for the acceptance of European thoughts [which must occur] prior to trade with Europe and [accepting] its products" (Adamiyat 1970, 165).

To achieve such "preparation" and cultural transformation, Akhundzadeh focused on two closely related issues. Reasoning that the subtle complexity of the Arabic-Persian script, which stemmed from its use of connected letters, had hampered the spread of literacy among Islamic peoples, he proposed first the modification of the Arabic-Persian writing system and later the adoption of a modified form of Latin script.[20] He also raised the related issue of universal education as the most important means of modernizing Islamic countries. Keenly aware of the importance of the universality of modern education, Akhundzadeh roundly criticized those who would confine literacy to urbanites, depriving people who lived in the countryside. Just as in Prussia and America, he proclaimed, all men and women should receive education so that the public could benefit (Adamiyat 1970, 81). Alongside his emancipatory ideas on education, however, Akhundzadeh introduced the vitiating element of "force" or compulsion, which would be adopted by the Iranian educational system. The compulsory education he proposed was inspired by the decrees of renowned reformers such as Peter the Great and Frederick the Great and did not flow from the consensual will of the people:

> According to the law of Frederick the Great, the king, who is the defender of the country and protector of the nation, has the same authority over any child born to any of his subjects, as the father has over the child. Therefore if the king forces this child to learn reading and writing for [the child's] own good from age nine to age fifteen, this type of force cannot be called oppression, but indicates affection and love, which, as the saying has it, is called "coercive benevolence" [*towfiq ejbari*]. (Akhundzadeh 1978, 158)

One of the central concepts developed by Akhundzadeh was that of critique (*kritika*), for which he considered freedom of thought the sine qua non. He believed that, so long as human societies did not offer "freedom of thought to their individual members and forced them to be content with what their

---

20. For a full discussion of Akhundzadeh's proposals on reforming the Persian-Arabic alphabet and script, see Akhundzadeh 1978.

forefathers and religious founders [had] established . . . without using their reason in the affairs of the community . . . these individuals would resemble the horses in a mill, going around in a predetermined circle every day." With freedom of thought, however, eventually and gradually, "as a result of the interplay of discourses and of different ideas, truth would come into focus" (Adamiyat 1970, 142).

Akhundzadeh's notion of freedom is based on a profound and radical notion of subjectivity, which he, more than any other Iranian thinker then or since, articulated in terms of a confrontation between human subject and monotheistic deity. He questioned what he viewed as the master-slave relationship in monotheism as antithetical to any notion of justice and equality; he considered the concepts of heaven and hell oppressive and wrathful and therefore unbefitting human nature (Akhundzadeh 1985, 183). He also accused the creator of "never acknowledging the power of our understanding because we are his slaves" (Akhundzadeh 1985, 88). The authoritarianism of despots, whether celestial or terrestrial, had resulted in an abject and sycophantic attitude among the people of the East toward authority (Akhundzadeh 1985, 52–53).

Akhundzadeh then turned his critique back to humans by characterizing the God of monotheism as a projection of our own passions and abominations, desires and quests for status and prestige, and our own vengefulness (Akhundzadeh 1985, 108). For these reasons, he advocated human reason over revelation, thus reversing, in his estimation, the process by which the guardians of religion had retarded and "imprisoned" reason for thousands of years (Akhundzadeh 1985, 94). What Akhundzadeh proposed as the content of this human reason was essentially a positivist view of modern science. Reflecting this view, he lamented that the God of Islam, instead of informing Muslims about America, steam, and electrical power, told them about Bilqis, the City of Sheba, and the story of Solomon and the Hoopoe (Hudhud) (Akhundzadeh 1985, 88). He called upon Muslims to transform their worldview from one based on religious-metaphysical beliefs to one based on the natural sciences. Addressing his imaginary correspondent, Prince Jalal Al-Duleh, Akhundzadeh wrote:

> So long as you and your coreligionists are not informed of the science of nature and astronomy, and so long as your knowledge of supernatural events and miracles among you is not [based on] scientific principles, you and they will always believe in supernatural events, miracles, magic, talismans, fairies, jin-

nis, saints, peris, and such delusions and will remain ignorant forever. (Akhundzadeh 1985, 94)

Most important, Akhundzadeh believed that the natural sciences should be our guide and our criteria for questions pertaining to the practical-ethical sphere. He argued that every religion consisted of beliefs, devotions, and practical-ethical matters. The last were the main purpose of all religions and the first two were secondary (Akhundzadeh 1985, 220–21). Until now, we had needed the first two to attain the third, but if we found a means to achieve our practical-ethical goals without subservience and enslavement, then we did not need the beliefs and devotions; needless to say, this means was provided by the modern European sciences, which had obviated the need for both beliefs and devotions (Akhundzadeh 1985, 222). In this way, Akhundzadeh delivered practical-ethical concerns, which he had just liberated from religion, into to the clutches of another type of determinism, science.

To illustrate his ideas, Akhundzadeh drew on a brief period of Isma'ili history.[21] He told the story of Hasan Ibn Mohammad (known as "Ala Zekratol-salam"), who, as the leader of the Isma'ili heterodox sect in the late twelfth century, declared the Sharia (divine law) annulled, decreed the unveiling of women, and banned polygamy (Akhundzadeh 1985, 134–37). These measures constituted, for Akhundzadeh (1985, 32), the essential foundation of what he called "Islamic Protestantism," by which he meant a religion in which "God's rights [huququllah] and the worshipper's duties [takalif ibadullah] are annulled, and only human rights remain."

At the core of Akhundzadeh's thought is his pantheistic ontology. First, he rejected the notion of a transcendental creator and creation fixed in a master-slave relationship: "The universe is but one complete force, one complete being." Instead, he advanced the pantheistic notion that all parts of the being, whether emanating or emanated, particular or universal, were equal: "The 'origin' and the 'end' are the same; neither the 'origin' nor the 'end' has priority over the other" (Akhundzadeh 1985, 95–96). Therefore, all "particles" of this unified "being" were equal and none had any authority over the other. No miracles willed by any of these particles could be performed because the relations between these particles of being were governed by an eternal and omnipotent

21. A sect within the "extreme" Shiites founded in late eighth century, the Isma'ilis were famous for their heterodox views and practices. See, for example, Daftari 1992, 1995; Lewis 1985.

law, which determined all the events in this world (Akhundzadeh 1985, 96–97). Thus, too, because even emanation was not by free will and because any notion of free will would negate the possibility of equality between the universal being and the particular, Akhundzadeh (1985, 102–3) denied the possibility of free will: "In reality, the universal and the particular are but one being, which is manifested 'without willing' [*bela ekhtiyar*] in infinite multiplicity and in different forms only in accordance to the said principle and under its own laws and conditions." In a footnote, he further explained that necessity (*jabr*) was the lack of will on the part of the universal (*vojud koll*) in its emanation, and those who interpreted necessity in any other way had not understood (Akhundzadeh 1985, 103).

Hegel had used the concept of pantheism to arrive at subjectivity and freedom. Akhundzadeh used the same idea to arrive at the necessity and determinism of the laws and principles of which the scientific laws constituted the concrete form. It is therefore no accident that Akhundzadeh, in discussing these rather abstract issues, also alluded to the physical laws governing events in the universe. For example, he considered the sun and the moon as "particles" of the universe; as such, they were subject to the eternal law that determined the state of all other "particles" (Akhundzadeh 1985, 97)

This duality at the ontological core of Akhundzadeh's discourse manifested itself in altogether concrete forms. Perhaps the most sinister manifestation of Akhundzadeh's positivism was what might be called "enlightenment from above," an approach to modernity that called for an enlightened despot such as a Peter the Great or Frederick the Great to put the house of Iran in order and to bring it modernity. As Iranian history would later clearly reveal, this role was fulfilled by the Pahlavi monarchs but at the expense of the emancipatory aspects of modernity. Perhaps the most ironic unintended consequence of Akhundzadeh's discourse was that, in attempting to create a human subjectivity through his radical views on Islam, he alienated his potential audiences, the majority of whom were devout Muslims. He seems to have been aware of such a consequence, but refused to tone down his rhetoric because, as he put it, his work would then be as ineffective as that of Rumi, Shabestari, Jami, and other Sufi thinkers before him (Akhundzadeh 1978, 184). In a similar vein, because they were not primarily based on a notion of citizenship rights, defining Iranian nationality in contradistinction to the alterity of the Arabs, Akhundzadeh's views on Iranian nationalism portended the eclipse of freedom and democracy.

Thus, in Akhundzadeh, we again encounter the duality of potentially emancipatory ideas (constitutional government, liberal universal education, and women's rights) side by side with their negation (practical-ethical positivism, racist nationalism, and enlightenment "from above" by a Great Man).

Talebuf: A Discourse of Conflict and Reconciliation

The themes bearing on universalizable subjectivity are more developed in the thought of Talebuf than in that of the other Iranian intellectuals discussed thus far, although, as we will see, Talebuf also exhibits a strong positivist tendency now and then. This tendency is also accompanied by another—to acknowledge and attempt to resolve the contradictions emerging in Iran's early encounter with modernity. Writing in the late nineteenth and early twentieth centuries, he was perhaps more exposed to these contradictions and therefore more aware of their complexities than earlier thinkers had been.

Abd al-Rahim Talebuf (1832–1910) was born into a middle-class family of artisans in Tabriz; his father and grandfather were both carpenters (Adamiyat 1984, 1). His background and later success in business in the Caucasus may also have helped shape his more complicated and less dogmatic views on modernity in Iran. At the age of 16, he left Iran for Tbilisi and studied in modern schools of the Caucasus, later settling in Tamar Khan Shureh in Dagestan. He would write a total of eleven books, all of them after the age of 55 (Afshar 1978, 19–20; Adamiyat 1984, 3). Talebuf's writing had a direct impact on the Constitutional Revolution. Although elected to the first Majlis (Parliament) in 1906 as a deputy from his birthplace of Tabriz, for reasons that are not entirely clear, he did not attend.

Central to Talebuf's discourse, as to Akhundzadeh's, is the notion of critique (*kritika*). He began his famous three-volume work *Ketab Ahmad* (The book of Ahmad) by stating that our humanity started the moment we started to question and seek the nature of things (Talebuf, 1893, 2).[22] He also attributed a nation's openness to progress to the practice of critique "in the practical-discursive sphere of natural interests" (Talebuf 1968, 100). Closely related to

---

22. Talebuf's *Ketab Ahmad ya Safineh Talebi* (The book of Ahmad) was published as two volumes in 1893 and 1894 in Istanbul. Both volumes discuss science and technology as they were known to him in easily understood language and in a style strongly reminiscent of Rousseau's *Emile*. In 1906, Talebuf added a third volume, with the subtitle *Masael al-Hayat* (The questions of life), in which he paid greater attention to moral-practical and philosophical issues.

Talebuf's notion of critique is his concept of freedom, which he considered an essential category in human affairs and an end in itself: "Freedom [*azadi*], unlike our other discourses or practices, is not a 'means' to produce an end, as for example walking is to travel. . . . [E]verything we see is a means to an end except freedom [which exists] only for freedom . . . hence we call it an abstract term" (Talebuf 1906, 95–96). This "abstract term" found its concrete expression in right, which was "born with the human" and remained with the human "from the day of birth to the day of death" (Talebuf 1906, 73). At this point, Talebuf was faced with the question of grounding his concept of right. For this purpose, he proposed the Persian term *mani*, which seems to be very close to the concept of subjectivity.[23] Derived from the Persian word *man*, meaning "I," *mani* may be translated as "ipseism" or "egoism." Although traditionally *mani* and its Arabic equivalent, *ananiyat*, have had the same negative connotation that "egoism" has in English, Talebuf used the concept of *mani* in a positive sense, one more aptly translated as "selfhood": "In order to produce right, we have one source and one origin . . . which is constituted of my selfhood [*mani*], your selfhood, and his or her selfhood. The origin [lies] in our language by means of which we express the right" (Talebuf 1906, 74).

Talebuf's discussion of right and freedom was not confined to the individual level: he extrapolated from the individual to the universal of collectivity. The cornerstone of his extrapolation lies in what he called the "collision" of the right of the self with the right of the other (Talebuf 1906, 73–74). Indeed, only through the collision of these rights did we arrive at universal rights, without which mutual happiness was not possible (Talebuf 1906, 74–75). After right was transmitted from particular to universal, it created a selfhood (*mani*) for the collectivity. This view of individual and collective subjectivity led Talebuf to define the concept of law (*qanun*), which in Iran had served as little more than the bureaucratic codification of despotism, in terms of the rights of both the individual and the collectivity: "Law [*qanun*] means the systematic articulation of

23. In *Izahat Dar Khususe Azadi* (Explanations regarding freedom), Talebuf grounded his conceptualization of freedom in terms of a natural right: "Whether in Arabic *huriyat*, in Persian *azadi*, or in Turkish *uzdenlek*, [freedom] may be defined as natural freedom [by] which all men by nature and birth are free in all acts and words and except for their commander, that is their will, there are no impediments in their deeds and words. God has not created any force external to man to impede him; and no one may dispose of our freedom, let alone give it or take it away from us" (Afshar 1978, 88).

specific principles of civil and political rights and restrictions pertaining to the individual and the collectivity, through which every person would be secure in property and life and equitably responsible for wrong acts" (Talebuf 1968, 94). Talebuf was careful to distinguish between law (*qanun*) as organized despotism (*montazam*), for example, in tsarist Russia, and law as derived from popular sovereignty (Adamiyat 1984, 39).

Talebuf took an enlightened approach to the question of nationhood and nationalism, one conducive to universal emancipation and unmarred by chauvinism. Defining freedom as "common spiritual capital . . . that individual Iranians have gradually accumulated and deposited in a vault called the nation" (Afshar 1978, 89), Talebuf extended his concept of nation to include not only intranational but also international rights. The same selfhood (*mani*) that existed in an intranational collectivity should also apply to the international community (Talebuf 1906, 75–76). To that end, he suggested creating a league of nations to resolve international disputes and conflicts (Talebuf 1893, 144). Later, in *Masael al-Hayat* (The questions of life), Talebuf refined his suggestion: such a league was to be a socialistic federation of nations where all the inhabitants of the earth would be treated as the members of one family (Talebuf 1906, 91).

Talebuf's theorizing on the concept of freedom was not confined to mere abstractions. He divided freedom into three principal spheres: life, opinion, and speech. From these, he derived secondary freedoms, such as freedom of election, freedom of press, and freedom of assembly, which in turn gave rise to tertiary freedoms (Talebuf 1906, 97). Interestingly, he used the metaphor of monetary assets to describe the "possession" of opinions: every person had a legitimate right to protect opinions and should not be forced to "exchange" them unequally or to give them away (Talebuf 1906, 97–98).

Among the conflicts engendered by the process of modernity, the conflict between the individual and collectivity constituted for Talebuf a case in point. When the individual's right "collided" with that of society, even though the individual's right was essential and immune from annulments, it could be suspended: "From the combination of two rights a third right may be created" (Talebuf 1906, 79). He gave the example of eminent domain as a legitimate case where, coming into conflict with that of the collectivity, the right of the individual might be suspended (Talebuf 1906, 77). However, Talebuf attempted to preserve both rights by differentiating their extents rather than their principles, which he held to be "symmetrical"; he then proposed a legal system based on popular sovereignty and majority vote to strike a balance between the extents of these two rights (Talebuf 1906, 80, 84).

Talebuf also attempted to reconcile the notion of popular sovereignty and its corollary, positive law, on the one hand, and divine law, on the other. Although he never explicitly addressed the issue in terms of a conflict, his new and extensive use of interpretation of religious beliefs represented an implicit acknowledgment of the conflict between the two spheres and hence also of an attempt to reconcile them. Although he thought of positive law as deriving from popular sovereignty, he described the Sharia (divine law) as the "foundation" of law in Iran, which he saw as the consummation and enforcement of divine law (Talebuf 1906, 84). Earlier, in the second volume of *The Book of Ahmad*, Talebuf had affirmed that "if we enact laws for ourselves, its basis would be the pure Sharia and the sacred explicit text [*nusus*] of the Quran" (Talebuf 1894, 11). What made reconciliation between the two spheres possible was Talebuf's equation of the people's will with the will of God: "The law that is enacted for the reform of public character by the votes of the majority will have the effect of celestial words," he wrote in *The Questions of Life*, "because the voice of the people is the voice of God" (Talebuf 1906, 137).

At the core of Talebuf's thinking on conflict lies a conflictual ontology, which itself reflects the conflict between orthodox monotheism and heterodox pantheism in Islam. In *Masalik al-Muhsinin* (The paths of the blessed), Talebuf (1968, 131–32) recounts the genesis of the universe in terms of creation and emanation at the same time, using the first person singular as the voice of the creator:

> In the center of my eternal and Protected Divinity, I created a nebulous moving light, which, because of extreme heat under my command, at times separated a part of itself and projected it into space, the same part then became mobile also and assumed a spherical shape until the space was filled with moving spheres. . . . From the movement of the spirit of spirits, I created light and heat and assigned them to educate the beings. . . . I assigned the earth, one of the small planets of the visible sun, as the habitat of man.

In contrast to the "creationist" tone of this passage, Talebuf (1968, 130) spoke of the universe and beings in terms of pantheistic emanations a page earlier: "Particles of beings testify to the Unity of God [*vahdat allah*] because beings are constituted of particles and every particle according to its capacity is both the one and carrier of unity."

As we have seen, theorists whose ontology was grounded in a pantheistic metaphysics tended to arrive at a theory of human subjectivity and its universalizability. Here, by presenting an ontology that is at once pantheistic and monotheistic, it would seem that Talebuf is attempting to bridge the gap between the two approaches and thus to resolve the conflict between positive law grounded in popular sovereignty and divine law. Faced with the problem of where to place human subjectivity vis-à-vis divine subjectivity, Talebuf invokes a theme from the Quran, according to which the human is given the mantle of God's vicegerent on earth as a limited subject (Talebuf 1968, 144–45).[24]

In an imaginary debate with an orthodox mullah in *The Paths of the Blessed*, Talebuf discusses the conflict between positive law and divine law quite concretely. When the mullah raises the question of the redundancy of positive law, given the elaborate injunctions of the divine law, Talebuf retorts that "these injunctions were the very best and the most proper of all laws of civilizations and religions of the world a thousand years ago. But they have no [application] to a hundred years ago, let alone to our age" (Talebuf 1968, 94). He then advises the mullah to "set aside those injunctions of the Quran that were enacted for a specific time and are inapplicable now and instead enact new and applicable laws" (Talebuf 1968, 95). From his view that all the universe, except the Necessary Being and its word, the Quran, was "incidental" (*hadeth*) and therefore subject to change, he arrived at the incongruent conclusion that, even though the Quran itself was not subject to change, those of its injunctions belonging to the "incidental" sphere nevertheless were.

Talebuf was one of the first theorists to become aware of the potential conflict between modernity and national identity. He chastised the "Westernized" (*mofarang*) Iranians, who apishly imitated Western dress and languages (Talebuf 1894, 22–23). In a famous passage from *The Paths of the Blessed*, he admonished Iranians to preserve their Iranian identity and not to be deceived by the glitter of the West. The purpose of learning was

24. As we will see in chapter 4, ever since Talebuf, the view of humans as God's vicegerents has been adopted by religious theorists facing the same dilemma on subjectivity. See the Quran 2:30 and also 17:70.

to become familiar with the management of the [affairs of] the country; to realize the [meaning of] love for the country; to worship the shah; to respect
your tradition and not accept anything from any country except science, industry, and beneficial information; do not imitate; be always and everywhere
an Iranian and realize that the East is different from the West—the sun rises in
one and sets in the other. This simple reason is enough to distinguish us from
them. (Talebuf 1968, 194)

Talebuf seems to have been also quite aware of the discontent of modernity.
He warned about the false utopia promised by "civilisation" (he used the French
word), whose "diabolic miasma" one could smell and whose monstrous lack of
consciousness and empathy one could see through as soon as one became familiar with its agents. He also saw the manifestation of the selfishness of modernity in the mass poverty, homelessness, and prostitution to be found in
European cities of his time (Talebuf 1958, 93). Yet, despite these criticisms,
Talebuf recognized that he could not reject modernity. In the third volume of
The Book of Ahmad, his fictitious son, Ahmad, who has grown up well versed in
modern science and philosophy, debates with another fictitious character, Agha
Abdulhah, who argues against the process of modernizing in Iran, observing
that the goal of the West is to conquer the markets and territories of other parts
of the world through military might, at the cost of turmoil, conflict, and car-
nage unprecedented in human history (Talebuf 1906, 50–55). Ahmad responds
by saying that the struggle among humans is "natural": our substance consists of
two conflicting urges—the urge to protect our own interests and the urge to reject the other's (Talebuf 1906, 56–57). Near the end of the debate, Ahmad con-
cludes that "preservation of the self" and "the right of existence" are naturally
given; to make his point, he mentions the rivalry between Cain and Abel. The
wars of the nineteenth century were an outcome of the struggle to preserve
one's own interests, a struggle that would eventually result in the creation of nations with a sense of rights in the international arena (Talebuf 1906, 64–68).
Thus, by analyzing the struggle for domination inherent in subjectivity, Talebuf
arrives at the creation of rights, which he then extrapolates to nations and the
gradual emergence of international rights.

Talebuf's considerable theoretical sophistication regarding the concept of
rights led him to recognize how limited citizenship was when confined to the
legal and political spheres. For this reason, he advanced the idea (for the first

time, it would seem, in modern Iranian history) that there could be no citizenry unless the land were distributed among the peasantry. This recognition represents the beginning of Iranians' felt need to expand and deepen the concept of universalizable subjectivity as citizenship.

Talebuf's discourse was enriched by his dialectical approach to the paradoxes he seems happy to have lived with. Thus he strongly believed in modern science yet did not dismiss the possibility that an Indian yogi might "violate" principles of physics (see Talebuf 1968, 228–29). In a similar vein, he considered freedom and necessity, human volition and destiny (taqdir) to belong to the same mixed bag of life (Talebuf 1968, 65, 150).

Although the most intricate discourse thus far—and the most conducive to universalizable subjectivity—Talebuf's is not completely free of elements of positivist subjectivity. Indeed, at times his views of the law seem very much in tune with those of the positivists, who considered the law as a mere codification of arbitrary rules (Talebuf 1894, 80–81). At times, he is also a strong proponent of "enlightenment from above," as when he elaborated on the Japanese model of "modernity" to be implemented in Iran.[25] Thus his thinking was subject to the duality discussed at the beginning of this chapter, although to a lesser degree than that of the other theorists discussed thus far.

Talebuf was among the first to raise the question of subjectivity and the struggle against imperialism, just as the Eastern nations were becoming aware of their subjugated status and the need to close ranks to fight against domination and to gain their rights (Talebuf 1906, 89–90). But, as we will see in the next section, this important theme was most elaborately developed by Jamal al-Din Afghani as the champion of the anti-imperialist struggle.

Afghani: Anti-imperialism and Subjectivity

Seyyed Jamal al-Din Assadabadi, known as "Afghani," was a major political thinker and activist whose personal legend and discourse have had a lasting influence on the nativist anti-imperialist struggle, not only in Iran, but in countries and communities all across the Islamic world. As we have seen, a large part of the discourse on and practice of modern subjectivity in Iran was a reaction to

25. Among all the written constitutions available, Talebuf chose to translate and append to the end of his book the late-nineteenth-century Japanese constitution, according to which the emperor was assigned the role of enlightened despot. See Talebuf 1906, 136–51.

Western imperialism. This reactive subjectivity was in turn strongly represented by the discourse on positivist sciences, militarism, rationalized order, bureaucracy, and chauvinist nationalism. All these elements of reactive subjectivity had their origins in the West itself. Afghani's discourse took the reactive as well as the critical and emancipatory elements of Western subjectivity and recast them in an Islamic mold, as the most effective means of fighting imperialism. In the course of such a remolding, Afghani's discourse would succumb to a series of contradictions, with crucial consequences for the emancipatory dimension of subjectivity.

Seyyed Jamal al-Din Assadabadi (Afghani) was born in 1838, most likely in the village of Assadabad near the city of Hamedan in western Iran (Keddie 1972, 10–11).[26] His father, though a farmer, seems to have been a learned man, who taught his son at home. When Afghani was about ten, his father took him to the town of Qazvin and then to Tehran to study. Later, he studied in the Shiite cities of Iraq, although not under Murtaza Ansari, the leading Shiite Mojtahed there, as Afghani would later claim (Keddie 1972, 14–17). It was during this period that he was thoroughly instructed in the traditional Islamic sciences; he was also taught Islamic philosophy and Sufism, two subjects considered by many to be on the verge of heresy. During the same period, he seems to have attracted the hostility of some of the ulema, perhaps partly because of his unorthodox views and behaviors, such as eating during the fasting month of Ramadan (Keddie 1972, 16–17). At about the age of 18, Afghani journeyed to India, where he developed his profound anti-imperialist sentiments as a result of firsthand observation of British colonialism in that country (Keddie 1968, 11–12). It was here that he also became familiar with Western thought and modern science and, according to one contemporary account, underwent a thorough conversion to atheism; he would remain an atheist, albeit privately, for most of the rest of his life (Keddie 1968, 12–13).

After a trip to Mecca in the mid-1860s, he went to Afghanistan to serve the emir of Afghanistan as an advisor, a position he secured by counseling the emir to ally himself with the Russians to fight against British interests. Soon after the defeat of the emir by his half brother, Afghani was expelled from Afghanistan and moved to Istanbul, where he came in contact with the mostly secularist intellectuals of the Tanzimat period and, in 1870, was appointed to the council of

---

26. Seyyed Jamal al-Din's birthplace has been a subject of disagreement, partly because he wished to be considered a Sunni Afghan, hence his common name, "Afghani."

education (Keddie 1968, 15–16). Later that year, accused of heresy for a public lecture, he was exiled to Cairo, where he stayed until 1879, when he was once again expelled. It is during this period that he attempted to create an anti-imperialist ideology that would appeal to the Muslim elite and masses alike. Although he became more cautious in addressing the faithful directly in heterodox terms (Keddie 1972, 19), for his elite audience, he reintroduced classical Islamic philosophy, which the Sunni world had abandoned as heretical. He revived this philosophy, with its deep nativist roots, to address the scientific and political-practical spheres without having to borrow from the imperialist West.

After his expulsion from Egypt, he went to the Muslim-ruled principality of Haidarabad in India, where he befriended some of the followers of Ahmad Khan, who advocated European-style modernization for India and Muslims. Afghani soon turned against Ahmad Khan, however, and wrote a treatise refuting the principles of his teachings. In 1882, Afghani left Haidarabad for London; from there, he went to Paris, where he collaborated with Arab intellectuals in their pan-Islamic and anti-British efforts by writing articles for Arabic journals. During this period, he criticized Ernest Renan for essentializing the backwardness of Muslims, but at the same time, Afghani expressed his own heterodox and critical views on religion in general and orthodox Islam in particular.[27] When his two-year-long attempts to negotiate with the British on the question of Egypt and the uprising of the Mahdi in Sudan met with no success, Afghani went to Tehran in 1885. Alarmed by Afghani's anti-British ideas, Naser al-Din Shah asked him to leave Iran in 1887. After two years in Moscow, Afghani returned to Iran, where his instigations against the government and the British resulted in his humiliating expulsion, then exile in London. There he joined Mirza Malkum Khan in his campaign against Naser al-Din Shah's autocratic rule (Keddie 1968, 28–29). At the invitation of Sultan Abulhamid II, Afghani went to Istanbul again in 1892; the sultan enlisted him in a propaganda campaign appealing to the Shiite ulema to support the Sultan's pan-Islamic aspirations. After a few years, however, relations between the Sultan and Afghani soured, and Afghani came under the Sultan's suspicion. In the last years of his life, Afghani was stripped of his political power and influence by the sultan,

---

27. Ernest Renan (1823–1892) was a French philosopher of religion in the tradition of the French rationalist Enlightenment with whom Afghani engaged in an exchange over the nature of Islam. See Keddie 1968.

who nevertheless prevented him from leaving Ottoman territory. He died of jaw cancer in 1897.

Underlying Afghani's discourse is a strong assumption that the modern world requires that human agency be expressed in "activism, the freer use of human reason and political and military strength" (Keddie 1968, 3). That the critical component in his approach to modernity was weightier than the positivist component makes sense in view of Afghani's commitment to the heterodox "Islamic" philosophy. "If someone looks deeply into the question," he averred, "he will see that science rules the world. There was, is, and will be no rule in the world but science" (Afghani 1968a, 102). But a few pages later, he qualified his statement by saying that

> a science is needed to be the comprehensive soul for all the sciences, so that it can preserve their existence, apply each of them in its proper place, and become the cause of progress of each one of those sciences. [Such a science is] philosophy [falsafa] because its subject is universal. It is philosophy that shows man human prerequisites. It shows the sciences what is necessary. It employs each of the sciences in its proper place. If a community did not have philosophy, and all the individuals of that community were learned in the sciences with particular subjects, those sciences could not last in that community for a century . . . that community without the spirit of philosophy could not deduce conclusions from these sciences. The Ottoman government and the Khedive of Egypt have opened up schools for the teaching of the new sciences for a period of sixty years and until now they have not received any benefits from those sciences. (Afghani 1968a, 104)

What is of crucial importance is that Afghani grounded his conceptualization of philosophy in the idea of reasoning and critical argumentation: "The father and mother of knowledge [elm] is reasoning [borhan], and reasoning is neither Aristotle nor Galileo. The truth is where there is reasoning" (Afghani 1968a, 107; translation slightly modified). In *Fawaid Falsafa* (The benefits of revelation), Afghani took his argument one step further by contending that philosophy was but a preparatory stage for the achievement of philosophy. In other words, revelation was a base that would lead the way to a subjectivist epistemology based on philosophy. He argued first for the centrality of critical faculties in humans: "Philosophy is the escape from the narrowness of animal sense

impression[s] into the wide area of human perception. It is the removal of darkness of bestial illusions with the light of natural intelligence; the transformation
of blindness and lack of insight into clear-sightedness and insight" (Afghani
1968b, 110). He then discussed the role of Islam and the Quran in preparing
the pre-Islamic "savage" Arabs to embrace the philosophical traditions developed by more civilized nations:

> In sum, in that Precious Book [the Quran] with solid verse, [God] planted the
> roots of philosophical sciences into purified souls, and opened the road for
> man to become man. When the Arab people came to believe in that Precious
> Book, they were transferred from the sphere of ignorance to knowledge, from
> blindness to vision, from savagery to civilization, and from nomadism to set-
> tlement. They understood their needs for intellectual and spiritual accom-
> plishment and for gaining a living. (Afhgani 1968b, 114)

The Arabs eventually realized that they could not develop further without the
help of other nations: "Therefore, notwithstanding the glory, splendor, and
greatness of Islam and Muslims, in order to exact and elevate knowledge, [the
Arabs] lowered their heads and showed humility before the lowest of their subjects, who were Christians, Jews, and [Persians] until, with their help, they
translated the philosophical sciences from Persian, Syriac, and Greek into Arabic. Hence it became clear that their Precious Book was the first teacher of philosophy to the Muslims" (Afghani 1968b, 114).

In discussing human action, Afghani seemed almost to adopt a Faustian
view of subjectivity. He recognized that human material needs (food, water,
shelter, health) had to be satisfied through science and technology (Afghani
1968b, 110; 1958, 118). Yet he considered critical philosophy to be the foundation of science and technology: "[Philosophy] is the foremost cause of the
production of knowledge, the creation of the sciences, the invention of industries and the initiation of crafts" (Afghani 1968b, 110; 1958, 118). Furthermore,
the satisfaction of material needs simply enabled us to pay attention to our souls
(Afghani 1968b, 111; 1958, 119). The most explicit statement of Afghani's critical thinking appeared, however, in an article published on May 18, 1883, in
Journal des Débats (Paris), refuting Ernest Renan's attack on Islam. Afghani
demonstrated the baselessness of Renan's racist attitudes and of his charge that
Islam was inherently against modern civilization, even as he praised the superi-

ority of critical (scientific and philosophical) thought over revelation (Afghani 1968c, 81–87).[28]

Such arguments constituted Afghani's critical "first discourse," addressed to the enlightened Muslim elite and written in highly abstruse and philosophical language. As we have noted, however, he also developed a parallel, more accessible "second" discourse, which was motivated by his anti-imperialist goals, and which stood in marked contrast to his critical "first" discourse.

Afghani's "second discourse" is most sharply expressed in "The Truth about the Neicheri Sect and Explanation of the Neicheris," written in 1881, well before he wrote the essays belonging to his "first" discourse.[29] In this famous essay, Afghani depicted an anti-imperialist collective subject, possessing political and military power embodied in an Islamic nation that could stand up to Western hegemony. He identified the concept of "social solidarity" as the linchpin of this collective subject, which the West, through agents such as Ahmad Khan, was trying to subvert. Drawing on Ibn Khaldun's parallel concept of *asabiyah*, Afghani's concept of social solidarity explained the longevity of a civilization or nation in terms of the beliefs that bonded its members or citizens together and that protected it from external invasion and internal disintegration.

The "Neicheris" (materialists), whether unorthodox or critical thinkers, whether Socialists, Communists, or nihilists, were bent on destroying the social solidarity of nations, Islamic and non-Islamic alike (Afghani 1968d, 140). What made social solidarity possible, in Afghani's analysis, was religious faith and specifically faith in a transcendental deity, who would in the next world mete out rewards and punishments as recompense to individual believers for what they had done or failed to do while living on earth (Afghani 1968d, 167). The religious faith that undergirded the social order and social solidarity had three components, which Afghani called "Religion's Three Beliefs": (1) the belief that "there is a terrestrial angel [human], and that he is the noblest of creatures," (2) the belief that one's community "is the noblest one, and that all outside [one's]

---

28. Interestingly enough, "Answer of Jamal al-Din to Renan" (Afghani 1968c) has never been translated from the original French into Persian, thus denying Afghani's Iranian audience ready access to his heterodox thoughts.

29. The Neicheris were the followers of Ahmad Khan (1817–1897). Derived from the English word "nature," *neicheri* was used by Afghani as a generic term for someone holding unorthodox or atheistic views. See Keddie 1968.

community are in error and deviation," and (3) the belief that "man has come into the world in order to acquire accomplishments worthy of transferring him to a world more excellent, higher, vaster, and more perfect than this narrow and dark world" (Afghani 1968d, 141). The first and second beliefs were necessary for a sense of collective subjectivity vis-à-vis nature and other social collectivities (Afghani 1968d, 142). The third belief, however, represented

> the best impulse towards civilization, whose foundations are true knowledge and refined morals. It is the best requisite for the stability of the social order, which is founded on each individual's knowledge of his proper rights, and his following the straight path of justice. . . . It is the only belief that restrains man from all evils, saves him from vales of adversity and misfortune, and seats him in the virtuous city on the throne of happiness. (Afghani 1968d, 144)

In contrast to this collectivist notion of agency, the most effective means by which the Neicheris and other unorthodox thinkers undermined social solidarity was by introducing individual subjectivity, rendered by Afghani as "égoïsme" (he used the French word), which denies all belief in the rewards and punishments of the afterlife. "And [because, owing to] these corrupt opinions, each of [the people corrupted] believed that there is no life but this one, the quality of égoïsme overcame them. [This] quality . . . consists of self-love to the point that [for] personal profit . . . a man having [it] would consent to the harm of everyone in the world" (Afghani 1968d, 151).

It would be wrong to conclude that Afghani rejected the concept of human subjectivity as such. What he and, as we will see in the following chapters, other religious theorists in the second half of the twentieth century proposed, however, might be best described as "mediated subjectivity," which I define as "human subjectivity projected onto the attributes of the monotheistic deity, such as omnipotence and omniscience" (for more on "mediated subjectivity," see chapter 4). In the Islamic discourse, this concept is usually expressed with the notion of the human as God's vicegerent (in Arabic, khalifato'llah). Although Afghani did not explicitly discuss this notion, the ontological underpinnings of his discourse are nevertheless powerfully informed by it.

The subjectivity attributed to God and that attributed to the human converge in Afghani's thought in an article entitled "Qaza va Qadar" (Destiny and providence). Afghani contrasts the concept of providence (God's destiny) to that of necessity (jabr) by stating that, though providence sets the general principles of phenomena, human volition also plays an important role in determining events (Afghani 1969, 144–47).

Belief in providence, as opposed to the concept of necessity (jabr), would result in the "creation of courage and initiative, bravery and chivalry and [would] encourage man to engage in daring acts which the fainthearted would fear" (Afghani 1969, 142–43). A person who thus believed in God's destiny as well as humans' free will and ability to fulfill that destiny would "never fear death in the defense of the people's and nation's rights and superiority. Nor would such a person be intimidated by death in rising up to fulfill what God has assigned to him" (Afghani 1969, 143). Afghani concluded that their belief in providence and their rejection of "necessity" accounted for the success of early Muslims and for their domination and superiority over other nations, which later Muslims needed to emulate (Afghani 1969, 144–47).

Although Afghani, in the tradition of many Muslim classical philosophers, believed that freedom for the Muslim masses was impossible as things stood, his "second discourse" pointed out the need for an indigenous form of subjectivity, raised in native Iranian soil, to make resistance to Western hegemony possible.

The Constitutional Movement and the Fundamental Law

On the practical level, the duality of positivist and universalizable subjectivity in Iran is reflected in the reforms intermittently undertaken by the Qajar high state bureaucrats in the second half of the nineteenth century and later in the Constitutional movement, which culminated in the Constitutional Revolution (1906) and in the Qanun Asasi (Fundamental Law), as the constitution was called.

After Amir Kabir's dismissal, the task of state and social reform from above was neglected for a while, but was soon pursued again, albeit less vigorously than in Amir Kabir's time, by the modernizers in the top echelons of Qajar bureaucracy. Most significant are the efforts of Mirza Hussein Khan Mushir al-Duleh, known as "Sepahsalar"; his reforms reflect greater emphasis on the positivist aspects of modernity, even though his efforts to bring change to the practical-cultural and political spheres cannot be neglected. Sepahsalar (1825–1880) was born into a middle-class family. His father, a state bureaucrat, sent his two sons, Hussein Khan (Sepahsalar) and Yahya Khan, to France to study. Sepahsalar became Iran's ambassador to the Ottoman Empire when he was only thirty-nine and stayed in that post for twelve years, until 1869, when he returned to Iran to be appointed head of the Judicial Office, Religious Endowments, and the Ministry of War, in that order. He served as prime minister from 1870 to 1872. After his resignation, forced upon him by the ulema and by corrupt members of the court elite adversely affected by his reforms, he served as governor of different provinces, war minister, foreign minister, and advisor to the crown prince, until his death in 1880, under suspicious circumstances.

Among the first, modern, steam-powered factories established by Sepahsalar were armament and arsenal factories, as well as a cast iron foundry imported from Europe in 1874 (Adamiyat 1977, 319).[30] He also ordered the importation of electric and gas light factories from Europe in 1878 (Adamiyat 1977, 320). The idea of railroads, seriously pursued by Sepahsalar and other reformers of his time and a national obsession until it was realized during Reza Shah's rule, was enthusiastically accepted by the ulema, who were not so keen on the other aspects of modernity in Iran.[31] Sepahsalar's attempts to rationalize and organize the state bureaucracy were also warmly received by Naser al-Din Shah: "I desire nothing but the organization [*nazm*] of the state [and] I consider you as its organizer. Your protection and the organization of the state [are] incumbent upon me to whatever degree that is necessary. Any person who obstructs and disturbs the organization, be he our own son, will be rejected" (Adamiyat 1977, 210).

Symbolic of the rationalization of the bureaucracy under Sepahsalar's reforms, regular business hours were instituted in the state bureaucracy (*darbkhaneh*) for the first time in Iran (Adamiyat 1977, 450). Before this reform, most of the ministers had run state offices from their private residences and at their convenience. Sepahsalar and his close associate, Mirza Yusef Khan Mustashar al-Duleh, were responsible for establishing the first court system in Iran, which not only administered secular justice, but also involved itself in the drafting of

---

30. The very fact that Sepahsalar's reforms were well within the framework of the Qajar state bureaucracy places them more in the direction of the positivist rationalization than emancipatory aspects of modernity. On the positivist side, rationalization and economic development are inevitable and necessary aspects of modernity, but their overarching domination of sociopolitical emancipation arrests the development of democratic aspects of modernity.

31. To promote his project for railroads, Sepahsalar solicited the opinion of Haji Mulla Sadeq, the grand orthodox jurist of Qom, who enthusiastically expressed his support for such a project, which might "under God's providential grace" turn Iran "into a flower garden and lift the distress, the dejection of the masses of people each of whom would engage in a vocation" (Adamiyat 1977, 328).

laws perceived as threatening by the clerical establishment (Adamiyat 1977, 172–78).

The positivist streak in Sepahsalar's reforms found explicit expression in his newspaper article "Elm va Jahl" (Science and ignorance). There he attributed the conquering power of Western nations to their science and technology, implying that a country such as Iran needed, first and foremost, to rationalize its bureaucracy and develop its productive forces (Adamiyat 1977, 148). Yet among Sepahsalar's reforms were those more in line with the emancipatory aspects of modernity, reforms that contributed to the emergence of a public sphere in Iran, such as the (successful) promotion of newspapers as a relatively open forum for the exchange of ideas.

Before we address the central theme of this section, the Constitutional movement and its crystallization in the Fundamental Law, we need briefly to consider some of the political and social literature produced immediately before or during the Constitutional Revolution. Although this literature addressed the same themes that concerned the thinkers of two previous generations, some of the concepts were refined and brought into a sharper focus by the later theorists and propagandists of the Constitutional movement.

By way of refining the concept of citizenship, for example, new words were introduced for "citizen." Before the advent of modernity, the ordinary citizens of Iran were referred to using the Arabic word ra'iyat (literally, flock of sheep). The Persian word taba'e (literally, follower) was later introduced (quite likely by Sepahsalar) to mean "citizen," for which it is still the most common word; this was followed, on the eve of the Constitutional Revolution, by the introduction of the Arabic word madaniun, a direct translation of citoyen, the French word for "citizen" (Adamiyat 1976, 215). Mirza Hussein Khan Mushir al-Mulk refined the concept of nationality by defining it in terms of the "concurrence of the ideas and aspirations of citizens" (Adamiyat 1976, 208). And Mirza Mustafa Khan Mansural-Saltaneh refined the concept of human subjectivity, introducing the Persian-Arabic words fa'el mokhtar to designate "subject" in his Fundamental Rights or the Principles of Constitution: "In the opinion of modern philosophers, only humankind, because of its concrete existence, [is] a subject [fa'el mokhtar] . . . whereas the state does not have concrete existence" (Adamiyat 1976, 216).

One of the most influential books of this period was The Travelogue of Ibrahim-Beg, a work of fiction by Haji Zein al-Abedin Maraghei, a merchant, promoting the ideas of popular sovereignty as the basis of government. More important, the book also reflects the duality between positivist and emancipatory aspects of modernity. Thus, although Maraghei discussed the concept of the law in terms of the rights of citizens, he also referred to law in terms of rational codification, regulation, bureaucratic organization, and order (Maraghei 1965, 81–83).

The Constitutional Revolution was the result of the coalition between disparate social forces—more or less secular intellectuals, reformist state officials, bazaar merchants, and certain clerics—that came together to overthrow the old regime and institute a new one by drawing on the intellectual heritage discussed thus far in this chapter. The intellectuals were a relatively new social force to emerge in response to Iran's encounter with modernity. The reformist position of certain state officials was also part of that response even though the bureaucracy had existed in Iran for millennia. The merchants owed their class consciousness and class solidarity to the development of Iran's infrastructure and means of communication (telegraph, newspapers, modernized postal system) in the last quarter of the nineteenth century. Their interest in revolutionary politics stemmed from Iran's gradual integration into the imperialist world economy, which, though benefiting a few big merchants, encroached on the traditional privileges of most (Abrahamian 1982, 58–60). The motivation of the clerics participating in the Constitutional movement was more complex, however. Some of the most energetic and effective participants in the movement were quite unorthodox activists, who wore the clerical garb and used the pulpit as their forum but were secret Sheikhis, Babis, or Azalis, all considered "heretical" tendencies (see Bayat 1981). Others were orthodox mullahs, who participated in the movement because they believed that restricting monarchical despotism would increase their own power and prestige. These were soon disillusioned; when the new monarch, Mohammad Ali Shah, attempted to overthrow the Constitutional Majlis (Parliament), they sided with him, although some of the more or less orthodox mullahs, such as Tabatabai, remained loyal to the movement at least for a time.

The events and personalities involved the Constitutional Revolution of 1906 go well beyond the scope of this chapter. A brief outline will suffice for our purposes here.[32] The immediate, precipitating cause of revolutionary activities was a drastic rise in food prices in 1905, brought about by a poor harvest, a cholera epidemic, the Russo-Japanese War, and the subsequent revolution in

32. For detailed histories of the Constitutional Revolution, see Nazem al-Islam Kermani 1967; Dowlatabadi 1982; Malekzadeh 1949; Kasravi 1951; and Browne 1910.

Russia (Abrahamian 1982, 81). Inflation prompted the government to raise taxes on Iranian merchants and to withhold repayment of its debts to them. The economic crisis gave rise to three increasingly intense public protests, leading to the revolution of August 1906 (Abrahamian 1982, 81). During the second protest, in December 1905, triggered by the government's public beating of two highly respected and elderly bazaar merchants for alleged hoarding, the protesters demanded, among other things, enforcement of the Sharia and establishment of a "house of justice" (*edalat khaneh*) (Abrahamian 1982, 82). During the course of the third protest, which lasted three weeks during the summer of 1906, a great number of protesters, representing different guilds and provinces, took refuge in the British league compounds in a northern suburb of Tehran. Their ranks were joined by the later anti-Constitutionalist mullah Sheikh Fazlollah Nuri and by the modernist intellectuals of the Darolfonun polytechnic. During this protest, in a crucial shift largely influenced by the modernist intellectuals of Darolfonun, the demand for creating a house of justice was turned into a demand for establishing a national representative parliament (*majlis melli*) (Abrahamian 1982, 84–85). After a bloody confrontation between government forces and revolutionaries on August 5, Mozaffar al-Din Shah (r. 1896–1907) signed a declaration promising to convene a parliament and appointed Muslin al-Duleh, a politician with liberal tendencies, as the prime minister (Abrahamian 1982, 85).

The first Majlis was inaugurated in October 1906, and the deputies immediately set about drafting a constitution or Fundamental Law, which in a ratified supplement gave most of the power to the legislature, at the expense of the shah, and which was signed by Mozzafar al-Din Shah on December 30, just five days before he died (Abrahamian 1982, 88–89). The new shah, Mohammad Ali Shah first refused to accept the new constitution as supplemented; he denounced the leading Constitutionalists as heretics. But soon, because of large public protests in many cities across the country, he backed down, changing his mind in December 1907, but again backing down in the face of public protest by pro-Constitutionalist forces (Abrahamian 1982, 94–95).

In June 1908, however, the shah staged a coup, bombarded the Majlis, arrested thirty-nine of the Constitutionalists, and executed four of his most outspoken opponents. Although the counterrevolution seemed to be succeeding in Tehran, at least for a time, in the provinces it was a different story. Within a year, the revolutionary forces, beginning in Tabriz, the capital of Azarbayejan province, had defeated the royalist forces, and with the help of some of the tribal armed troops marched on Tehran on July 13, 1909, ending the civil war. Soon the Majlis was reconvened. It deposed the shah and declared his twelve-year-old son, Ahmad, to be the new shah. It also set up a tribunal, which tried and executed five outspoken opponents of the movement, including Sheikh Fazlollah Nuri (Abrahamian 1982, 97–100).

The dualistic appropriation of modernity by Iranian intellectuals in the late nineteenth and the early twentieth century can also be seen in the Constitutionalist movement, something only recently recognized by scholars of Iran's modern history and sociology.

> The Constitutional Revolution . . . was both a nationalist revolution and a democratic revolution and has commonly been recognized as such. This characterization, however, does not do justice to the teleology of the Constitutional Revolution in that it leaves out a primary goal—*the* primary goal for many of the participants—of that revolution: the reform of government, creating a strong state capable of overcoming Iran's backwardness. (Amir-Arjomand 1988, 35; emphasis original)

One can find the institutional manifestations of the democratic trend in the Constitutional movement in the numerous associations (*anjomans*) created in the late nineteenth century, which flourished during the first decade of the new century and culminated in the creation of the Majlis. Although the positivist tendency was present in the statism and developmentalism of the associations and the Majlis, at least in the beginning, it did not dominate these institutions.[33] Rather, it was the executive, theoretically subservient to the legislature but actually independent of it, that increasingly manifested this tendency, which was clearly visible in the appointment by prominent Constitutionalists of the heavy-handed and pro-absolutist Amin al-Sultan to be prime minister of the new constitutional government in 1907 (Amir-Arjomand 1988, 42), and which came into full force with the advent of Reza Shah, as we will see in chapter 3.

To the duality of positivist and universalizable subjectivity reflected in the text of the constitution and its supplement, a third, religious dimension was

---

33. By designating the associations (*anjomans*) as the institutional nuclei of the more democratic trend, I do not intend to ignore the role that some "progressive" associations played in contributing to the chaos that increasingly engulfed Iran at this time, thus paving the way for the opposite trend to take over.

added, namely, the religious debate that had, since Afghani, shifted Iran's discourse on modernity toward the theological. Thus, according to Article 35 of the supplement to the Fundamental Law, sovereignty was divided between three entities, God, the people, and the shah: "Sovereignty is a trust confided, as a Divine gift, by the people to the person of the shah."

This symbolic tripartite division of sovereignty in the text of the Fundamental Law and its supplement gave, at least on the theoretical level, overlapping and sometimes mutually contradictory powers to the people, the shah as head of the executive, and the clerics. According to Article 2 of the Fundamental Law, "The National Consultative Assembly [Majlis] represents the entire people of Iran who participate in the economic and political affairs of the country." According to Articles 15 and 46, the creation of laws of the constitution was the prerogative of the Majlis; these laws, upon ratification by the shah, had to be executed. But, according to Article 45, thirty of the Senate's sixty members were to be appointed by the shah.[34]

The supplement to the Fundamental Law reflected the struggle between the secular and religious elements within the movement and between Constitutionalists and those religious personages who at one point or another supported absolutism. The second section of the supplement contains articles pertaining to the rights of the people and, as such, might be considered a bill of rights. Thus, according to Article 8 of the supplement, Iranians were to enjoy universal and equal rights before the state, that is, under secular law. But the universalistic spirit of this principle was violated by Article 58 of the supplement, which barred non-Muslims from holding cabinet positions. Moreover, under a crucial provision in Article 2 of the supplement, a committee of five Mojtaheds was given veto power over laws passed by the Majlis to ensure that they were in conformity with Islam.[35]

The contradictions in the constitution of 1906 are rooted in the ideological dispute between the forces of Constitutionalism and anti-Constitutionalism, a dispute carried on largely as a religious discourse immediately before and during the revolution. The two central figures in the dispute were both high-caliber theologians. One was the great Mojtahed of Tehran, Sheikh Fazlollah

34. The provisions of these four articles remained on the theoretical level: the Senate was not convened for another four decades, and, with the advent of Reza Shah and of his son, Mohammad Reza Pahlavi, the constitution was all but shelved.

35. The five-member committee was never convened.

Nuri, who, as we have noted, was on the side of the absolutists. The other was Mirza Mohammad Hussein Naini (d. 1927), who lent his theological skills to the cause of the Constitutionalists. Before concluding this chapter, it is instructive to discuss their theoretical debate over opposing positions on modernity derived from the same source, namely, Islam.

As a Mojtahed, Naini was active both in Iran's Constitutional Revolution and in Iraqi politics.[36] His *Tanbih al-Ummah va Tanzih al-Millah* (The awakening of the community and refinement of the nation) was published in 1909, just as the physical and ideological forces of Constitutionalism and anti-Constitutionalism joined battle. The paired concepts of freedom and equality constitute the foundation of the pro-Constitutionalist argument of Naini. He criticized the anti-Constitutionalist forces for portraying the "innocent" (*mazlum*) principle of freedom as corruption and the dissemination of heresy. Freedom and equality, Naini maintained, constitute the mainstay of any polity, and therefore the protection of the state and the monarchy. But the anti-Constitutionalists have tried to depict freedom and equality as license and immorality. As he explained in his rather arcane prose, it is "because the substance of happiness and national life, the limitation of the monarchy, the responsibility [that] strengthens [the monarchy,] and the protection of national rights [are] based on these two principles [that the anti-Constitutionalists] have turned these two great Divine Gifts into such obscene features" (Naini 1955, 37).

To rebuff his absolutist critics, Naini argued that the reasons for the rapid progress of early Islam were freedom and equality, to include equality between the ordinary person and the caliph, which constituted the justice found in the early Islamic state (Naini 1955, 49). Naini then criticized the conservative ulema, who, however many rules they derived from the slightest remarks of the Shiite imams, were unable to recognize that freedom and equality constituted the core of the teachings of Islam. He attributed the progress of Westerners to their appropriating these Islamic principles, and the retrogression of Muslims to their forgetting them (Naini 1955, 59–60).

Naini's approach to the question of freedom for all is closely connected to his views on the restriction of absolutism and on the Muslims' developing consciousness of their rights:

36. For a biography of Naini, see Hairi 1977.

At this juncture . . . the era of Muslims' retrogression has reached the final point and enslavement under the rapacious and tyrannical whim of oppressors has expired. . . . All Muslims, through the good guidance of spiritual leaders informing them of the requirements of their religion regarding their God-given freedom, have [liberated] themselves from the despotic rule of national pharaohs and have become conscious of their legitimate national rights and their [rights] to participate and be equal in all affairs with the oppressors. (Naini 1955, 3–4)

In a bold departure from traditional views of government, Naini condemned the despotic and "proprietary" role assumed by the state and the ruler, as "owners" of everyone and everything (Naini 1955, 8). Moreover, he expanded his condemnation from terrestrial despotism to "celestial despotism," believing the celestial to be more dangerous and more difficult to fight against because it controlled hearts and souls (Naini 1955, 27).

Of crucial importance is the central role played by consciousness in Naini's discourse against despotism. Referring to despotism as a "corrupt plant," Naini believed its "origin . . . is merely the lack of knowledge of the people regarding the responsibilities of ruling [saltanat] and the common rights of the species; and its foundation is based on lack of responsibility and accountability and liability" (Naini 1955, 10). Against the absolutist position of denying the people a say in governing, he argued that, in Islam, government was based on consultation (shura) and, because they paid taxes, the people had to have a say in the running of their affairs (Naini 1955, 87–89).

At the core of Naini's discourse was the concept of defiance (iba), which he ingeniously derived from Islamic and particularly Shiite tradition. The Shiites' third imam, Hussein Ibn Ali, challenged the tyrannical rule of the Muawiyeh and was martyred for it in 680. Naini called what the imam had done an "act of defiance" (iba) (Naini 1955, 24–25). In giving a positive connotation to a concept traditionally having mostly negative overtones, Naini transformed it into the grounding for his concept of freedom. This grounding brings Naini's "freedom" very close to "subjectivity," yet is derived from and couched in terms of venerated Shiite as well as Islamic tradition. He considered "God-given freedom," that is, liberation from "plant existence" and the "morass of bestiality," to be one of the most important goals of God's prophets (Naini 1955, 28). Moreover, he thought that subjectivity was only possible when universalized because absolutism was the negation of subjectivity and universality combined. The "intimidation, terror, and persecution" practiced by absolutism were intended to "uproot the pure plant of defiance [iba] and freedom [huriyat], preventing its dissemination to the public" (Naini 1955, 117–18).

These rather abstract notions constituted a foundation for Naini's discourse on social and political principles. One such principle was the idea of rights for the people of the East and its importance for their struggle against Western imperialism. He pointed out that the British ruling classes had to behave responsibly toward their own people because the latter were "awake" and knew their rights. But toward their Indian "slaves" their behavior was despotic because the Indians were in a deep slumber and lived in a state of senselessness (Naini 1955, 44). He also explicitly called for dropping the Islamic requirement demanded by some of the absolutists and for convening a Majlis whose deputies would be responsible to all citizens of the country as the electorate (Naini 1955, 15).

Naini advocated the separation of powers, justifying it not only in terms of Islamic tradition but also in terms of Iran's pre-Islamic history, thus creating a secular precedent (Naini 1955, 102–3). During the course of the ideological battle between the modernists and the antimodernists, the thorny issue of extending the principle of universality to the non-Muslim minorities within the nation was raised (Martin 1989, 129). The absolutists rejected any notion of extending equal citizenship rights to the religious minorities who had lived in Muslim societies but who were considered inferior to Muslims and had to pay a special tax (jazyah), namely, Christians, Zoroastrians, and Jews. Naini's liberal views called for the participation of "non-Islamic sects" in the electoral process by electing one from among their ranks because, even though they were not expected to be loyal to Islam, they would have good will toward their fatherland (vatan, namely, Iran) and that would be sufficient for participation (Naini 1955, 98). In a similar vein, Naini viewed freedom of the pen and speech as a God-given freedom necessary for liberation from despotism (taghut), for raising consciousness of the people, and for restoring their usurped rights (Naini 1955, 123–24).

One of the most difficult problems that the Constitutionalists faced was the question of positive law and its implications for divine law. The opponents of Constitutionalism pointed out that positive law, created by human agency as legislation, stood in opposition to divine law, whose principles and texts were immutable. Naini responded to this objection by pointing out that Islamic law consisted of two distinct categories. The primary laws, based on the Quran and other known Islamic principles, were unchangeable; the secondary laws, in contrast, were subject to change, depending on temporal and spatial circumstances, making them the proper sphere for legislation.

Whereas Naini derived from Islam a discourse (albeit not always consistent) in support of modernity, his archrival and detractor, Sheikh Fazlollah Nuri (who was executed in1909), working with the same material, arrived at an opposite position. At the time of the Constitutional Revolution, Nuri was probably the leading theologian in Tehran, with a large following. He had studied in the prestigious Shiite shrine cities of Iraq for many years, before returning to Tehran sometime in the 1880s. He had participated in political protests such as the one in 1891–92 against a tobacco concession to the British and later another against governmental loan policies (Martin 1989, 58). He had even briefly supported the cause of the Constitutionalists immediately before the culmination of the Constitutional Revolution and the declaration of acceptance of a constitutional regime by Mozzafar al-Din Shah on August 5, 1906. Nevertheless, he soon led the ideological assault in the war waged by the new shah, Mohammad Ali, against Constitutionalism.

At the core of Nuri's argument against Constitutionalism were the "evil" principles of freedom and equality based on universality within the nation-state. In contrast to Naini, Nuri thought the entire edifice of Islam was based on submission (ubudiyat) and not on freedom.[37] He also rejected the modern principle of universality within the nation-state because it would make Muslims and non-Muslims equal. "Islam is founded upon submission [ubudiyat]," he wrote, "and not freedom, and the edifice of its laws based upon discrimination and generalization reflecting differences and not equality; hence, according to the Law of Islam, we should hold equal those whom divine law holds equal and treat differently those classes that Islam holds different from other classes" (Nuri 1983, 59). There is, however, an important twist in Nuri's discussion of universality. He did not object to the principle of universality as such, but rather to its modern manifestation in the nation-state. Thus he advised non-Muslims seeking equality with Muslims simply to accept Islam (Nuri 1983, 60).

Nuri's fiery opposition to freedom in general was specifically directed against freedom of speech and press, which he condemned as promoting the

---

37. Ubudiyat is derived from the Arabic root 'abd, meaning "slave"; its cognate, ibadat, means "worship of God." Thus, according to Nuri, ubudiyat (submission) characterizes the existential state of humans vis-à-vis God, which forecloses any possibility of freedom.

dissemination of the blasphemous views of heretics and infidels, and therefore negating divine law in many respects (Nuri 1983, 60).[38] He attacked law created by humans by deriding modern legislation as vacuous and by criticizing the very idea of secular positive law (*qanun*). He argued that the forgers of secular law had created an order from their "imperfect," human reason and had gone along with it merely to satisfy their appetites. In their secular order, punishment was the only method of enforcement, and there were no heartfelt goads to obedience (Nuri 1983, 111). Nuri's argument against a representative parliamentary system was rooted in the Shiite theological position that, during the absence of the infallible imams and the occultation of Imam of the Age, the running of the affairs of the community devolved to the ulema as deputies of the Imam of the Age (Nuri 1983, 67). Thus he confined the legitimacy of representation and deputyship only to this Shiite formulation, rejecting popular sovereignty exercised through parliamentary representation.

Nuri's impact on Iran's encounter with modernity was considerable: he managed to insert in the supplement to the Fundamental Law as Article 2 the requirement that all laws passed by the Majlis be in conformity with Islam and that a committee of five Mojtaheds with veto power be designated to ensure this conformity. After the defeat of the absolutists and the hanging of Nuri, however, the discourse on modernity in Iran waned, becoming dormant for the next few decades, only to be rekindled in the 1960s (as we will see in chapter 4).

Deepening the Discourse of Subjectivity and Social Democracy

While the intellectual scene in Iran was deeply involved in a debate over modern political thought, in the radical branch of the Constitutional movement, intellectuals and political activists attempted to expand and radicalize the concept of subjectivity. In doing so, they wished, on the one hand, to go beyond the political sphere, to which subjectivity had been confined, and to penetrate the economic sphere, and, on the other, to go beyond Iran's urban middle classes and to enlist the peasants and the newly created urban working class.

Although radicalization of subjectivity was immanent in the concept of universalizable subjectivity, its expansion and radicalization had been resisted,

---

38. Nuri specifically warned that freedom of speech would result in the publication of the "French Voltaire's" books, which are full of imprecations against the prophets, and in the publication of Bab's and Bahaullah's writings (Nuri 1983, 268).

mainly because of class interests. During the course of the Constitutional movement, however, two factors caused that situation to change. One was the influence of Socialist and Marxist thought, filtering into Iran via the radicalism of Russia and Caucasia. The other was the limited but significant awareness of conflicting class interests among the participants in the Constitutional movement. Later in Iran, as in many other countries, the radicalization and expansion of subjectivity would be reduced to a quest for a collective subject, thereby negating the very principle of subjectivity.

We can find references to the concepts of social and economic justice in the late-nineteenth-century writings of Malkum Khan, Kermani, and Talebuf, even though these references were not developed into major themes. Nevertheless, they constitute the beginnings of the deepening and radicalization of modern social thought in Iran. The issue of selling state lands to the peasants, for example, had been raised by Malkum Khan a half century before the Constitutional Revolution (Adamiyat 1976, 273). Kermani had discussed themes pertaining to equality in wealth, restriction of ownership, elimination of social privileges, and securing social rights for workers (Adamiyat 1976, 270). Sismondi's 1819 book *Nouveaux principes d'économie politique*, translated into Persian in the 1880s, had also influenced the radicalization of the discourse on modernity in Iran (Adamiyat 1976, 271–73).

However, it was only in the early years of the twentieth century that ideas bearing on social and economic justice and the inadequacy of merely formal democracy were considered in depth in the Iranian discourse on modernity. At the climax of the Constitutional Revolution, in a series of articles in the influential newspaper *Sur Esrafil*, Ali Akbar Dehkhoda (d. 1955) correctly recognized that, because landless peasants comprised the bulk of Iran's population, as long as they did not own the land they cultivated, talk about political rights and freedom would be meaningless. Indeed, he considered ownership of land to be the sine qua non of freedom for the peasants (Adamiyat 1976, 275). Dehkhoda also believed the peasants were justified in resorting to violence to restore their "usurped national rights," although he advocated first offering the landlords compensation for their lands through the creation of a national agricultural bank (Adamiyat 1976, 276–77).

From the early twentieth century on, Iranian radical thought and praxis were closely connected to, and fed by, radical thought and praxis in Russia and especially in Caucasia. Founded in 1904 and a branch of the large Social Democratic Party of Caucasia, the Hemat Party was one of the first political parties to be established in Baku (Adamiyat 1975, 13). In 1905, the Iranian Social Democratic Committee was also formed there; branches of the Social Democratic Party were soon established in different cities inside Iran, including Mashad, Tehran, Tabriz, and Rasht, having close connections, and sometimes overlapping memberships, with many of the associations (*anjomans*) during the Constitutional Revolution.

In this period, before Marxist, Leninist, and Stalinist ideology had caused the sclerosis of Iranian radical thought, two approaches toward political democracy were evident in these radical circles. The first approach viewed social and economic justice in terms of the expansion and unfolding of the newly established political democracy and its institutionalization in the Majlis and the constitutional state apparatus. It was perhaps best represented by Mohammad Amin Rasulzadeh (d. 1954), a central figure in the Hemat Party, who created a Social Democratic discourse in the region in opposition to the Marxist-Leninists and the Bolsheviks. By contrast, the second approach viewed political democracy as antithetical to any notion of social and economic justice. Its advocates usually resorted to violence and had established terrorist organizations parallel to their political organizations.

Chapter 3 will explore the development of radical thought in Iran in the larger context of the eclipse of universalizable subjectivity, on the one hand, and the search for a collective subject, on the other.

3

The Eclipse of Universalizable Subjectivity and the Quest for a Collective Subject

Before proceeding to the central themes of this chapter, we should briefly review the sociopolitical conditions in Iran for the period between the establishment of the constitutional parliamentary system in 1909 and the advent of the Reza Shah regime in 1925. It was a time of chaos and disintegration, brought about by civil war, by foreign intervention and military occupation, by extreme political factionalism and conflict, by feuds among tribes and their domination of politics, and by the emergence of separatist movements asserting their newly discovered ethnic rights. A growing awareness of Iran's technological and economic backwardness vis-à-vis Europe and the United States led Iranian intellectuals to move away from a dualistic approach to modernity and toward a wholehearted embrace of its more positivist aspects.

After the Civil War of 1906–9 and the defeat of the absolutist forces, Iran increasingly became the object of domination and intervention by foreign forces, especially those of Britain and Russia. The Anglo-Russian agreement of 1907 effectively divided Iran into a northern, Russian zone of influence and a southern, British zone. In October 1910, British forces, invading from the Persian Gulf, occupied Shiraz and Esfahan in central Iran, ostensibly to quell tribal rebellions and bloodshed. In November of the same year, Russian forces occupied the Caspian cities of Rasht and Anzali in the north (Abrahamian 1982, 108–9). During the First World War, Ottoman troops occupied the western parts of Iran and German agents set about arming the tribes (Abrahamian 1982, 103).

As we saw in chapter 2, some of the tribes were instrumental in the victory of the Constitutional forces in the Civil War. But after the restoration of the Majlis, the domination of the political scene by the Bakhtiyari tribe and the resultant rivalry among the different tribes and tribe factions led to further chaos, insecurity, and pillaging, used by the British as the pretext for their occupation of central Iran. The rivalry among political factions within and without the Majlis also resembled feuds. In 1910, a year after its convening, two political parties emerged in the second Majlis (together with their affiliated outside organizations): the Democratic Party (Ferqeh-ye Demokrat), representing radical intellectuals, rooted in the associations (*anjomans*), and connected, through Caucasia, to Russian radicalism; and the Moderates (Etedalion), representing the ulema, merchants, and high-ranking bureaucrats, who were mostly pro-Constitutionalist, but whose ranks were increasingly joined by the conservative and sometimes reactionary landlords, tribal chiefs, and erstwhile absolutists. The conflict between the Democrats and the Moderates came to a convulsive climax when four members of the armed faction of the Democrats assassinated the highly influential cleric and veteran of the Constitutional Revolution Seyyed Abdullah Behbahani in 1909. Some of the leaders of the Democrats, such as Seyyed Hasan Taqizadeh (1878–1969), who were implicated in the assassination went into exile, and armed clashes broke out between the supporters of the two political parties in the capital (Abrahamian 1982, 106–7).

By 1920, partly in response to the foreign occupation of Iran and to their discovery of ethnic rights, and partly as localized efforts to salvage what they could from the collapsing situation, there emerged local and often radical separatist movements, the three most prominent of which were the Jangal (Jungle) movement in the forested areas of northern Iran, the Khiabani movement of Tabriz in Azarbayejan, and the Pesiyan movement led by Colonel Pesiyan of Khorasan in western Iran.[1]

These disintegrating and chaotic forces set the stage for the eclipse of the emancipatory aspects of modernity and for the overarching triumph of its positivist aspects. Iran's dualistic encounter with modernity, in which universalizable and positivist subjectivity existed side by side, gave way to the dominance of positivist subjectivity in culture, society, and the state, arresting the development of civil society—an inevitable phenomenon, considering the conditions of the period.

---

1. In addition to these three most prominent movements, there were separatist outlaws, such as Nayeb Hussein Kashi in the city of Kashan, who ruled breakaway towns, cities, and regions (Amir-Arjomand 1988, 59).

Intellectuals and the Eclipse of Universalizable Subjectivity

"All Iranians with a grain of awareness," Ahmad Kasravi would write in 1942,

> are saddened by the backwardness of their country. . . . What lies at the root
> of this drastic decline? At the beginning of this century, reformers could claim
> that the main culprits were the despots who had a vested interest in keeping
> their subjects ignorant and unenlightened. After twenty years of constitu-
> tional government, however, we cannot in good conscience give the same an-
> swers. We now know that the main blame rests not with rulers, but with the
> ruled. Yes, the chief reason for underdevelopment in Iran, perhaps in most
> Eastern countries, is disunity among the masses. (Abrahamian 1980, 112)

Kasvari's statement reflects the general disillusionment among intellectuals
with the development of civil society in Iran after the Constitutional Revolution, and their gradual drift toward a monolithic nationalism and toward embracing the positivistic aspects of modernity. The most important theme to
emerge in the period was national unity (*vahdat-e melli*), heralded by intellectuals
of diverse persuasions at home and abroad as a means to halt and reverse the
disintegration of the country. Three magazines—*Kaveh* and *Iranshahr* (published
in Berlin) and *Ayandeh* (published in Tehran)—were instrumental in disseminating the central idea of national unity and related subthemes (Entekhabi, 1993).
As early as the close of World War I, Taqizadeh, the radical Constitutional activist who had been exiled for his involvement in the assassination of Behbahani, took up the theme of national unity in his magazine, *Kaveh*, established in
Berlin in 1916. For Taqizadeh, the mission of *Kaveh* was "the dissemination of
European civilization in Iran, campaigning against fanaticism and serving to
preserve Iran's nationhood and national unity" (Entekhabi 1993, 192). The contrast between Taqizadeh's earlier assessment of the vitality of national life as a
Constitutional activist and his later views is instructive in this regard. In his
1906 essay, he wrote:

> Today the nations of the world are divided into two types according to their
> political orientation. Some are "living" nations and some "deceased." . . . Some
> people would say that a nation is alive [if it] possesses law [*qanun*], and dead [if
> it does not]. Others would assume that the life and death of a nation depends
> on formal political independence. And another group believes that [it de-
> pends on] perfection of the instruments of war and defense. But none of these

[positions] is correct. The spiritual life of nations that can be considered eternal and perpetual consists of the *individual* national awareness that has been implanted in the makeup of [their members]. This means that, as the life and vigor of a living body is mediated by the vitality of each of its individual members and even the life, health, natural fervor, and perfection of all its cells—in the same way national life also depends on the independence of each individual member, who possesses independent awareness, movement, and natural and innate fervor. [Such] individuals are in no need of an external protector, pivot, center of fervor, [external] source of duty, and leader. This means that the actions of each member [of society] must be based on belief in a universal imperative [*wujub a'ini*]. . . . To put it more plainly, in the army of a nation, the individual soldier should not look up to the standard bearer; his heart should not be annexed to the collectivity, and he should not expect the backing and support of the leader and chief. Each member of that nation and each individual of that collectivity [must] be a complete and proper nation . . . a mobile cannon, a clamorous bomb . . . his veins and organs [must be] fed by the blood of self-dignity and "subjectivity" [*hakemiyat*] and his character developed with the stock of love of independence and nobility. (Taqizadeh 1974, 337–38; emphasis added)

Such grandiloquence in describing the concept of universal subjectivity stands in sharp contrast with Taqizadeh's later pronouncements. Thus, regarding Iran's newly formed regime under Reza Shah, he wrote, "The four pillars of this independence and civilization, in my opinion, are national unity, security, reform of the bureaucracy, especially the treasury, and reform in the principles of national sovereignty and national representation" (Taqizadeh 1974, 37).

The same emphasis on the concept of national unity had been promulgated by Mahmud Afshar in his magazine, *Ayandeh* (Future):

National unity is today one of the most important international questions and realities. Whether we want it or not, in the future our nation will enter this political current, and this reality will one day become the mainstay of our state politics, as it has become the axiom of most states, especially the [Ottoman state]. Every politician must be well aware of this because national unity is the common border between domestic and foreign policy. (Afshar 1926, 564)

Earlier, in a preface to the first issue of *Ayandeh*, Mahmud Afshar had proclaimed national unity as the goal and intention of his magazine. He defined national unity in terms of political, ethical, and social unification of the peoples living within the contemporary boundaries of Iran (Afshar 1925, 5). Unity entailed not only preserving Iran's political independence and territorial integrity but also universalizing the Persian language, abolishing regional differences in clothing and mores, removing the decentralized sovereignty of local magnates (*mulak al-tavayef*), and homogenizing the different ethnic and tribal groups (Afshar 1925, 5).

Thus the idea of national unity implied a strong and centralized state. Indeed, writing in 1926, Taqizadeh asserted that creation of a strong central government was the essential prerequisite for reform and progress, for freeing the country from foreign pressure and intervention, expelling the foreign occupying forces, establishing security, and divesting the once-sovereign local magnates of their power (Taqizadeh 1974, 44–45).

In the intellectuals' schema for the transition to positivist modernity, the central and strong state required a strong personality, an "enlightened despot" to implement the switch to positivist reforms. In a 1923 article in the magazine *Iranshahr*, edited by Hussein Kazemzadeh (1883–1962), who would later adopt "Iranshahr" as his surname, this idea is bluntly expressed by a certain Aljay Afshar, who believed that a Peter the Great could be "a thousandfold" more effective than "committees, meetings, and commissions." Significantly, she claimed that most Iranians could not relate to the "truth" of Constitutionalism, republicanism, and freedom:

> I believe that Iranians would not sweep their front doorstep, would not light their front door light, would not give their yard's rubbish to the municipal scavengers by their own hands. An enlightened and open-minded reformer is needed to sweep our front doorstep every morning by force; light our streetlights by force; reform our clothing and make it uniform by force; reform our education by force; prevent the intrigues of the Majlis by force . . . purge our imperial court by force . . . prevent clerics from meddling in politics and politicians [from meddling] in spiritual affairs by force; *select, by force, [members] of the Majlis* from among those who can tell the Pasteur Institute from a cowshed; organize our coffeehouses, dairy shops, grocery shops, and apothecary shops by force. We need an enlightened reformer to make education for men and women compulsory by force and [we need] the power of the bayonet and whip . . . to determine even the hours of our sleeping and awakening and eventually to lift the veil of illusion from before our eyes by force. (Afshar 1923, 139–40; emphasis original)

Aljay Afshar concluded her article with the anguished question, What if a "Lenin, a Mikado or a Kemal Pasha" could not be found to "salve our pains" and "impose happiness" on us? (Afshar 1923, 140).[2]

Unification of the country entailed creating a unified national military, on the one hand, and expanding and streamlining the national bureaucracy, on the other (Taqizadeh 1974, 38). In a 1927 article, Taqizadeh proposed a 12- to 15-year development plan for Iran, in which he allocated 25 percent of the country's annual budget to the military in the first year, to be increased to 32 percent by the end of the proposed period (Taqizadeh 1974, 81–114, esp. 96). These ideas were translated into reality by the bureaucratic military regime of Reza Shah, which, by 1941, could boast of 127,000 men under arms and a bureaucracy 90,000 strong (Abrahamian 1982, 136).[3]

In the deepening eclipse of emancipatory modernity, Iranian intellectuals became almost obsessed with industrialization, science, technology, and the ideology of developmentalism. In the first issue of *Ayandeh*, a certain Badi' al-Zaman Khorasani wrote a long ode on the railroad, praising its advent in classical Persian poetic style (Khorasani 1925, 26–27). Taqizadeh, for his part, called for the training of Iranians to replace foreign technicians, who had traditionally provided Iran's technological needs (Taqizadeh 1974, 48). By 1934, he was urging Iranian schools to devote 70 percent of their curriculum to modern natural sciences (Taqizadeh 1972, 229).[4]

Another essential element in the transition to a positivist approach to modernity was the emergence of a monolithic nationalism. Among previous generations of Iranian intellectuals, nationalism had consisted of a duality, with

2. To be sure, Aljay Afshar was only one of many who expressed similar views at this important juncture. I have chosen her because she put these ideas most forcefully and bluntly.

3. Amin Banani estimated the number of men that could be mobilized by the end of Reza Shah's rule as 400,000. See Banani 1961, 57.

4. The trend toward ever greater emphasis on the natural sciences reached its highest point during the rule of Mohammad Reza Pahlavi in the 1970s, when philosophical and liberal arts subjects were virtually absent from school curricula and when universities devoted themselves to the production of engineers and medical doctors, to the virtual exclusion of fields more related to critical thought. The exclusionary bias against such fields has continued under the Islamic Republic, with the government vigorously discouraging the study of social sciences and humanities as "nonessential" by cutting off the stipends of Iranian students pursuing these subjects abroad and, in the early 1980s, by prohibiting them even from using their own private funds to pay for their studies.

nostalgic notions about Iran's past—especially its pre-Islamic past—and Iranian identity, on the one hand, and democratic notions about the rule of law and popular sovereignty, on the other (Entekhabi 1993, 186). During this period of transition, however, a nostalgic nationalism that cast Arabs and Turks as the "other" gradually eclipsed any democratic notion of nationhood that might, at least partly, ground itself in citizenship rights. The magazines *Kaveh, Iranshahr,* and *Ayandeh* were instrumental in this development (Entekhabi 1993, 191), each publishing numerous articles on one or another aspect of ancient Iranian civilization, all glorifying Iran's pre-Islamic past. The titles alone of articles published in *Iranshahr,* for example, give a clear sense of the near obsession with Iran's pre-Islamic glories and the efforts to construct an Iranian identity based on ancient history (Entekhabi 1993, 195).[5]

It was also during this period that the new, nostalgia-driven nationalism was associated with the revival of pre-Islamic Iranian monarchy. The crisis of Iran's monarchy brought on by the disintegration of the state in the 1920s had raised a clamor for republicanism. Yet republicanism could not serve the course of the new nationalism, which had closely linked Iran's past glories with those of the monarchy; indeed, the marriage between nostalgia-driven nationalism and revived ancient monarchy would exclude any grounding of nationalism in citizenship rights.

Support for the shift to a unipolar, positivist approach to modernity came from disparate quarters. The ulema, at least at first, supported the reforms of Reza Shah and his efforts at positivist nation building. Indeed, as the strongest opponents of republicanism, they insisted on preserving the monarchy by transferring it from the Qajar to the Pahlavi Dynasty. They were joined by the Socialists, under Rasulzadeh, who voiced their desire for a unified and strong state to carry out necessary social reforms (Adamiyat 1976, 305). Even the Communists supported centralizing the state apparatus after the defeat of the Gilan Soviet Republic in northern Iran by Reza Khan (his title before he became the new monarch) in 1923 (Ghods 1989, 74).

The convergence of the clamor of intellectuals for unification and the nation-building efforts of Reza Khan, which gave rise to Iran's unipolar approach to modernity, found clear expression in a meeting between Reza Khan, who was

5. Consider the following titles: "Stone Cuttings of the Sassanid Period," "Education in Ancient Iran," "Khaqani and the Ruins of Madaen," "Cuneiform in Iranian Tablets," "The War Committee of Darius II," and "Ancient Industries of Iran." See Entekhabi 1993, 195.

at the time the prime minister, and the members of the Young Iran Association (Anjoman Iran Javan) in March 1921, shortly after its establishment. Reza Khan had summoned the association's members to learn the nature and purpose of their organization. Founder Ali Akbar Siasi explained that they were patriotic young men who were in agony because of Iran's backwardness and wished to close the gap between Iran and European countries. After carefully reading the charter of their association, Reza Khan assured them that what they "expressed in words," he "would carry out in practice" (Siasi 1988, 76–77).

One of the few voices opposing the eclipse of democratic thought and institutions was that of Mohammad Mossadeq, the future liberal prime minister of Iran, who would again try to restore democracy to Iran in the early 1950s, but who would fall victim to a coup staged by the CIA. In 1925, Mossadeq opposed transferring the monarchy to Reza Khan; he warned that a powerful monarch unaccountable to any form of popular sovereignty would violate the principles of the constitution, for which so much blood had been shed during the Constitutional Revolution (Mossadeq 1925, 228–33).

Despite Mossadeq's warning and largely unaware of the consequences, Iranian intellectuals and statesmen proceeded to shift from a dualistic to a unipolar approach in their appropriation of modernity in Iran. Perhaps the most eloquent manifestation of this shift was an article written by Ali Akbar Davar, a Majlis deputy at the time and later Reza Shah's minister of justice (who, after falling out of favor with the shah, would commit suicide). The solution to the crisis facing Iran, Davar wrote in "Bohran" (Crisis), lay in abandoning concerns with democracy and pursuing a "rational" economic course of development. Using the Iranian staple bread (nan) as a metaphor for the economic situation, he directly addressed Iran's democratic thinkers and reformers:

> The Foundation of our crisis is economic. . . . What is to be done? Think about bread. A poor nation, by the decree of nature, is condemned to all these afflictions . . . You thought that the principles of national sovereignty could be shoved down poor people's throats—that is why all of your effort and attention was spent on the discourse of freedom and equality—and at the same time, you wanted to spread foreign constitutionalism [all over Iran] by the "good offices" of the statesmen of the previous dynasty. Today, it seems, there is no room for doubt. You saw that you were in error and received no results. . . . In the opinion of better-qualified scientists, the production of wealth is the foundation of the ethics, culture, and politics of the nations of the world. . . .

If you really want to reform the general conditions, revive and renew economic life. . . . In short, seek bread [and] freedom will follow by itself. (Davar 1926, 8–9)

Although it is hard to imagine a future for any Third World country without economic development, modern technology and science, and even an active state—the material basis without which modernity cannot take root—to pursue them as the overarching priority at the expense of the universalizable aspects of subjectivity is to arrest the development of democratic institutions and principles. Such was the case in Iran after Reza Shah came to power in 1921. With the eclipse of universalizable subjectivity, sociopolitical thought in Iran became imbued with nationalism, "antimaterialism," and utopianism, on the one hand, and with Marxist-Leninism, on the other.

The Antimaterialist, Utopian, and Nationalist Discourses of Iranshahr and Kasravi

Hussein Kazemzadeh (1884–1962), later called "Iranshahr" after the famous magazine he published, was born to a religious family in Tabriz. His father and brother practiced traditional Persian herbal medicine. He himself went to Istanbul to study modern medicine at the age of 20, but, because of events surrounding the Constitutional Revolution in Iran, decided to study law instead. Having received his baccalaureate in political and social sciences from a college in Louvain, Belgium, in a single year, he spent the next few years in Paris, then taught Persian in Cambridge, England. In 1915, he went to Berlin to join Iranian patriots involved in organizing a military force to repel foreign occupation forces from Iran. He spent two years in Iran and Turkey participating in these efforts before returning to Berlin, where he would live for the next nineteen years, publishing his magazine *Iranshahr* from 1922 to 1927. He left Germany in 1936; he would spend the rest of his life in Switzerland, where he wrote many of his books and essays in Persian and German. During these final years, Iranshahr became aloof from the sociopolitical thought of his native country, serving instead as the spiritual leader of a theosophical group in Switzerland.[6]

Unlike that of many other nationalists of his period, Iranshahr's discourse

6. The biographical sketch of Iranshahr's life is taken from his nephew Kazem Kazemzadeh Iranshahr's account. See Iranshahr 1984.

on nationalism contained a critique of the West. His time in Europe had left him dissatisfied with Western materialism. As early as 1924, Iranshahr took modern Western civilization to task for its predatory, dominating ethos and for its conquest of others; he warned Iranians against establishing modern civilization, which was being "imported into Iran by bayonet and at the expense of the blood of Iranian youth" (Iranshahr 1924, 449).[7] In 1926, while acknowledging the contribution of the Enlightenment to the development of human rights and freedom of thought, he criticized the West's extreme materialism, corporealism, and spiritual alienation of God's grace, all of which had resulted from the vacuity of human reason, a situation he hoped would somehow be resolved in the future (Iranshahr 1926, 204–5).

Iranshahr's search for a remedy culminated in a conceptual dichotomy between the mind or the spirit, on the one hand, and the body, on the other. "Our error," he wrote, "stems from our lack of knowledge that we are constituted of soul and body and [that] the soul is the primary and the body is the secondary. [The spirit] is the commander and the body the receiver of command and at its service. . . . But we strive for the satisfaction of our body because we consider it to be our happiness, and forget our souls altogether" (Iranshahr 1956, 24). According to Iranshahr's "hierarchy of perfection" (marahel u'ruj), being "evolved" through a series of states, from the inanimate, to the plant, to the animal, to the human state, to the realm of spirit (malakut), and to the realm of power (jabarut) before finally arriving at the realm of meaning (lahut) (Iranshahr 1956, 45).

Modern Western civilization, Iranshahr reasoned, had gone in the wrong direction. True, the nations of the West had developed their rational power and had surpassed other nations, but because they had used this power against the natural path of "perfection" (u'ruj) and had used their "animal power" to plunder and dominate the weak, the powerful hand of providence had punished the West and had inflicted revolutions and bloodshed upon it. Some Western thinkers had realized the sad state of modern civilization and, believing the demise of this civilization to be inevitable, had tried to raise their people's consciousness (Iranshahr 1956, 51–52).

Iranshahr's mind-body dichotomy provided the ontological grounding for his utopian nationalism, whereby the downplaying of the realm of "body" and

---

7. Iranshahr's profound misgivings about Western civilization are quite logical when we consider that he witnessed World War I in Europe firsthand. I am grateful to Mehrzad Boroujerdi for drawing my attention to this point.

"matter" left little room for the development of individual subjectivity. Although he did not explicitly elaborate this connection, his discourse clearly contained the seeds of departure from the synthesis between individual subject and collectivity and moved toward the surrender of the individual to the collectivity. Thus, in a 1923 article in *Iranshahr*, he writes: "Each of the individuals . . . of a nation may have a different and individual objective. . . . But [each has] a common and general, that is, social and national, objective that is superior to individual objectives and annihilates them" (Iranshahr 1923, 67–68). He exhorts his fellow Iranians to be just like moths who annihilate themselves in the flame of a candle and who know no love but the love of nationalism and Iranianness (Iranshahr 1923, 76).[8]

Although, after the eclipse of democratic thought and institutions, in which he played a crucial part, his direct influence inside Iran would be relatively limited, Iranshahr broached significant themes that were later elaborated by those who stayed in Iran. Thus Ahmad Kasravi continued and expanded Iranshahr's discourse on nationalism, exercising a considerable influence that persists in Iran to this day. His work and personality were multifaceted and met with widely differing assessments. Some considered Kasravi to be the foremost theorist of modernity, whereas others considered him a "dangerous iconoclast" who tried to undermine the very foundations of tradition in Iran; still others saw him as the historian of the Constitutional movement. Abrahamian (1980, 100), for his part, regarded Kasravi as the "integrative nationalist of Iran." Indeed, Kasravi was all of these—a historian of the Constitutional movement, familiar with its ideas, a theoretician and activist in the unification and integration, and a foremost theorist of utopian nationalism in Iran.

Seyyed Ahmad Kasravi (1890–1946) was born into a clerical family in Hukmavar near Tabriz. His father, though he was an orthodox (*mutishar'i*) mullah, maintained good relations with the less dogmatic mullahs, namely, the Sheikhis and Karimkhanis, in his hometown (Kasravi 1962, 13). Because Kasravi was expected to continue the clerical line of his family, his upbringing was highly disciplined and he received a traditional religious education. Later, in 1915, while teaching Arabic at an American missionary school, he would also study English (Kasravi 1962, 60). During this period, he developed a sympathy for the Constitutional movement; indeed, he would begin work on his history

---

8. Iranshahr is here alluding to an image from classical Persian poetry, in which the moths "annihilate" themselves in the flame of their beloved, represented by the candle.

of the movement while employed by the Ministry of Justice (1920–30), whose mission under Davar was to secularize and codify legal procedures in Iran. Forced to resign his position as judge in the Ministry of Justice in 1930 because he had ruled against Reza Shah and in favor of the cultivators in a land dispute, Kasaravi practiced law privately, developing and disseminating his ideas on utopian nationalism until his assassination by an Islamist group in 1946.

Kasaravi lived in an era when disenchantment with liberal democracy in Europe soon would give rise to Fascism and Nazism, on the one hand, and to Bolshevism and, later, Stalinism, on the other, whose effect on radical movements and thought on the international scene would spell the end of democratic socialism and make itself felt in countries such as Iran, although only after a delay of some years. Thus the early work of Kasravi was affected by the Constitutional movement, grounded in the liberal democratic tradition, whereas his later work, influenced by events in Europe, distanced itself from this tradition.

Varjavand Bonyad (The sacred foundation), first published in 1943, contains many of his philosophical views. In it, Kasravi criticizes Western modernity and the violence prevalent in Europe, especially the bloodshed during the Second World War. The "movement of science" or progress, he argues, has wreaked havoc in its European birthplace; indeed,

> it has given rise to much harm. In Europe, which is the cradle of this movement, ever since these sciences have become prevalent and new gadgets for living . . . are employed, life has become so much more difficult, to the point that many people escape not only the sciences but also civilization and seek to return to the simple life of the nomadic era. In Europe there is either war, insecurity and slaughter for the youth or unemployment and poverty for the masses. (Kasravi 1961, 87)

Although Kasravi was not a pious man and would lose his life because of his attacks on Shiism, as a committed antimaterialist, he would attack "materialism and atheism" until his death (Kasravi 1944, 79). Like Iranshahr, he proposed a mind-body dichotomy, in which the mind (*ravan*) stood for "reason, thought, understanding, modesty, humility, and similar commendable characteristics," whereas the body (*jan*) represented "evil qualities," namely, caprice, avarice, envy, wrath, spite, ostentation, sycophancy, and tyranny (Kasravi 1961, 31). Furthermore, the body and mind were opposite essences, always in conflict. When one side grew stronger, the other side became weaker. The person whose mind was in control over the body kept the body in line and averted desire (*hava*) and other evil qualities. Conversely, when the body became dominant, base qualities would take over, and truth would be shunned (Kasravi 1961, 32). This is what happened in Europe, where,

> as the sciences advanced, the blunder of materialism occurred, and this blunder became a great deception, with [grave] consequences. The pundits who considered the universe [to consist of] merely this tangible material system, did not view man but as corporal and sensual. They believed the wellspring of man's wants and deeds, just like [that of] the animals', to lie in selfishness and thus [they] believed conflict and struggle to be inevitable. (Kasravi 1961, 38)

To overcome the problems of the modern world and rectify the tragic consequences of materialism, Kasravi laid down the principles of a cosmology that closely resembles the seventeenth- and eighteenth-century notions of Deism. Thus *The Sacred Foundation* begins with the words "the world is an orderly and organized system." Indeed, Kasravi's cosmology is dominated by this notion of order and organization:

> This is a systematized world in which needs are satisfied. It rotates and does not rest; It is never impaired. If we observe the rotation of the earth and the stars, if we look into the birth of humans and animals, if we consider the growth of trees and plants, they are all based on an order and everything has its place. The [reason why] the sciences have advanced so much and each has created a great space for itself [is that], more than anything else, they discuss the order and orderliness of the world. And the more they advance, the more the order and greatness of the world comes to light. (Kasravi 1961, 3)

Having raised the issue of order, Kasravi must address the related problem of meaning. If there is order in the universe, there must also be a purpose. Without elaborating, he asserts, "There is a purpose, [indeed] a great and valuable purpose" (Kasravi 1961, 4–5). Order and meaning, in Kasravi's discourse, require an active agent responsible for the creation of the universe. To be sure, as the human species, we belong at the top of the hierarchy of creation, but the ultimate will belongs to the creator (Kasravi 1961, 8). Accordingly, Kasravi (1961, 24) assigns humans the role of "overseer" (*jahanban*) of the orderly world created by God: "Just as a gardener who plucks the weeds, trims the trees, and grows beautiful flowers, humans should treat the earth in the same manner."

Kasravi's orderly cosmology found its earthly social function in the need for religion, which in turn was necessary for social order and social solidarity. Thus, despite his reputation for being "iconoclastic" and "antireligious," Kasravi called for religion to serve the cause of social integration: "Many see no need for religion. But there is much need for it. Religion is the high road of life. If it did not exist, each group would take up a different path and become misled and dispersed. If it did not exist, each person would seek his own interests, and the social bond would be disrupted" (1961, 75).

The upshot of Kasravi's preoccupation with order and social integration was the formulation of an extreme puritanical rationality in which the category of "reason" as order enjoyed the highest status. Kasravi became infamous for his extreme criticism of those elements of Persian culture he found at odds with his notions of order and "rationality." Throughout his works, he denounced mysticism, intuition, poetry, metaphysics, and lyrical and Dionysian ideas as these were expressed in Persian poetry and even in philosophy. He even organized book burnings, in which those books he and his followers deemed harmful to a rational social order were destroyed. There was no place in his extreme "disenchanted" world for imagination (*pendar*), which

> is one of the basest human faculties. It is a bane [*asib*] in the world. All confusions arise, more than anything else, from imagination. . . . Sciences must be followed and their results must be accepted. . . . Following imagination and speculation [*gaman*] and speaking of unfathomable categories to mislead people. . . . Those following this path must be warned and if they do not reform and persist, they deserve death. (Kasravi 1961, 164–65)

Such a tightly ordered cosmology had little room for the development of autonomous, self-willing subjects and the consensual congregation of their wills in intersubjectivity. Indeed, like many of his predecessors and contemporaries, Kasravi reduced human subjectivity to a Faustian level of developmentalism: "God has created people and entrusted the earth to them to trim it, decorate it, develop it . . . so that they [may] establish cities, gardens, and fields [and] so that they may make the water flow, construct roads, fight disease and evil" (1961, 22). Kasravi held to this Faustian view of human agency despite his criticism of instrumental rationality as surrendering to the realm of the body; indeed, his developmentalism, subsumed in the orderly nature of the universe, is in harmony with his cosmology.

The question of citizenship rights is more complicated in Kasravi's discourse. Throughout his career, he would advocate various democratic citizenship rights and freedoms. In an essay written shortly before his assassination, he argued that constitutional democracy was the best form of government (Kasravi [1945], 51). More significantly, he wrote that "Constitutionalism is not mere existence of laws and the Majlis. Constitutionalism has a more sublime meaning. Constitutionalism means that a people wants to run its own affairs; wants no one else to rule over it" (Kasravi [1945], 41). Nevertheless, despite his emphasis on the democratic rights of the collectivity, he excluded the rights of individual subjects as citizens. Such an exclusion is rooted in Kasravi's ontological view of society, whose foundation he believed to be the same as that of the family (Kasravi 1961, 45).[9] He expressed this idea more explicitly in a later passage of the *The Sacred Foundation:*

> Because people live in a social setting, their interests and losses are tied together. Ineluctably, there must be a path that all individuals can follow, and [thereby] know their limits. Otherwise . . . conflict would arise and the social bond would break. If you establish a school or organize an association you would have to write a charter for it. How could it be that hundreds of millions of people would live together and would not need a charter or a path? Indubitably, there must be a path. Now the question is whether people by themselves can make that path. . . . It must be said that they cannot. If people could know [the difference between] good and evil and benefit and harm, what need would there be for the path? Obviously they cannot make a path on their own. (Kasravi 1961, 76)

Kasravi's record was at its worst when it came to women's rights. Although he advocated certain limited rights and freedoms for women, such as the right to vote and the freedom to study, he essentially viewed them as second-class citizens, created by God to raise children and take care of the home for men (Kasravi [1945], 54–55). Thus he denied women the right to be elected to public office and to serve as judges (Kasravi 1961, 237). In conjunction with the patriarchal structure that informed his discourse, the denial of women's rights can be traced to granting rights first and foremost to the "nation" as a collective en-

---

9. Theodor Adorno has argued that identifying society with the family constitutes the essence of the surrender of subjectivity to the collectivity (see Adorno and Horkheimer 1972; see also "Adorno: The Dialectic of Modernity" in the appendix).

tity. Indeed, he went so far as to demand that every Iranian "worship" the fatherland (Kasravi 1961, 126).

Though significant in itself to sociopolitical thought in Iran, Kasravi's discourse also served as a bridge for many young Muslims, disillusioned with the political limitations of their faith but unable to make the break on their own, to shift to secular ideologies such as Socialism and Marxism in the 1940s and 1950s (Dabashi 1993, 46). The next three sections will discuss some of these ideologies in the context of Iran's encounter with modernity.

Socialism and Universalizable Subjectivity: The Marxist Quest for a Collective Subject

In its attempt to deepen and expand subjectivity, leftist thought constitutes a crucial ingredient of Iran's sociopolitical discourse in the twentieth century. I use "leftist" to describe two trends, closely related at the beginning but later distinct and often antithetical. Reflecting the international split between democratic socialists and Marxist-Leninists, the radical discourse in Iran started as a common critique of the shallowness and limited scope of the Constitutional movement in Iran.

The Communist Party of Iran (Ferqe-ye Komonist-e Iran; abolished in 1937) sprang from the Justice Party (Ferqe-ye Edalat) during the latter's first major conference in the Caspian port city of Anzali in June 1920. The new Communist Party immediately called for a series of ultraradical measures, such as immediate and radical land reform, violent overthrow of the bourgeoisie, the British imperialists, and the monarchy, the pursuit of militant trade union policies, and close alliance with Soviet Russia (Abrahamian 1982, 115; Zabih 1966, 29). Soon, however, the party toned down its rhetoric and adopted a more pragmatic approach.

In their party organ, *Setareh Sorkh* (The Red Star), the Communists criticized liberal democracy for its inability to emancipate the masses of Iranian people. In a 1929 article published in *The Red Star*, the author attacked the parliamentary system, as such, for not facilitating the emancipation of the people of Iran:

> The seventh Parliament in Iran entirely corroborates and proves the view of
> the Communist Party of Iran regarding the principles of parliamentarianism
> [namely, that] parliaments in general can never be the real representatives of

the people and can never protect the interests of the toiling classes. Moreover, as long as the present property relations remain and the state apparatus remains in the hands of the nobility and the bourgeoisie, it is absolutely impossible that the masses could make full use of their illusory and nominal "freedom." (Chaqueri 1993, 20)

The same article likened the merely legal and nominal freedoms granted by the constitutional system in Iran to taking the thirsty to a deep well without giving them the means to draw water (Chaqueri 1993, 21).[10]

The major theme addressed by the Communist Party of Iran was land reform: unless land could be distributed among the peasantry, the party argued, emancipation of Iran's predominantly agricultural society would be meaningless. Calling the Constitutional Revolution a "bourgeois revolution," another article in The Red Star criticized the movement for not solving "the peasants' problem, which is the problem of the majority of the nation, even though it was its most important responsibility and its historical mission" (Chaqueri 1993, 55).

What The Red Star considered liberation, however, was not the liberation of each individual member of society as an autonomous subject of modernity. Rather, analyzing the struggle for liberation in collective terms, as was typical of Marxism internationally, it asserted that "what distinguishes us from all the known and unknown revolutionaries in Iran, from Mirza Aqa Khan [Kermani] to Ehsanollah Khan and the rest of revolutionaries, old and new, is, first and foremost, our clear and firm understanding of the class nature of our struggle" (Chaqueri 1993, 60). Furthermore, in their response to this article, the writers' board of The Red Star pointed out that

as the bourgeois revolutionaries are concerned with protection of their own class interests, [so] the Communist Party is the representative of the working class and struggles for the interests of workers, their definite emancipation, and the creation of the dictatorship of the proletariat. Because the interests of the workers and their emancipation are completely related to the interests and freedom of the majority of the great mass of toilers in society, therefore, in this

10. The Red Star was sophisticated enough to realize that, under Reza Shah, parliamentary elections in Iran were a sham, with the shah hand-picking every deputy himself. Nevertheless, the 1929 article represents a critique of the parliamentary system in general.

struggle, the proletariat and the proletarian revolutionaries not only achieve the interests and liberation of the proletariat, but also liberate human society and the world as such. This constitutes the principal difference between proletarian and bourgeois revolutionaries. (Chaqueri 1993, 63; emphasis original)

To complete the Marxist distortion of universal subjectivity, *The Red Star* added the Marxist-Leninist principles of "vanguardism" and "democratic centralism" to their discourse, thereby "particularizing" the already collectivized subjectivity.[11]

This distortion was challenged by Mohammad Amin Rasulzadeh (d. 1954), an old hand in the Iranian and later the Turkish Socialist and pan-Turkish movements, and one of the main organizers of the Democratic Party outside the Majlis immediately after the victory of the Constitutionalists (Abrahamian 1982, 103). Rasulzadeh published *Iran-e Nou* (New Iran) in the early 1910s, which rapidly became the most widely circulated newspaper in Tehran (Abrahamian 1982, 104). He was born in Baku and studied political science in the modern schools of the Caucasus. Sent to Iran by the Social Democrats of Caucasia to participate in the Constitutional movement in Gilan, after the defeat of Mohammad Ali Shah and the restoration of the constitution government in 1909, he became involved with the Democratic Party in Tehran. Under pressure from the Russian Embassy, he was expelled from Iran in 1911 (Adamiyat 1975, 96–97). He spent two years in Istanbul before returning to Baku under a general amnesty granted by Russia in 1913. In Baku, he participated in the Social Democratic Party Musavat. After the October Revolution in Russia, he became involved in the struggle of the Autonomous Socialist Republics of the Caucasus against the centralizing attempts of the Soviets. With the collapse of the autonomous regime in Baku and the occupation of that city by the Red Army in 1920, Rasulzadeh was arrested and sent to Moscow, from which he escaped in 1922. After living in a number of different European countries, he settled in Turkey in 1947.

Rasulzadeh's challenge to the Communist discourse belongs mainly to the period of his disillusionment with the Bolsheviks. But even as a Marxist neophyte who attacked private property as the cause of all trouble in human history and who subscribed to the Marxist thesis of "immiseration" and the

---

11. Its distortion and pursuit of a collective subject notwithstanding, we should acknowledge the role of the Communist Party of Iran in raising the consciousness of Iran's peasants and small working class, especially in the oil-producing Persian Gulf area.

inevitability of revolution, he grounded his concept of class struggle in his desire to expand and deepen the emancipatory moment of modernity. All constitutional governments and republics having some type of popular sovereignty, he reasoned, had wrested this sovereignty from the privileged classes by force: social struggle had always existed (Adamiyat 1975, 100). The subjectivity of modernity was still in a particularistic state and needed to be universalized. Thus the constitutional laws of most countries had "given special privileges to special classes and [had] deprived the public of their rights. [Even in France] the people and democracy [were] not entirely liberated from the yoke of nobility and privilege. And still the property criteria . . . prevalent in elections and the Senate [and belonging] to the privileged classes exist[ed]" (Adamiyat 1975, 109). Rasulzadeh wrote explicitly of expanding and deepening subjectivity when he noted that the Socialists, "in addition to political equality, also demand[ed] economic and social equality" (Adamiyat 1975, 104). Yet, even in this period, Rasulzadeh believed in the principles of political democracy and parliamentarianism (Adamiyat 1975, 108, 116–17).

Indeed, soon after his disillusionment with the Bolsheviks, Rasulzadeh carried his social democratic critique of Marxist-Leninist thought to its logical conclusions.[12] In his essay "Ayande-ye Demokrasi" (The future of democracy), he questioned the absolutism of the collectivity as the sole function of the state: "The implementation of absolute national sovereignty is collective coercion [jabr] and despotism, which is not much different from personal despotism, as exemplified by [Soviet] Russia" (Adamiyat 1975, 73).[13] He maintained that democracy consisted of three independent principles—freedom, equality, and popular sovereignty—that only worked if they operated in a synthesis. He believed that if each of these principles became absolute and abstracted from others, then democracy could not be maintained (Adamiyat 1975, 174). In explicit terms, Rasulzadeh attempted to reconcile the individual and the collectivity, believing this could be accomplished through a fourth principle, cooperation,

12. After his escape from the Soviet Union in 1922, Rasulzadeh commented that "the Communists from the Left and the Fascists from the Right have made democracy the target of their lethal attacks" (Adamiyat 1975, 169).

13. Although I was unable to obtain copies of the original essays by Rasulzadeh used in this section, Fereydun Adamiyat (1975) quotes them extensively in his *Fekr-e Demokrasi-e Ejtemai dar Nehzat-e Mashrutiyat-e Iran* (The idea of Social Democracy in the Constitutional movement of Iran), which I have used instead.

which maintained the equilibrium of contemporary society (Adamiyat 1975, 180). He also recognized the principle of private ownership, provided it did not interfere with the rights of the collectivity (Adamiyat 1975, 180). He even gave a philosophical interpretation to the connection between the concept of rights and the concept of democracy, believing it stemmed from the "synthesis and combination of individualism [fardiyat] and universalism [koliyat]" (Adamiyat 1975, 181).[14] Thus, he concluded, democracy consisted of "equality of rights arising from the combination of principles of individual freedom and popular sovereignty" (Adamiyat 1975, 182).

Rasulzadeh's metaphysics represented a radical departure from that of Marxism-Leninism. According to his subjectivist ontology of freedom, man, "not content with his life . . . cherishes in his soul the changing of conditions of the realm of necessity and . . . achieving the realm of freedom" (Adamiyat 1975, 198). Although, in this respect, he differed little from classical Marxism, reflecting the mature European tradition of democratic socialism, he rejected Marx's reduction of subjectivity to human labor:

> The idea of establishing a worldly paradise devoid of any historical contextuality is an illusion. . . . History is a road without an end. Its beginning and [ultimate end are] unknown, [but] it always moves in the direction of betterment. The image that makes that possible is that humans in the end will become, as much as possible, free, [self-]willing, and perfected beings. (Adamiyat 1975, 241)

In another but related essay, he also wrote that,

> by rejecting the idea that all values refer only to labor, and that no one else but the laborer has the right to live . . . we do not intend to inflame class antagonism artificially. European Socialism, after much experience, is convinced of the bankruptcy of the abstract notion of [class struggle], a question that revolutionary Socialism has raised without regard to its social and historical context . . . We oppose the dictatorship of class. (Adamiyat 1975, 241)

By rejecting class dictatorship and the "fetishism of labor" inherent in the Marxist reduction of subjectivity to labor, Rasulzadeh was one of the few radi-

---

14. Rasulzadeh used both the Persian words fardiyat and koliyat and their French equivalents, individualisme and universalisme, in his original text.

cal thinkers in Iran to disavow the ruinous quest for a collective subject. Unfortunately, however, the influence of Rasulzadeh on Iranian sociopolitical thought was much overshadowed by that of the Tudeh Party.[15]

The Tudeh Party and Modernity

By the early 1930s, the Communist Party of Iran was, for all practical purposes, dissolved. Most of its members were in jail, killed, or exiled to remote areas inside Iran, or had fled the country. In June 1931, Reza Shah introduced a law banning all organizations with a "collectivist ideology" (Zabih 1966, 62; Abrahamian 1982, 154).

While the old Communist Party was declining in Iran, a new generation of young Marxist intellectual activists was coming of age. These new Marxists were markedly different from their predecessors in a number of ways. Most were highly educated, middle-class young men who had studied in Western Europe and not in Russia; unlike the older generation of Marxists, most spoke Persian rather than Turkish or Armenian. In 1935, they formed a "study group" to discuss and propagate Marxist ideas without explicitly referring to their activities and studies as "Marxist," for fear of being suppressed. This group was later called the "Fifty-Three" after the fifty-three members who had been arrested and imprisoned in 1937 (Abrahamian 1982, 155). Late in 1941, the remaining members of the Fifty-Three banded together to form the Tudeh Party. The foundation of the party's ideology was laid by a German-educated university professor named Taqi Arani, who would greatly influence the development of "revolutionary socialist" thought in Iran.

The central figure of the Fifty-Three, Taqi Arani (1902–40) had studied in Berlin from 1922 to 1928 and received his doctorate in chemistry there. In 1935, he founded the group's theoretical magazine, *Donya* (The World), a forum for philosophical and theoretical aspects of Marxism. Arani wrote a number of books on physics, chemistry, biology, and psychology, as well as theoretical books and essays on science and on the scientific-materialist interpretation of Marxism. The titles of some of his works reveal much about his theoretical outlook: *Usul-e Madi va Manteqi Elm* (The material and logical principles of sci-

15. The eclipse of Rasulzadeh's influence on Iranian sociopolitical thought by "revolutionary socialism" might be explained in part by his anti-Iranian positions when he was involved in the pan-Turkish movement in 1920s. See Entekhabi 1993, 197.

ence), "Jabr va Ekhtiyar" (Necessity and free will), "Mashinism," (Machinism) "Hunar va Materialism" (Art and materialism), and "Erfan va Usul madi" (Mysticism and the principles of materialism) (Chaqueri 1983, 5). Arani's deeper scientific interpretation of Marxism, his heroic defiance of Reza Shah's regime, and his subsequent death in Reza Shah's prison combined to produce a lasting impact on generations of Iranian Marxists.

Personally defending the Fifty-Three when they went on trial in 1938, in his speech before the court, Arani revealed the classical Marxist approach to "liberal" revolutions as a preparatory and necessary, but incomplete, stage in the liberation of the entire society:

> The current constitution of Iran is the product of a . . . revolution for which thousands of Iranian youths in every corner sacrificed their blood to obtain a few articles of law. This revolution . . . is still incomplete and its product, insofar as justice is concerned, is [also] incomplete because its principles were created from the intellectual influence of Montesquieu, Voltaire, and Rousseau on French law and [on the] laws of other countries including those of Iran. . . . It is [also] obvious that, insofar as justice is concerned, Iran's constitution is still very incomplete and must be perfected in the same [revolutionary] manner in which it was [originally] achieved. (Arani 1963, 109–10)

In his attempt to ground the concept of rights in labor, Arani was led to expand the idea of citizenship rights. In the same defense speech, he argued that

> right, which is engendered as early as the appearance of man and his society, comprises of the entirety of the freedoms of one individual or a legal person. The right of the individual vis-à-vis other individuals creates the concept of duty. Real justice and right comprise the protection of those rights and duties which in proportion to the structure and natural and logical development of the individual and society must be accorded to them. The first and most essential of those rights is the right to life and freedom, that is, the equal rights and duties of individuals relative to their share in the toil of production and consumption and the regulation of the process of production and consumption. (Arani 1963, 109)

The prevailing laws in Iran were nothing but "fossilized" and "transparent" formulas enacted by the ruling classes, and therefore devoid of justice. Because labor constituted the primary grounding of right and because the majority of the people of Iran owed their existence to their labor, only laws that protected the interests of the masses could be considered legitimate, or so he seemed to imply (Arani 1963, 109).

It was no accident that Arani referred to "the masses" (*tudeh*) instead of "the proletariat" in his defense speech. Because of the Anti-Communist Law of 1931, he and his cohorts avoided using well-known Marxist terms, although his choice of an alternative term reveals his interest in a collective and undifferentiated subject, an interest clearly articulated in Arani's more philosophical essays. In his article "Honar dar Iran Jadid" (Art in modern Iran), Arani argued against the autonomy of art and artists. He believed that art merely reflected social life, and that the artist merely "recognized" but did not create. In what could have been a working definition of Socialist Realism, Arani asserted that "the artist, in the last analysis, is a social product. His spirit and the spirit of his work are determined by the economic forces of his time" ([1983], 54).

It was his deterministic denial of individual subjectivity that served as the link and common denominator between Arani's quest for collective subjectivity and his deeper (and until recent years highly influential) materialist-scientific interpretation of Marxism. In Arani's epistemology, for example, the "human sciences" were subsumed under the physical sciences, in turn subsumed under "dialectical materialism":

> The chain of the exact sciences is a continuous string . . . which begins with the most materialist and therefore most exact sciences, namely, the natural sciences (physics and chemistry). This chain continues with the observation of the special material changes in the physical and psychological state of living beings (biology and psychology) and finally . . . discusses mankind and the human sciences according to the principles of dialectical materialism. (Agahi 1964, 20)

Positivism and labor fetishism combined in Arani's discourse to deny any possibility of creative thought. "It is only with the brain," he wrote in "Mysticism and the Principles of Materialism," that "we can think." The brain, however, was matter, and thought was simply one of the effects of this matter. Experience proved that if material conditions, such as light, temperature, humidity, and so on, changed, there was also a change in the structure and functioning of the living being. The brain followed the same principle. But, Arani added, society was also an external determinant of thought. Because society was the largest apparatus containing all of human communications, and because communications were mediated by labor, thought was also determined by the externalized hard force of matter and labor (Arani [1970?], 3).

Arani ([1970?], 4) believed that "dialectical materialism," embodying the "materialist" grounding of thought, represented the "highest peak" of achievement in the history of human belief systems. He even attributed the emergence of the modern era entirely to "material" factors such as trade, industry, and manufacturing (Arani [1970?], 45).

Arani's materialist discourse, by denying free will, culminated in the negation of human subjectivity. In his article "Necessity and Free Will," he concluded that, because "the soul and life are the determined effects of the special system of matter . . . man's volition is not free and is dependent upon the external circumstances and conditions of his life" (Agahi 1964, 23).

It is interesting to note that, just like Kasravi, Arani intended to "disabuse" the Iranian "masses" of their superstitions by disseminating his ideas of "dialectical materialism." Thus, in "Mysticism and the Principles of Materialism," he wrote: "The goal of publishing this article is to raise the consciousness of the masses to the diseases of mendicancy [dervish], seclusion, contentment, opium, madness, apotheosis . . . to encourage people toward material life and struggle for the preservation of life" (Arani [1970?], 4). When Arani's life came to an abrupt and tragic end, the task of promulgating "dialectical materialism" devolved to the next generation of Iranian Marxist-Leninists.

The Second Generation of Marxist-Leninist Thought and Modernity

Taqi Arani died in prison in 1940, apparently from being deliberately infected with typhus; the remaining members of the group of Fifty-Three were released from prison in 1941, after the Allies forced Reza Shah to abdicate and go into exile. The party these members formed, Tudeh (literally, the masses), has ever since exercised an enormous influence on Iranian sociopolitical life. During its legal and clandestine existence inside Iran between 1941 and 1953, the Tudeh Party closely followed the Soviet line, especially with regard to foreign policy, although in its more pragmatic and eclectic theoretical orientation and ideology, as these were publicly manifested, it hewed more to a typical Marxist-Leninist line.[16]

Only in 1953, however, when the party was finally disbanded and its leader and major theoreticians exiled, did Tudeh's theoretical discourse reach the level of maturity that would have such an impact on Iran's intellectual life. Among the leading theoreticians contributing to *Donya* (The World) in the two decades following its revival in 1960, Ehsan Tabari, Abdulhussein Agahi, and N. Qaziani were most prominent, with Ehsan Tabari serving as indisputable central philosopher of the party.

Born in Sari into a upper-class landed family in Iran's northern province of Gilan, Ehsan Tabari (1917–1989) studied law at Tehran University, where he met Taqi Arani. He later studied in Britain, then worked for the Anglo-Iranian Oil Company in Iran. As a junior member of the group of Fifty-Three, Tabari was sentenced to three years' imprisonment in 1937. He soon assumed a leadership role in the Tudeh Party. In 1948, after the state suppressed internal dissent and the party for its involvement in the separatist fiasco in Azarbayejan, he took on the tasks of theoretical clarification and ideological indoctrination of the cadres, moving the party more and more in the direction of Marxist-Leninist thought. A prolific author, Tabari produced numerous books and essays on topics ranging from philosophy to Iranian history and culture.

Tabari's discourse covered many years and was subjected to all the turbulence stirred up by the Twentieth Congress of the Communist Party in the Soviet Union, where Tabari lived for a time in exile, and by de-Stalinization. Underlying most of Tabari's abstract discussions, however, is a single theme: universal empowerment of the Iranian masses. Paraphrasing Engels in an article entitled "Marksism va Umanism" (Marxism and humanism), Tabari expressed the classical Marxist critique of modernity:

> When bourgeois society became firmly established in the nineteenth century, it aroused a [sense of] bitter despair because it was the caricature of those brilliant promises of the revolutionary "enlighteners." Instead of liberty, equality, fraternity, and the promised elevation of human dignity, modern society and

16. The complete history of the Tudeh Party has yet to be written. But Abrahamian's 1982 book *Iran Between Two Revolutions* remains an excellent source of information on the history of the Tudeh Party and its impact on Iranian politics.

exploitation in capitalist society led to the decline of human dignity and to moral degeneracy. The antihuman nature of the bourgeoisie was ever more forcefully revealed. (1964, 43)

Marxism, Tabari contended, reciting the classical Marxist formulas, overcame the abstraction of humanism when it criticized Feuerbach and the "realist Socialists" for their belief in the fixity of human nature. For Tabari, Marxism demonstrated that human nature was historical and that only through class struggle, the elimination of exploitation, and the creation of collective ownership of the means of production by the proletariat could freedom, equality, and fraternity be realized. "It is only through the emancipation of labor from capital," Tabari wrote, paraphrasing Marx, "that the universal emancipation of man is possible. It is only within the freedom of the collectivity that the freedom of the individual may have any meaning" (1964, 46–47).[17]

In a different article but the same larger context, Tabari broached the Marxist concepts of alienation and commodity fetishism. What had deprived humans in the modern era, he argued, was the alienation of labor's power and its transformation into the control and domination of humans through the "fetishism of commodities" (Tabari 1963, 90–91).

Tabari resolved to restore this lost subjectivity to all mankind. Extolling the virtues of human subjectivity, he wrote: "In the battle of man with nature and with death, man is more powerful. Yea, man is the ultimate victor. Man may not uproot the 'hellish thorn' of death, but he will enrich the dynamic substance of life so that death will appear but a mere pale shadow before it. History is replete with the victories of many a Prometheus and a Sisyphus" (Tabari [1977?]a, 384).

What seems to have engaged much of Tabari's attention was the issue of who should be the carrier of subjectivity—the individual or the collectivity. Indeed, he would wrestle with this issue in many of his theoretical writings. In his article "Mokhtasat Jahan va Duran Ma: Chashmandazi az 'Omdehtarin Masael" (The characteristics of our world and time: A perspective on the most important issues), he wrote, "The freedom of individuals, the freedom of peoples

17. In "Marxism and Humanism," Tabari engaged in an ideological debate with the Chinese theoretician Chou Yang over de-Stalinization and the critique of the cult of personality in the context of "bourgeois humanism" versus "proletarian humanism." Tabari argued that "bourgeois humanism" should not be opposed to "proletarian humanism," but should instead be considered its preliminary stage.

[*khalq-ha*]—these two phases disclose the content of the momentous struggles of our eventful era" (Tabari [1977?]b, 405). He even advocated greater freedom for the individual in the post-Stalinist era:

> After the Stalinist period, what direction should Socialist society face? Collective and scientific leadership in the government and the economy should replace bureaucratic organizational styles, personal methods, abstract [icon-making] and scholastic illusions. Economic life should be organized in such a way that, while preserving the priority of the interest of the collectivity, the arena for the expression of initiative is not circumscribed and the flame of individual enthusiasm is not suppressed. (Tabari [1977?]b, 410)

In a rare moment in the history of Iranian Marxist thought, Tabari ([1977?]c, 440) recognized the individual as the carrier of subjectivity and expressed concern for the crushing of the individual subject under the "weight of the species." He even attempted to reconcile the individual and the collectivity, a reconciliation he relegated to some vague future Socialist society:

> The combination of independent individual life with the collective communal life is based on the voluntary consent of each individual. The power of the collectivity should never crush individual personhood, and the independence of the individual should never harm the order and discipline of collective coexistence. Finding the correct balance between these two opposite and dialectical poles is one of the most complicated problems, whose solution is predicated upon the solution of a mass of other economic and social problems. Capitalism has never been able to solve this problem; it has created chaos or despotism, or both at the same time. Even Socialism, despite its achievements, under pressure by capitalism and the present level of development of man, has been unable to solve this problem entirely. (Tabari [1977?]c, 440)

Such a new approach by Tabari toward the recognition of the individual as at least a partial carrier of subjectivity necessitated a new and revisionist attitude toward the conceptual framework of dialectical materialism. Within the framework of a critique of capitalism, probably influenced by Georg Lukács,

Tabari emphasized the process of capitalist reification.[18] By imposing an un-healthy competition and the arms race, he argued, the "criminal" capitalist sys-tem had turned science and technology against humanity everywhere and in everyday life. After the liberation from capitalism, there would be no need for a hasty transformation of nature. One could take hold of the "helm of the ship of scientific, technological and economic progress and navigate in a direction that would not lead to the domination of souls by objects. Rather, the opposite [could take place]" (Tabari [1977?]c, 442–43). Tabari even proposed a dynamic and "dialectical" relation between the "base" and "superstructure," which would result in the emancipation from necessity imposed by nature and society:

> A Marxist observes in human history, just as in natural history, a progressive movement which stems from the particular laws of social structure. That is to say, it is not possible to find scientific and convincing reasons for this phe-nomenon only in the laws of biology and [physical] anthropology. The con-stant change in the forces and relations of productions, the transformation in the sphere of meaning in society—that is, the political and ideological super-structure which originates in the base but in turn influences it—creates a com-plicated dynamic mechanism in history which causes the progress of historical stages and socioeconomic formations in the direction of man's increasing domination over material and social necessity [jabr]. (Tabari 1975, 8)

This development allowed Tabari to reconsider, for example, the role of mystical thought in traditional Iranian culture and its impact on contemporary intellectual processes. Unlike Kasravi and Arani, Tabari believed that Iranian mystical tradition and thought contained emancipatory elements, that a dis-tinction had to be made between the poems of Hafez and Rumi, on the one hand, and the "self-negating" and "corrupt" poems belonging to the same tradi-tion, on the other (Tabari 1961, 78).

Seemingly influenced by French Existentialism, Tabari departed farthest from the "dialectical materialism" of other Iranian Marxists. In his essay "Barkhi Andishe-ha va Daryaft-ha dar Bareh Adami va Marg" (Some thoughts and per-ceptions on man and death), he wrote:

18. Even though Tabari makes no explicit reference to any of Lukács's works, it is not unrea-sonable to assume that he was aware of the main points of Lukács's discourse and critique and thus engaged with some aspects of them.

Between human life and a world that creates our understanding, reason, and passions, on the one hand, and the mute world of elements and their chemical interactions, on the other, there is no qualitative resemblance. The haphazard turning of elements is quite different from the network of emotional interactions. Man is let loose in the desert of existence to realize his essence by transforming the strange and alien world [he encounters] into a pleasant home. (Tabari [1977?]a, 384)

Tabari's relative departure from orthodox Marxist-Leninist positions becomes even more apparent when his views are compared to those of some of his colleagues and contemporaries. Abdulhussein Agahi, for example, published his articles next to Tabari's in *The World,* attempting to demonstrate the priority of matter and structure by frequently quoting the "eternal words" of Lenin.[19]

Tabari was unable to dissociate himself completely from the tenets of Marxism and Marxism-Leninism, however. As a good Marxist, he firmly believed in collective ownership and in the proletariat as the collective subject of history. On numerous occasions he emphasized the priority of the collectivity over the individual subject.[20] This frame of mind is eloquently captured in a metaphoric passage where, to redeem our individual mortality, Tabari ([1977?]a, 389) surrendered the individual to the universal "ocean" of history:

We can correctly assume the content of human life to consist of thinking, striving, and struggling in the direction of progress in universal human history. In this process, we gradually attain a kind of eternal existence, a kind of a great victory because if it is true that I am a sound in the thunder of history, a leaf in its forest, a drop in its ocean, and a ray of its sun, then my existence, my suffering, my struggle is not futile. . . . If death is absolute annihilation in regard

19. See, for example, Agahi's articles in various issues of *Donya* (The World) in the early 1960s, especially "Barkhi Anaser-e Dialektiki va Madi dar Afkar Abdulrazaq Lahiji, Saheb-e *Guhar-e Morad*" (Some dialectical and material elements in the thought of Abdulrazaq Lahiji, author of *Guhar-e Morad*) and "Enteqadi bar Enteqad az Falsafe-ye Materializm Dialektik" (A critique of the critique of the philosophy of dialectical materialism).

20. When Tabari attempted a reconciliation between the individual subject and the collectivity, he delegated the task to some distant future utopian Socialist society. See, for example, his essay "Shahr Khorshid: Bahsi Falsafi va Ejtema'i dar bare Ayandeh Ensan" (The city of the sun: A philosophical and social discussion about man's future) (Tabari [1977?]c).

to our particular individual existence, it is only relative in regard to our collective existence. Here the absolute is the progressive movement of history.

The sixties and seventies were a period of relative sophistication for Iranian radical discourse and theory, although without much achievement in the practical and political spheres. While the theorists of the Tudeh Party were engaged in these relatively abstract discussions from abroad, however, inside Iran, the "New Left" Marxist-Leninist guerrilla fighters were calling for action.

The Marxist Guerrilla Movement: Praxis and Subjectivity

The period from 1953 (when the CIA-sponsored coup toppled the democratically elected government of Mohammad Mossadeq, reinstalling Mohammad Reza Pahlavi as shah) until 1963 was marked by increasing consolidation of the Pahlavi regime and by U.S. domination of Iran, intermingled with sporadic activities by the opposition. After 1963, however, especially after the summer uprising of that year by supporters of Ayatollah Khomeini and its bloody suppression, the shah's regime extended the tentacles of state power into every corner of civil society. Relying on the increasing oil revenues and on receiving geopolitical support from the United States, the rentier regime of Mohammad Reza Pahlavi banned all political expression and severely curtailed political participation by all classes and groups in society.[21] The political repression by the shah's regime and the conservatism and inaction of the Tudeh Party prompted a group of young Iranian radicals to start a guerrilla movement whose spirit can be captured in one word—"praxis."[22]

Even as it downplayed the importance of theory, the Marxist guerrilla movement developed its own theory of praxis.[23] The two central figures who were responsible for the development of the movement's theoretical positions

21. On the concept of "rentier state" in Iran, see Skocpol 1982.

22. In February 1971, theory became praxis when a group of thirteen young men armed with light weapons attacked the Siahkal Gendarmerie station in the forested mountains near the Caspian Sea, sparking eight years of guerrilla warfare against the regime, in which a total of 341 fighters, mostly belonging to Marxist groups, lost their lives. See Abrahamian 1982, 480–81.

23. Here I will discuss only the Marxist guerrilla movement and not the Islamic groups, partly because of limited space and partly because of the close resemblance between their discourse and that of Ali Shariati, which I will discuss in chapter 4.

were Bizhan Jazani (1937–1975) and Mas'ud Ahmadzadeh (d. 1971). Born in Tehran and involved in political activity from the age of 10, Jazani was imprisoned in the 1950s for being a member of the Tudeh Party. He studied political science at Tehran University, graduating in 1963. He was one of the founders of the Organization of the Iranian People's Self-Sacrificing Guerrillas (Sazaman-e Cherikha-ye Fedai Khalq-e Iran), known simply as the "Fedais." Captured in 1968 by the shah's secret police, the SAVAK, Jazani was kept in prison until 1975, when he was shot to death, allegedly while attempting to escape (Zabih 1986, 118–19; Abrahamian 1982, 483–44). Ahmadzadeh was born in Mashhad and, while still in grade school, engaged in political activities in the National Front, the political organization associated with Mossadeq. Although he seems to have held strong religious views during these years, after entering college in Tehran in 1967, where he majored in mathematics, he was exposed to Marxism-Leninism and established a secret circle devoted to the discussion of the works of Che Guevara, Regis Debray, and the theories of urban guerrilla warfare by the Brazilian revolutionary Carlos Marighella. Ahmadzadeh was captured and executed in 1971. His essay *Mobarezeh Mosalahaneh: Ham Esterategi, ham Taktik* (Armed struggle: Both a strategy and a tactic; published posthumously in 1978) constitutes one of the most important theoretical works of the Marxist guerrilla movement.

Assessing what he considered to be objective conditions for the launching of a revolutionary working-class movement, Ahmadzadeh expressed regret that, unlike tsarist Russia in Lenin's time, where revolutionary intellectuals could establish spontaneous connections with the workers and therefore organize a revolutionary movement, the extreme political repression in Iran in the seventies did not permit such a possibility. Indeed, the harshness of the police state had deprived workers of even trade union consciousness, let alone the political consciousness necessary for revolutionary action (Ahmadzadeh 1978, 31–35). What was even worse, both Ahmadzadeh and Jazani argued, the conservatism, conformism, and inaction of the leadership of the Tudeh Party had resulted in the slaughter of devoted and sincere members of the party (Ahmadzadeh 1978, 12; Jazani 1976, 39).

To remedy the inertia created in "the masses" by these two factors, Jazani and Ahmadzadeh proposed praxis (*pratik*) as the motor of the revolutionary movement they were determined to start. Jazani described praxis in terms of the priority of action in the formation of theory:

For us, not fearing to act, not fearing to commit possible errors, and attempting to overthrow the present conditions with sincerity and courage will provide the means of arriving at perfectly correct tactics. In fact, it is only through praxis [pratik] that our theories are developed and corrected. Spinning our wheels in the theoretical phase, fear of action, and sinking into mere [discussion of] strategic issues would only lead us to opportunistic conservatism. (Jazani 1976, 4–5)

Both Jazani and Ahmadzadeh downplayed theoretical issues in their task of building a revolutionary movement. Quoting Mao Tse-tung, Jazani stated that it was only by participating in revolution, by immediate experience, that revolutionary knowledge and method could be achieved. He also observed that the goal of all political-military movements had been to battle against the people's enemies, not to increase the political consciousness of the members—thus demonstrating the "undeniable superiority of praxis over theory"(Jazani 1976, 5). Extending the theories of Regis Debray to the Iranian context, Ahmadzadeh proclaimed that in Iran, as in Latin America, being a revolutionary was not defined by formal membership in a party but by action (Ahmadzadeh 1978, 49). Unlike the nineteenth century, when grand theorists such as Marx were needed to respond to the theoretical needs of the movement, today there was no such need. Because the content of the revolution had already been clarified and a general method for action achieved, therefore the formulation of a particular theory of revolution depended on revolutionary action rather than theory (Ahmadzadeh 1978, 89).

What constituted the core of praxis for Jazani and Ahmadzadeh was armed struggle and military action against imperialism and its domestic lackeys. Ahmadzadeh exhorted Iranian Communists to replace "the weapon of critique" with the "critique of the weapon" (Ahmadzadeh 1978, 81). Even an existing party was, in his analysis, unnecessary if not actually harmful for the movement because a political organ to carry out tasks of revolutionary leadership would be created in the process of armed struggle (Ahmadzadeh 1978, 55). The most important merit of the military action, according to this analysis, was that, even as it exposed the myth of the invincible, omnipotent state, it also reversed the inertia of "the masses." Paraphrasing Debray, Ahmadzadeh (1978, 40) contended that, by action, "we should demonstrate that the stability and security of [the regime] is but a deception." Jazani assigned the role of sparking of such consciousness among the people to a guerrilla movement, which would by its heroic acts assume the mantle of vanguardism abandoned by the old Communist parties, revealing the vulnerability of the regime and encouraging the repressed masses to join the movement (Jazani 1976, 7).

Indeed, the goal of the praxis advocated by the guerrilla movement was the empowerment of the oppressed people of Iran. Of critical importance was "the problem of transition of the armed struggle from the levels confined to the vanguard, to the level of the masses" (Jazani 1976, 6). Ahmadzadeh joined Jazani in suggesting that empowerment of the masses, the sole means of bringing about social change, could be achieved only by raising their consciousness, which ultimately necessitated the spread of a military-action orientation among them (Jazani 1976, 41).

These conceptual positions entailed altering some of the ontological assumptions in classical Marxist theory, which grounded subjectivity and therefore emancipation in human labor (see appendix). Following their French and Latin American mentors, without actually abandoning the classical Marxist economic grounding for subjectivity and emancipation, the theorists of Iran's Marxist guerrilla movement attempted to shift that grounding from labor to action, especially military action. Thus, Jazani wrote, "[just] as ignoring economic conditions, disregarding attachments of the masses to the economy and resorting to empty propaganda is deviation from 'Marxism,' so undoubtedly is separating 'Marxism' from its revolutionary characteristic and mass revolutionary fervor also an unforgivable deviation" (1978a, 8). Elsewhere, he declared that "what caused the appearance of protest movements [in Iran] in the years following the war (1942–46) was not the change in the productive relations of society but the transformation in the superstructure and the subjective conditions" (Jazani 1978b, 17). Ahmadzadeh (1978, 52) went even further:

> In the process of revolutionary struggle, the economic struggle is increasingly losing its significance. This is the result of the increasing victory of politics over economics. It is the result of domination by the class enemy with the most repressive equipment under conditions of suffocation and terror. It is the result of domination by global imperialism and the fact that this global domination is experiencing the process of its expiration.

In transforming Marx's grounding of subjectivity, the theorists of the Marxist guerrilla movement reduced subjectivity to a single dimension, that of military action. Under the assumption that military action could lead to subjectivity and therefore to emancipation, they, like the generation of Iranian Marxists before them, sought liberation in the collectivity of "the masses." Aware that military action might be misinterpreted as the "petit bourgeois" tendency toward individual action and glorification, they once again sacrificed the individual subject to the collectivity. Thus, even as he warned against the potential for hero worship in the feats of individual guerrilla fighters, Jazani identified emancipation with the amorphous and undifferentiated collectivity of the masses:

> This is not an individual struggle so that a "hero" may change the course of history by "derring-do" and thereby emancipate the people. The armed movement is the starter of a mass movement. The Leninist principle that "without workers all bombs are potentially powerless" has been accepted by the armed movement without any qualification. For this reason, the armed movement's sole goal in [pursuing] military action has been the mobilization of the masses. The ultimate value of the armed struggle lies in the ability to direct the masses in the battle against the regime. (1976, 34)

For all his purported sophistication in dialectical methodology, Jazani failed to realize that reducing the people of Iran to level of "the masses" and creating a "cult of personality," which he had tried to avert, were two sides of the same coin.[24]

By denying the principle of subjectivity implicit in his critique of the link between individual subjectivity and what he construed as "idealism," Jazani returned to the old Marxist-Leninist materialism. In his article "Ravanshenasi Ejtema'i" (Social psychology), he attributed subjectivity and the "mind" only to the individual: "In principle, if by 'psychology' is meant the study of the impacts of objects on the subject or on the conditions and activities of the mind, it should be noted that the society and the collectivity possess neither subjectivity [zehn] nor mind [ravan]. These phenomena, whether in their idealistic or scientific definitions, belong to the individual" (Jazani 1978c, 4). But because such a psychology was at odds with his ideal as collectivity, he denounced it as "bourgeois" and sought to derive consciousness and self-motivation from the

---

24. For an interesting analysis of the genesis of mass society in modernity and the relationship between creation of the masses and charismatic cult of personality, see Moscovici 1985.

collectivity, while reducing psychology to its biological and physiological aspects (Jazani 1978c, 4).

In the attempt to reconcile subjectivity and universality, classical Marxism committed two fundamental errors: (1) it reduced subjectivity to one of its many dimensions, namely, human labor; and (2) it annulled the individual as the carrier of subjectivity, positing the collectivity as the subject of history writ large. Indeed, by denying its carrier, the individual, Marxism negated the very notion of modern subjectivity. The Marxist guerrilla movement in Iran, by grounding subjectivity in armed struggle and by making the amorphous "masses" its carrier, committed similar reductionistic errors. To be sure, the praxis-dominated Marxist guerrilla movement of the 1970s represented the acme of "revolutionary" Marxism in Iran and had an enormous impact on the sociopolitical discourse there. Nevertheless, for the reasons discussed above, even if the Marxist guerrillas had achieved political success, they would have faced great difficulties in coming to terms with modernity. The movement known as the "Third Force" (Niru-ye Sevum) would take a different path.

The Third Force

In 1947, after the failure of the separatist movement led by the Democratic Party of Azarbayejan, a group of dissenters broke away from the Tudeh Party. Among these was Khalil Maleki (1901–1969), one of the original members of the group of Fifty-Three imprisoned with Taqi Arani by Reza Shah.[25] A few years later, Maleki joined Mozafar Baqai to create the Toilers' Party, whose program called for establishing a genuine constitutional government, adopting social and economic reforms, and freeing Iran from "all forms of imperialism, including Russian imperialism" (Abrahamian 1982, 256). The party's youth newspaper, *Niru-ye Sevum* (The Third Force), was especially popular among college students in Tehran (Abrahamian 1982, 256). When Mossadeq proposed nationalizing Iran's oil industry in the early 1950s, Baqai withdrew his party's support of him. As a result, Maleki broke away from the Toilers' Party to found his own organization, which he named the "Third Force" after his newspaper. Constituting the left wing of Mossadeq's National Front coalition, formed for

25. For a survey of this group and some the ideas of their members, see Abrahamian 1999, 48–72.

the nationalization of oil, the Third Force espoused the cause of a "social democratic revolution" that would bring about extensive reforms such as distribution of land and voting rights for women (Abrahamian 1982, 277). Even as the
Third Force fought against internal despotism and its Western backers, it denounced Soviet imperialism and the Soviets' blind loyalists within the Tudeh
Party. Its discourse had an important influence on sociopolitical thought in Iran,
contributing to the emergence of the all-important theme of the "return to the
self," to be examined it in the next section.

The central figure in the Third Force, Khalil Maleki was born into a religious merchant's family from Tabriz. His father was active in the Constitutional
Revolution. Maleki received his primary and secondary education in Arak and
in Iran's Azarbayejan province, then studied at the German technical school in
Tehran (Katouzian 1983, 22). In 1928, he went to Germany to study chemistry
on a state scholarship. Probing into the suspicious suicide of an Iranian student,
he soon came into conflict with the officials of the Iranian Embassy in Berlin,
was branded a "Communist," lost his stipend, and had to return to Iran without
finishing his doctoral dissertation (Katouzian 1983, 28). He registered at the
Teachers Training College in Tehran and became a teacher. Although he had
established contact with certain radical Iranian student circles while in Germany, it was not until his return to Iran that he frequented Taqi Arani's group of
Fifty-Three; he was imprisoned with them in 1937. Upon their release from
prison in 1941, the remaining members formed the Tudeh Party and recruited
Maleki. Though he would be very active in the party and hold sensitive positions, he was critical of its predominant Stalinist ideology and opposed its subservience to the Soviet Union. This criticism and opposition would lead to
Maleki's leaving the party and eventually to his establishing the Third Force.

Maleki took the Tudeh Party's leadership to task for their "necessitarianism," which amounted to a latter-day fatalism, that is, for believing in an "auto-
matic view of history" in their conceptualization of historical materialism
(Katouzian 1983, 63). In criticizing the party's determinist approach (one of the
reasons he broke with it), Maleki distinguished between two paths to the goal
of Marxism—his and the party's:

> In our opinion, party and social commitments must be based on discernment,
> intelligence, and correct understanding and analysis of events, especially the
> realization that our [human] intervention has an impact and as a social force

makes a difference in the process of events. The process of historical necessity is created by us, not by esoteric celestial or terrestrial forces. . . . This is the [essence] of two paths to the same goal and as the result of the collision of these two paths, unfortunately, the current schism [i.e., the split between Maleki and the Tudeh Party] takes place. (Katouzian 1983, 64)

Maleki believed in the "genuine" Marxist notion of "scientific historical necessity," by which he meant a limited sense of human agency in the process of history. In his view, the "hero" and the "genius" in history, without actually making and initiating history, nevertheless had an impact on it (Maleki 1995, 73). By contrast, he contended, the leadership of the Tudeh Party believed in "absolute historical necessity," which accounted for the party's passivity and inaction vis-à-vis international events, and for its following the Soviet line so submissively (Maleki 1995, 73, 78–79). Maleki even criticized Hegel for discounting the role of individuals in history by holding them powerless vis-à-vis the zeitgeist (Maleki 1995, 70–72).[26] Maleki's emphasis on the individual was one of the causes of the mutual disfavor between him and the Tudeh Party. Indeed, while still a Tudeh member, he had one of his articles censored by the party for discussing the role of the individual in history (Maleki 1983, 289). Maleki's contempt for those who surrendered their individual subjectivity to the collectivity was abundantly clear in his assessment of an Iranian member of the Soviet Communist Party he met while in prison in Iran: "He is a weak individual in relation to larger society and [even] the larger party. His individual reason, intelligence, and understanding vis-à-vis public opinion are naught. In brief, [he speaks] of public opinion in the same manner as a devotee speaks of his master or a Dervish who is annihilated in God [fanafillah] of his God" (Maleki 1983, 322).

Such a view of individual subjectivity prompted Maleki to decry the lack of individual freedom in the Soviet system. Though critical of the capitalist system, he was even more critical of the Soviet system for denying economic and political freedoms and for destroying individual freedom (Maleki 1983, 186).[27]

26. Much in agreement with the prevailing misunderstanding of Hegel in the West as well as in Iran, Maleki here seems to be unaware of the emphasis Hegel placed on the notion of subjectivity and the individual as its carrier.

27. Maleki specifically targeted the Soviet concept of "democratic centralism," which he considered a farce, having no democracy and unlimited centralism. See Maleki 1995, 132.

This did not mean, however, that Maleki would neglect the principle of universality. His concern with universal subjectivity is encapsulated in his aphorism that "every baker should be able to learn the art of governing and participating in government" (Maleki 1995, 230).[28]

As a Marxist, Maleki criticized the Constitutional Revolution for the incompleteness of its universality (Maleki 1995, 85). For this reason, he proposed that the democratic movement in Iran should take up the task of creating a society in which universal subjectivity in all its depth and breadth could develop:

> In my opinion, the most important historical task of the National Front is the creation of a "mass civil order" [madaniyat-e tudeh-i], so that every individual [member] of the nation could have a place there and according to his or her merit and talent would contribute to society and would enjoy the fruits of his or her toil. We can identify a society and a civilization in which there would be a logical and proper combination of the individual and society, a civilization in which society is not sacrificed to the individual, and also remember that society does not exist in itself but rather is made up of all individuals. (Maleki 1995, 230)

To present a balanced view of Maleki's discourse, I should mention that, though he bravely fought against Stalinism and Soviet Communism, he remained ambivalent toward Leninism (Ashuri 1991, 52). Even more important, it might be added, he remained loyal to most tenets of Marxism, while largely ignoring Marxism's unwavering pursuit of a collective subject. What is most important, however, is that Maleki's discourse helped to set the stage for the emergence of the "return to the self" theme, which would change the destiny of Iran. Near the end of his career, by attempting to steer away from both capitalist imperialism and Communist domination, Maleki arrived at a position that required an ideology designed specifically for the particular needs and circumstances of Iran. Maleki expressly called for the creation of a "social school" [maktab-e ejtema'i] rooted in the specific historical and cultural experience of Iran. He

28. Here one must differentiate between what Maleki meant by "mass civil order" and what might be construed as a populist approach. As Maleki makes clear in the passage quoted, the role of the individual is crucial to mass civil order, although there should be a "logical" combination of the individual and the collectivity, whereas, in the populist approach, the individual is usually sacrificed in the name of collectivity.

even recommended Islam as the source of social justice for that ideology, thus initiating the call for "authenticity" (Maleki 1995, 218–24).

Return to the Self

Without a doubt, Jalal Al-e Ahmad (1923–1969) played a central, crucial role in developing this theme, initiated by his close friend and colleague, Maleki, and his impact was pivotal in the intellectual life and the history of the Iranian nation.[29] The relationship of the two men went back to their membership in the Tudeh Party, their split from the party in 1948, and their creation of the Third Force a few years later. Although shortly after the establishment of the Islamic regime in 1979 Al-e Ahmad was blamed for Iran's retreat from modernity, the picture is more complicated, as I hope to show.[30]

Born into an esteemed religious family, Al-e Ahmad grew up under Reza Shah, when religion was in eclipse. Both his grandfather and father were locally well-respected and prominent clerics; he himself wore the clerical robe until his early twenties (Dabashi 1993, 42). In 1943, he went to the seminary in Najaf, Iraq, one of the most prominent Shiite centers for the study of theology, but returned to Iran after a few months to join the newly established Tudeh Party. In 1948, Al-e Ahmad joined those, led by Khalil Maleki, leaving the party, although he made it known that he was no mere follower of Maleki's group and parted from Tudeh on his own terms (Dabashi 1993, 48). In 1951, Al-e Ahmad joined Baqai and Maleki in establishing the Toilers' Party and, after the split between Baqai and Maleki in 1953, joined the latter to organize the Third Force.

After splitting from the Tudeh Party, Al-e Ahmad could not confine his political activity to mere party politics or to one particular party. He turned his considerable talents to many different fields, ranging from fiction to ethnogra-

29. Although a detailed discussion of the sociopolitical factors that impelled the intellectuals of Al-e Ahmad and Maleki's generation toward Islamic symbolism is beyond the scope of this volume, schematically, they can be summarized as follows: the disillusionment with liberal democracy, especially after the coup d'état of 1953; Iran's experience with the Tudeh Party; and the powerful and prevalent discourses that originated in the West, which celebrated notions such as "authenticity" and the idea of "organic intellectuals." For a discussion of the political and intellectual context of this period, see Gheissari 1998, chap. 5.

30. For an interesting indictment of Al-e Ahmad's role in Iran's alleged retreat from modernity, see Adamiyat, 1985.

phy, social and political essays, literary criticism, translation, and journalism (Dabashi 1993, 49–63). Behind his literary achievements was a unique prose style, whose short and often verbless sentences, like telegraphic messages, wasted no time in getting to the point, a style that made extensive use of folklore and everyday speech, and that was very likely intended to reach the largest segments of the social universal.[31]

Al-e Ahmad was among the first "postcolonial" thinkers to pay increasing attention to cultural issues in the confrontation between the imperialist West and the East. In striving to create an Eastern Iranian identity to protect Iranians from the erosive effects of Western cultural imperialism, he gravitated more and more to Islamic symbolism. But his significant reliance on religious symbolism and his efforts against Western imperialism did not, in the final analysis, lead him into an antimodern camp, even though he often appears to have fallen into that trap.

Gharbzadegi (literally, West-struckness) was the central concept in Al-e Ahmad's sociopolitical discourse and the title of his highly influential book, published in 1962. It has been variously translated as "Occidentosis," "Westmania," and "Westoxication." In point of fact, *gharbzadegi* was the Persian equivalent of *dysiplexia*, a Greek neologism coined by Ahmad Fardid, an Iranian philosopher who was influenced by Heidegger and who seems to have taken upon himself the task of introducing Heidegger's antimodern philosophy into the intellectual circles in Iran, where he promoted it throughout the sixties, the seventies, and even the eighties.[32] Although Fardid had coined *dysiplexia* and its

---

31. For a detailed, English-language biography of Al-e Ahmad and analysis of his works, see Dabashi 1993.

32. Ali Gheissari has provided a highly informative account of Fardid's original conceptualization of his Greek coinage *dysiplexia* and its Persian equivalent *gharbzadegi* (Westoxication). Fardid created *dysiplexia* from *dysis*, which means "the West," and *plexia*, which means "being struck by or afflicted with something." *Dysis* (like the Arabic *gharb*) refers both to the geographical West and to the place where the sun sets and darkness begins. Fardid's chief reproach of the West was not over its technology (or "the machine," according to Al-e Ahmad) but over the egocentric worldview of Western epistemology, originating in ancient Greece, which had as its object of study an existential separation between man as the knowing subject and the external world. The emergence of such a perspective, as opposed to the harmonious and illuminative perspective of Eastern philosophies, was the beginning of a period of universal darkness, which had since concealed the original unity and totality of Being (Gheissari 1989, 264–65; see also Gheissari 1998, 89, 177–80 [note 101]).

Persian equivalent to denote the antimodern constructs of Heidegger, Al-e Ahmad defined *gharbzadegi* quite differently, as

> the aggregate of symptoms afflicting the life, culture, civilization, and mode of thought of a people having no tradition to function as a fulcrum, no continuity in history, no gradient of [social] transformation, but having only what the machine brings them. . . . Thus Westoxication [*gharbzadegi*] is the characteristic of a period of our history when we have not yet conquered the machine and do not understand the secrets of its configuration and structure. (Al-e Ahmad 1977, 34–35)[33]

This definition, especially its first part, could easily be misinterpreted as a critique of modernity, the implied remedy to which would be a simple return to a premodern Iranian identity heavily overlaid with religion and fanaticism. Indeed, Al-e Ahmad himself unwittingly encouraged this misinterpretation by fulminating against the figures of the nineteenth- and early-twentieth- century Iranian Enlightenment (without understanding its dialectical nature) and by praising reactionaries such as Fazlollah Nuri (Al-e Ahmad 1977, 78–80). Such a misinterpretation has been the common reading of Al-e Ahmad's work; indeed, it has led many to place blame for the consequences of the Islamic Revolution largely on him.

A closer examination of Al-e Ahmad's writing, however, yields different results. In many passages of *Gharbzadegi* (Westoxication), he described the concept of Westoxication as the process of creating an "empty self." Borrowing the term "facelessness" (*bi-simayi*) from Maleki, he characterized Iranian youth as a "faceless crowd who have lost their religious anchors without gaining any sensibility of selfhood" (Al-e Ahmad 1977, 106). Using still other metaphors to describe the personality devoid of subjectivity and the destruction of Iranian subject, Al-e Ahmad faulted the Iranian educational system for creating "Westoxicated" (*gharbzadeh*) people, who are just like "faces on water" (*naqsh bar ab*). He also explained the concept of Westoxication in terms of "suspension" and "being on the fence." He criticized the members of the ruling elite for being just

---

33. In Daryush Ashuri's estimation, Al-e Ahmad was much more influenced by Sartre—even though he did not seem to have read Sartre's *Being and Nothingness*—than by Heidegger through Fardid. Ashuri also suggests that Al-e Ahmad misunderstood Fardid's Heideggerian sense of *gharbzadegi* (Ashuri 1995, 257–58).

like a "particle suspended in the air" or a "mote on water," for being "discon-
nected" from the roots of their society, culture, and tradition. A Westoxicated
(*gharbzadeh*) person, far from being "the connecting point between the ancient
and modern, between old and new," is rather "a thing without any connection
with past and without any understanding of the future. He is not a point on the
line, but a hypothetical point on a plane or even in the space, just like that suspended particle" (Al-e Ahmad 1977, 141). Westoxicated people had neither beliefs nor commitments. They were neither believers in God nor even atheists.
Going to their mosques as they would to movies or clubs, they were everywhere mere onlookers, always sitting on the fence (Al-e Ahmad 1977, 144).
Most important, Al-e Ahmad defined the Westoxicated person in terms of "inauthenticity," devoid of personality and subjectivity:

> The Westoxicated [*gharbzadeh*] person does not have a personality. He is an in-
> authentic [*bi-esalat*] thing. His self, his house, and his words smack of nothing.
> He is more representative of everything and everybody. Not that he is cosmo-
> politan, that he is internationalist. By no means. He belongs to nowhere rather
> than being cosmopolitan. [He] is an amalgam of an individuality devoid of
> personality and a personality devoid of character [*enferad bi-shakhsiyat va
> shakhsiyat khali az khasiseh*]. (Al-e Ahmad 1977, 146)

In the long rivalry between the East and the West, "we have ended up becoming the sweeper of the circus ring," and the West has become "the ringmas-
ter." "And what a circus!" he wrote. "A circus of pornography, stultification, and
arrogance in order to sponge [our] oil." Al-e Ahmad further argued that the
process of creating empty selves in Iran was aided by the technological domination of Iran by the West through their domestic henchmen.

> It is true that, as Marx said, we still have two worlds in struggle against one an-
> other. But these two worlds have acquired much vaster dimensions since his
> time and the struggle is much more complicated than the struggle between
> capital and labor. . . . Our time is characterized by . . . one world involved in
> making, developing, and exporting the machine [and by another] engaged in
> consuming, depreciating, and importing the machine. (Al-e Ahmad 1977,
> 26–27)

To fight against this unholy alliance between reification and imperialism, Al-e
Ahmad exhorted Iranians to put the Western "jinni of the machine" back into its

bottle and to make, and gain control over, the machine themselves (Al-e Ahmad 1977, 118).[34]

To fill the empty self and restore authenticity to it, Al-e Ahmad proposed a concept he referred to as "rushanfekri," a relatively recent Perso-Arabic coinage composed of *rushan*, meaning "enlighten," and *fekr*, meaning "thought." Whereas *rushanfekr* in modern Persian is roughly equivalent to "intellectual," *rushanfekri*, at least as used by Al-e Ahmad here, may be translated as "enlightenment." Indeed, explaining what he meant by *rushanfekri* in *Dar Khedmat va Khianat Rushanfekran* (On the services and treasons of intellectuals), he offered almost a textbook definition of the Western Enlightenment:

> We can say that *rushanfekri* is peculiar to the period in which human societies are no longer organized on the basis of blind obedience [*ta'abud*] or fear of the supernatural . . . in which the transformation in thought following the principle of experiment and progress in technology spreading among increasingly vaster human societies . . . has taken the element of fear out of natural phenomena and demonstrated that they have no influence on human destiny. In more general terms, *rushanfekri* is a period in which man is cut off from natural elements . . . and his destiny is separated from that of nature. [He] finds himself alone vis-à-vis his destiny, without any celestial or terrestrial support . . . forced to act relying on himself only, without any expectations from the Outside or the Sublime world . . . to choose, to be free and responsible. (Al-e Ahmad 1980, 30–31)

When humans were liberated from "necessitarianism" (*jabr*) and took their own destiny in their hands, they entered the "sphere of *rushanfekri*." Al-e Ahmad's ideas on this concept were discussed chiefly in *On the Services and Treasons of Intellectuals*, which he started after the religiously inspired uprising of the summer of 1963 was bloodily suppressed by the Pahlavi regime. Holding the secular intellectuals responsible for the failure of this uprising, Al-e Ahmad used the occasion to discuss the role of intellectuals in addressing Iran's sociopolitical

---

34. Al-e Ahmad's basically sound analysis of the alliance between reification and imperialism did not prevent him from making ludicrous pronouncements, for example, that the Constitutional Revolution was a plot by the British to wrest an oil concession from Iran (Al-e Ahmad 1977, 83). Similarly ludicrous were his suggestions that Timur Lenk (Tamerlane) destroyed the Islamic East at Europe's instigation (Al-e Ahmad 1977, 67–80). On the other hand, Al-e Ahmad (1977, 151) discussed the phenomenon of Orientalism some two decades before Edward Said did.

problems. Among the most important meanings he attached to *rushanfekri* was an ideal representing both the exact opposite of, and the antidote to, Westoxication. According to Al-e Ahmad, freedom and free thinking constituted the substance of *rushanfekri* (Al-e Ahmad 1980, 431). Believing therefore that the "foundation of *rushanfekri* [lay] in the dissemination of free-thinking and the freedom to ask questions" (Al-e Ahmad 1980, 243) put him at odds with dogmatic religionists (*mutshari'*), whom he excluded from being *rushanfekr*s because they, just like military personnel, only obeyed the "command" (*amr*). Al-e Ahmad presented a fascinating comparative ontology of different religious traditions regarding the relationship between God and humans. He contended that, in Islam, the relationship between humans and God was that of master and slaves, whereas, in Judaism, it was that between two rivals, as exemplified in the story of Jacob wrestling with Jehovah.[35] In Christianity, he argued, the relationship is that between father and children; in Buddhism, that of the unity between creator and created. He concluded that the relationship of master to slaves was one of the causes of the weakness of *rushanfekri* in the Islamic world (Al-e Ahmad 1980, 34).

Al-e Ahmad expressed some of his deepest ontological thinking on the subjectivity of the individual in an intimate analysis of his own existential problem of being sterile. Using the Persian metaphor that every child is a gravestone for his father, Al-e Ahmad "celebrated" his sterility, perhaps out of frustration, as signifying his radical freedom as an individual. In his essay "Sangi Bar Guri" (A stone on a grave), written in 1963 but not published until 1981, he interpreted his inability to connect his ancestors to his progeny as a break in the continuity of tradition, guaranteeing his individual freedom. Regarding his sterility as the negation of the past and tradition, he characterized the past and tradition as "nothing" (*hich*). But all this was salutary because it proved there was freedom for the individual: "If you knew how happy I am that I am the last gravestone for my dead [ancestors]. I am the one and the only end point of Tradition. I am the negation of future that would have been imprisoned by past. . . . At least I am left with the consolation that in this world there is freedom for the sole individual" (Al-e Ahmad 1981, 92–93).

Such a radical view of individual subjectivity, however, did not deter Al-e

---

35. Here Al-e Ahmad erroneously refers to Jacob wrestling with "a man" (Genesis 32:24 [King James Version], who in the West is popularly thought to be an angel, but who nevertheless symbolizes God) as "Jacob wrestling with Jehovah." See also Genesis 32:30.

Ahmad from advocating the dissemination of *rushanfekri* among the Iranian people. Indeed, it was his thinking with regard to the types of agents and the popular Islamic symbols to be used disseminating *rushanfekri* that gave rise to contradictory and controversial positions in his discourse. Like many of his predecessors, Al-e Ahmad contended that the of universalization and empowerment issuing from the Constitutional Revolution had been confined to the aristocracy (Al-e Ahmad 1980, 202–5, 402). He also faulted the Tudeh Party for its inability to reach deep into the social universal and its failure to disseminate *rushanfekri* among "the masses," despite its promising beginnings (Al-e Ahmad 1980, 415).

At the heart of three related dilemmas that Al-e Ahmad never managed to resolve completely was the failure, indeed the inability, of secular movements to disseminate *rushanfekri*, as he called the universalization of empowerment. Secular ideologies could not penetrate the depth of the social universal, he maintained, as Iranian history had proven time and again. To illustrate his point, he harked back to the sixth and eighth centuries B.C., to the success of Zoroaster's religious message and the failure of the secular reformer Geumat, respectively (Al-e Ahmad 1980, 152–58). But, at the same time, Al-e Ahmad found religion to be the greatest obstacle to disseminating *rushanfekri*. In particular, he criticized the Shiite expectation of justice (*intizar*) upon the advent of the promised Imam, a concept that was based on

> ignoring the present reality and living only by hope of that [promised] Day or relegating the solution of all problems to that [promised] Advent. Do you not think this is the greatest cause of [belief in] predestination [*qaza va qadar*]? This gives rise to negligence in acting and decision making, and to procrastination, which is the biggest obstacle in the achievement and dissemination of *rushanfekri*. (Al-e Ahmad 1980, 271)

Al-e Ahmad attempted to resolve this dilemma in a cursory fashion by invoking the Shiite principle of *ejtehad*, which had long been used to logically deduce secondary rules from the Quran and the Prophetic Tradition.[36] *Ejtehad*, he claimed without elaborating, could be used to address the issues and problems of a modern society (Al-e Ahmad 1980, 257).

The second dilemma Al-e Ahmad faced, of such pivotal significance that it

---

36. On the exercise of *ejtehad* in Shiite tradition, see, for example, Mottahedeh 1985.

has overshadowed the rest of his discourse, was who should disseminate *rushan-fekri*. He reserved his most caustic criticism for Iran's secular intelligentsia, whose greatest sin had been the rift and alienation from the social universal they had brought about by attacking the religious beliefs and traditions of the people. Upon cursory review, he dismissed the efforts of some of the major intellectuals of the nineteenth-century Iranian Enlightenment as "paltry" (Al-e Ahmad 1980, 272–76). Worse still, he accused most Iranian intellectuals of his day of being the pawns, if not the direct agents, of cultural imperialism:

> The intellectual in Iran is someone who in theory and practice, has a colonial approach in the name of a scientific approach. That means he discusses science, democracy, and freethinking [*azadandishi*] in an environment in which modern science is not established. Therefore, he does not know his indigenous people [well enough] to believe that they deserve democracy. Similarly, he exercises his freethinking not against the rulers but only against the traditional institutions (religion, language, history, ethics, and rituals) because exercising [it] against the rulers and colonial and semicolonial institutions is difficult. (Al-e Ahmad 1980, 50)[37]

Because of this colonial link, the contemporary intellectual in Iran "is still alienated from the people." And because he "is not in touch with the people," he "inevitably has no concern for them." Indeed, "as long as the Iranian intellectual is not familiar with his indigenous and local problems and does not try to solve them, the situation remains the same" (Al-e Ahmad 1980, 407).

In his sociological analysis of Iranian intellectuals, Al-e Ahmad drew heavily on the work of the Italian Marxist activist and philosopher Antonio Gramsci (1891–1937). Taking Gramsci's "organic" intellectual as his model, Al-e Ahmad conceived of the "indigenous" (*bumi*) or "self-same" (*khodi*) intellectual, who stood in direct opposition to the "Westoxicated" (*gharbzadeh*) and imperialist intellectual.

Because he considered the overwhelming majority of secular Iranian intellectuals since the nineteenth century to be Westoxicated (*gharbzadeh*), Al-e Ahmad undertook a desperate search for "indigenous" intellectuals to guide the

---

37. Al-e Ahmad also blamed the intellectuals for fleeing the front line with the coming of Reza Shah's dictatorship and the concomitant eclipse of what I have called "universalizable subjectivity." See Al-e Ahmad 1980, 321–22.

Iranian people to their liberation, a search central to the second dilemma of his discourse. Well aware of the obscurantism of the clerics and their negative attitudes toward *rushanfekri*, he nevertheless gravitated toward them as the primary source of indigenous intellectuals who, through their religious offices, were closely in touch with the people. Thus, on the one hand, he found the clerics "ineligible" to become "indigenous" intellectuals and therefore political leaders of the nation because they, like members of the military, belonged to the realm of "obedience" (*ta'abud*). On the other hand, he believed that "by the virtue of its defense of tradition, the Shiite clergy" was not only a "resistance force against the encroachments of colonialism whose primary target for pillaging is cultural and traditional," but also "a bulwark against the Westoxication of the intellectuals and the absolute submission of [our] governments to the West and its imperialism" (Al-e Ahmad 1980, 255). Al-e Ahmad was careful to stipulate, however, that if the clerics decided to participate in sociopolitical movements, they would have to abandon their idea of government based on revelation or else refrain from political activity altogether (Al-e Ahmad 1980, 271).

The third dilemma Al-e Ahmad faced was which "self" to return to. As we have seen, the central goal of his book *Westoxication* was to identify the substance with which to fill the "personality" emptied of subjectivity by imperialism. Basic to that substance was *rushanfekri*, or what Al-e Ahmad considered to be true enlightenment and freethinking. At the same time, he could not ignore how deeply Islam and loyalty to the Islamic heritage were ingrained in the consciousness of Iranians.

None of the three dilemmas Al-e Ahmad faced was easy to resolve. But the significance of his discourse lay in his opening the road for a return to a self that proved to be partially but not entirely at odds with the principle of subjectivity. The full force of this return to self became apparent in the religious discourse we will examine in chapter 4. But, for now, let us briefly consider the theories of two other thinkers, Ehsan Naraqi and Daryush Shayegan, who, though limited in their influence, explored important dimensions of the theme of return to the self.

The work of Ehsan Naraqi (b. 1926), a French-trained sociologist and UNESCO official, was popular in the 1970s, particularly among young college students sufficiently Westernized to be familiar with Western counterculture, yet yearning for an authentic identity. Drawing on his many years of living in the West and his experience there with social movements in the sixties and seventies, Naraqi's work largely reflected the Western countercultural critique of

modernity, even as it addressed issues raised by Critical Theory. Its most important contribution was to bolster the convictions of Iranian thinkers pursuing the
return to the self: no less an authority than the West itself was confirming what
amounted to the lost and maligned virtues of Iranians. Thus Naraqi's first book,
Ghorbat Gharb (The alienation of the West), published in 1974, discussed some
of the implications of such a critique for a country like Iran, trying to emulate
Western technological achievements. His next book, *Ancheh Khud Dasht* (What
the self had), published two years later, would develop this line of thought, ex-
ploring in greater detail the possibility of a return to certain elements in the "native" culture.

Naraqi urged his compatriots to understand and heed the message of the
Western countercultural movement (Naraqi 1974, 167). "Today, a sort of 'alienation' [*ghorbat*] has surrounded the Western man. Alienation from the self, from
one's home and finally from one's cohorts . . . has nothing to do with geographic
borders. This means," he warned, "that the 'East' may also become the 'West' and
the sense of alienation may also engulf the Easterners" (Naraqi 1974, 10).

Contrasting the East and the West, Naraqi stressed that the domination of
nature was at the core of Western alienation. In the Eastern way of life, "man did
not dare consider himself the master of nature. He did not find such impudence
in himself as to believe he could conquer nature. Having done just that ever
since the Renaissance, the Westerner has now come to see that nature has rejected him" (Naraqi 1974, 159).

Reflecting the central theme of Adorno and Horkheimer's *Dialectic of Enlightenment* (1972), Naraqi pointed to the paradox of modern humans, who, in the
very process of achieving subjectivity, had brought about the domination of
both nature and humankind itself: "In Western civilization, on the one hand,
man as a subject is involved in the act of appropriating and controlling nature.
On the other hand, nature and man himself—by virtue of being a part of nature—are considered as objects to be appropriated and controlled" (1976, 14).
He also articulated a principal thesis of the Orientalism of Edward Said (b.
1935): if Westerners have shown any interest in Eastern cultures, it has been not
to acquire any theory from them to improve universal human culture. Rather,
their goal has been to search for archetypes to confirm and validate their own
culture (Naraqi 1976, 156).

Although the scale of disaffection with Western culture was large enough
to encourage Iranians to return to their own cultural heritage, Naraqi never ad-

vocated abandoning modernity altogether. Acknowledging the need for science and technology, he criticized the ideology of developmentalism, which was part and parcel of the hegemonic discourse underlying the Pahlavi regime's efforts to gain legitimacy.

> The European and American model of economic development has paid more attention to increasing man's power vis-à-vis nature and has neglected the relations of man with man. In fact, its goal has been the struggle with nature and its conquest. . . . [In liberating] man from restrictions of nature . . . it has imposed other restrictions upon him. Today it has become evident that development is not a mere technical and technological problem [but that] human dimensions are also involved. . . . The conclusion to draw is that human freedom and the realization of human personhood must be the main goal of development. (Naraqi 1974, 114–15)

Thus Naraqi saw universal subjectivity as the main objective of his proposed new scheme for development. Even his advocated return to Islam was to be based on the combined principles of freedom and responsibility (Naraqi 1976, 140), although this critical requirement for the return, for the most part, did not register on his audience.

Despite their criticizing certain aspects of Iranian modernity, both Al-e Ahmad and Naraqi upheld the pillars of modernity. This was not the case with Daryush Shayegan (b. 1934), whose discourse directly spoke to Iran's intellectual appropriation of modernity, even though his direct influence, at least before the revolution of 1979, remained mostly confined to elite intellectual circles. Shayegan was born into a wealthy cosmopolitan family in Tehran. His father was a well-to-do merchant from Azerbaijan and his mother was a Georgian Sunni Muslim who traced her ancestry to the ruling families of Georgia. From an early age, Shayegan was exposed to several languages and cultures, learning Turkish and Persian at home, where he also became familiar with Russian, and soon learning French at the French missionary school in Tehran. At the age of 15, he was sent to a boarding school in London and then studied in different European countries. Upon his return to Iran in 1960, he began to explore Eastern philosophies, including the Persian Gnostic tradition and Indian philosophies. He developed a keen interest in the religious and mystical traditions of Iran and studied with some of the leading figures in that tradition; he also observed ritual Muslim praying and fasting.[38]

During the first phase of his thought, before the Islamic Revolution, Shayegan was very much influenced by Martin Heidegger, whereas, after the revolution, he took up positions that were almost the exact opposite of his pre-revolutionary ones. In his Heideggerian phase, Shayegan maintained that nihilism constituted the very foundation of modernity. In his book *Asia Dar Barabar-e Gharb* (Asia confronting the West), first published in 1977, he described modernity in terms of a destructive, violent, inevitable, ubiquitous, and descending movement in the history of the "spirit," which in its irreversible course left nothing stable. Nietzsche was, according to Shayegan, the first person to discover the movement of modernity and its mode of action (Shayegan 1992a, 23–24). Closely related to the anthropocentrism and vacuity of modern subjectivity, with added religious sensitivity toward "appetites," "nihilism gradually substituted man's reason for Divine Revelation, and in [its] later stages replaced reason with instincts and appetites" (Shayegan 1992a, 30).

For Shayegan, nihilism had two phases. During the first, which he called "passive nihilism," the congruence between value and end was destroyed. As a consequence, "the power of faith gradually weakens and values that have no affinity with the end start railing against each other, and the war of values begins." During the second, later phase, which he called "active nihilism" or "absolute negation," "the vacuous and the absurd appear. This period of decline is a period of neither this nor that. In other words, the declining phase in the West is a form of diseased consciousness that obeys neither terrestrial nor celestial [norms] and as a result denies everything" (Shayegan 1992a, 47).

Furthermore, Shayegan contended, the nihilism of the liberal age had evoked the totalitarian and authoritarian responses of the twentieth century. In the realm of thought, however, he saw two responses to the nihilism that constituted modernity. Borrowing a concept from Herman Rauschning, he called the first response the "de-realization of Reality" (Shayegan 1992a, 32). With this "response," which in fact was the extension of the logic of nihilism itself, every value and reality is undermined and questioned. Shayegan cited the works of Gilles Deleuze, Timothy Leary, Alan Watts, Wilhelm Reich, R. D. Laing, and Michel Foucault as examples of this type of response to nihilism.

The second response to nihilism, which met with his heartfelt approval,

---

38. The biographical information on Shayegan is drawn from Shayegan 1995.

Shayegan called the "righteous leap of great thinkers," by which he meant the metaphilosophical thought of thinkers such as Martin Heidegger, Karl Jaspers, and Paul Tillich (Shayegan 1992a, 36–38). Reflecting Heidegger's criticism of Western metaphysics going back to Plato's conception of the Idea and its characterization as subject-centered representation, Shayegan saw the historical emergence of subjectivity as having occurred at the expense of "Being" (Shayegan 1992a, 238). Without understanding its dialectical nature, he criticized human subjectivity as the central theme in modern philosophy that had given rise to domination and conquest in the West:

> Subjectivity in Fichte's philosophy is prior to Being, and Hegel considered it the origin of the movement of the Absolute Spirit. Schopenhauer made the will the foundation of his philosophy, and Nietzsche regarded the eternal return as the will to power. Will and want are the surging point in this way of thought and all later phases are to satisfy these. . . . And because will refers to power, imperialism, conquest, domination, and appropriation are inherent in [modern Western] culture. (Shayegan 1992a, 234)

Shayegan advocated the absolute surrender of individuality and subjectivity to universality, setting Hegel's notion of the emergence and unfolding of subjectivity against Heidegger's lament over the "forgetting of Being."[39] Indeed, he praised traditional Chinese civilization for its absolute surrender of the individual and subjectivity to the universal:

> The view that [the Chinese] had of nature and the origin is unrivaled. The principle of nonappropriation, nonaction, and submission to the bountiful forces of the Being . . . has been a distinctive characteristic of the ancient Chinese cosmology. The Chinese are the only people who invented gunpowder but did not make cannons; they invented the compass but they did not give in to [the urge] to discover new navigational routes and new continents, which was one of the facets of the Western Renaissance. (Shayegan 1992a, 60)

Shayegan concluded that traditional societies such as Iran should avoid the nihilism that was modernity. In the Asian mode of thought, the evolution of

39. Ironically, Shayegan seems to have missed the close affinity between the totalitarian ideologies he criticized and the surrender of the individual subjectivity to the totality of the universal or "Being."

subjectivity from Plato to Hegel had never taken place (Shayegan 1992a, 239). "Our" Asian civilizations, he argued, had no affinity with the latest aspects of Western nihilism such as Marxism, positivism, or any other modern Western ideology (Shayegan 1992a, 19).

Shayegan's critique of modernity referred to some of the most painful consequences of modernity: the reduction of thought to calculation and of ethics to utilitarianism, the dismissal of the essential forms of spirituality as metaphysics, and the radical transformation of the world from "hearth" to "mechanism." But, at the same time, he lamented the disappearance of some of the most oppressive institutions of premodernity:

> The disappearance of the hierarchical "esteem" system has caused the elimination of authority and obedience, which used to be the foundation of Asian social orders. In those social orders, there were links that connected children with father, wife with husband, [Sufi] follower with master, creature with creator, and community with religion. There were also intermediary links that, according to [their] status and authority, connected members of the family, urban community, nation, and religious community in their own respective spheres and thus created a pyramidal world in which each person had a definite place, each group an aspiration, and each people an order. But [modern] Western civilization has eroded this hierarchy and replaced it with the desire for democracy and freedom of every human according to the law. In reality, the law has replaced the caste system and the structure of responsibility found in medieval Western and Eastern societies. (Shayegan 1992a, 144)

In an ironic reflection of René Guenon's view of egalitarian society as the kingdom of the Shudras on earth, Shayegan looked upon the democratic aspects of modern society as "mass society" (Shayegan 1992a, 82).

Before the Islamic Revolution, Shayegan's audience was, in large part, the highly Westernized Iranian elite who had become disenchanted with modernity. After the revolution, however, Shayegan seems to have completely reversed his prerevolutionary positions. If, before the revolution, he was all for the universal or Being, in his book *Cultural Schizophrenia: Islamic Societies Confronting the West*, published first in France in 1989, he promoted the subjectivity of modernity without any attempt at reconciling it with universality.[40]

40. As Ali Banuazizi has observed, Shayegan's turnabout entailed an extreme dichotomization between modernity and tradition that is simply not conducive to a viable society in our time.

Shayegan's prerevolutionary discourse was the last and most radical development of the secular theme of the return to the self; as such, its audience was relatively small. As we will see in chapter 4, however, this theme was brought to its logical conclusion and was given a religious content by Ali Shariati, who appealed to a large audience among the Iranian people in the 1970s and 1980s.

See Banuazizi 1993. That Shayegan seems to be adopting a more "moderate" position, which attempts to make a synthesis between subject and Being, is indicated in his recent book *Zir Asmanha-ye Jahan* (Under the skies of the world; Shayegan 1995).

Islamic Discourses and Modernity

Part two focuses on Islamic sociopolitical thought in Iran during the last four decades of the twentieth century. Chapter 4 closely analyzes the works of the three main architects of the Islamic Revolution, Ali Shariati, Ayatollah Khomeini, and Ayatollah Motahhari, delving into the underlying metaphysical assumptions and sociological implications of their discourses to explicate the complex relationship of their thought to the tenets of modernity. Chapter 5 explores the unfolding of the Islamic discourse in the postrevolutionary period. Contrary to many Western accounts, the development of sociopolitical thought in Iran has not been halted by the establishment of an Islamic regime. The dynamics of the revolutionary Islamic discourse of the sixties and seventies have given rise to two distinct postrevolutionary discourses with opposite potentials for accommodating modernity. Chapter 5 examines the thought of the two intellectuals most closely identified with these discourses, Reza Davari-Ardakani and Hussein Hajfaraj Dabagh, known by the pen name Abdolkarim Sorush. It considers the sociopolitical implications of their discourses in light of Iran's urgent postrevolutionary need to cope with modernity and with the popular desire for democratic reforms and economic development.

4

Islamic Revolutionary Thought

The Self as Mediated Subjectivity

As we saw in chapter 3, a number of "secular" intellectuals responded to the call to return to the self initiated by Jalal Al-e Ahmad. Although Al-e Ahmad's invitation was also enthusiastically received by many religious groups and individuals, some religious figures, most prominent among them Ayatollah Khomeini, had long before, and independently of Al-e Ahmad, reached similar conclusions. As early as the mid-1940s, in a book entitled *Kashf al-Asrar* (Secrets unveiled), Khomeini had called for activation of the clauses in the 1906 constitution designed to guarantee the conformity of state laws with those of the Sharia (divine law).

Islamic revolutionary thought, as developed by its three main architects, Ali Shariati, Ayatollah Khomeini, and Ayatollah Motahhari, was a direct and indirect response to the discourse of modernity and to the course and consequences of the policies of positivist modernity implemented by the Pahlavi Dynasty.[1] Already in the 1940s, Khomeini had engaged both the positivist modern thought of Kasravi (discussed in chapter 2) and the policies of Reza Shah. The main thrust of the Islamic revolutionary discourse was to refute the discourse of modernity in Iran, to which the three Islamic theorists advanced serious challenges, going back to early Iranian thinkers and to the nineteenth-century importers of modernity. But in their own discourses, Shariati, Khomeini, and Motahhari were much influenced by the discourse they set out to challenge, incorporating certain of its crucial elements, which served to com-

---

1. Although Shariati, Khomeini, and Motahhari are considered the central figures in the Islamic revolutionary discourse that culminated in Iran's Islamic Revolution, other theorists and activists contributed significantly to the discourse as well. For an informative general analysis of their works, see Dabashi 1993.

plicate analysis of revolutionary thought and practices in Iran. The impact of Kasravi's brand of modern thought on Khomeini's, for example, can be gauged by Khomeini's prose style in *Secrets Unveiled*. Time and time again, Khomeini lapses into a style unmistakably reminiscent of Kasravi's, with its strong preference for "pure" Persian words over Arabic and Turkish loan words. Shariati, who had early in his life taken on modern European thought in the form of Marxism and existentialism, would "go native" in much of his more mature engagement of these European discourses. Motahhari's lifelong preoccupation with predestination and its impact on a dynamic civilization was also, as we will see later, motivated by his wish to refute certain Western observations about the putative prevalence of fatalism and predestination in Islamic thought. The development and vigor of the revolutionary Islamic discourse were not only a response to the strength and appeal of secular discourses and modernists, but also a reaction to their weakness and failure. Indeed, the weakness and ultimate failure of Iran's liberal-democratic, socialist, Marxist, and liberal nationalist discourses and movements, especially their failure throughout the twentieth century to mobilize the populace, were as important to the growth of the Islamic discourse and movement as the hegemonic challenge of secular discourses. The unique ability of the Islamic movement to mobilize the bulk of the population in Iran owed its success to the strong universalistic elements in its discourse. Indeed, the Islamic discourse appealed to and received support from secular movements and individuals primarily because it was able to reach and mobilize the social universal.

The developmental policies issuing from the positivist stance of the Pahlavis toward modernity and the consequences of those policies, prevalent especially during the reign of Mohammad Reza Pahlavi (1941–79), had a direct bearing on the nature and success of the Islamic discourse, as did the political events played out in the intersection of Cold War and domestic Iranian politics, especially after the CIA-sponsored coup d'état in August 1953. Reza Shah's reign (1925–41) had witnessed the rapid, deliberate undermining of the power and influence of the religious establishment by the state. The reduction of religious endowments, and in many cases their appropriation by the Ministry of Endowments, seriously threatened the economic independence of the clerical order. The establishment of centralized and state-controlled institutions of education and justice deprived the mullahs of their historically dominant roles in these important arenas. The introduction of a compulsory national conscription was also seen to curtail their influence among the populace, especially in the countryside. What the mullahs found most outrageous and humiliating, however, was the forced unveiling of women in 1936 and the compulsory imposition of European dress style on men, not least because of their own impotence before the state's use of brute force in its violation of public moral sentiments among the populace. Khomeini's career as an Islamic revolutionary ideologue should be traced back to this period. The period between 1941, when Reza Shah was forced to abdicate by the Allies, and 1953, when the Mossadeq government was overthrown, was marked by political democracy and chaos, during which the liberal nationalists led by Mossadeq and the Marxists led by the Tudeh Party both carried the day.

That was to end abruptly in August 1953, when the Pahlavi Dynasty was forcibly restored and the Marxist and nationalist movements decimated. These events gave the Islamic movement and its discourse a new lease on life. In the early 1960s, the religious nationalists, led by Mehdi Bazargan, were instrumental in establishing the National Resistance Movement, the first such movement against the fully developed dictatorship of the shah (Chehabi 1990, 31); the Islamic movement and its discourse came of age. In 1961, Bazargan (who would become transitional prime minister in 1979) also founded the Liberation Movement of Iran (LMI), a political organization of professional, middle-class Iranians with relatively liberal Islamic views on politics and society.[2] After the bloody suppression of the religiously inspired uprising in the spring of 1963, in which Khomeini and his followers played a key role, the shah's secret police, the SAVAK, extended its control to virtually all aspects of public life, independent political parties were banned, and literature, art, and political discourse subjected to widespread censorship, creating an ideological vacuum, which made the ascendancy of the Islamic discourse possible.

The shah's obsessive desire to suppress Marxism and Communism in Iran led to his regime's relative tolerance of Islamic discourse and activities in the 1960s and 1970s as counteracting the expansion of those ideologies. Consequently, in the two decades before the Islamic Revolution, Islamic associations (anjomans) flourished among the intelligentsia, some well organized, with their own publications and propaganda apparatuses. Most prominent among these were the Month's Discourse (Goftar-e Mah), a large public discussion group with its own journal by the same name, and the Husseinieh Ershad, an Islamic

2. For a detailed analysis of the role and discourse of the Liberation Movement of Iran (LMI), see Chehabi 1990.

center for political and social activities, in which Motahhari and Shariati were actively involved. A parallel development, though less important than the activities of the religious and middle-class intelligentsia, was the rapid growth of Islamic activities among the recent urban migrants in large cities. As a result of land reform in the early 1960s and the uneven industrialization of the economy in the 1960s and 1970s, the urban population nearly tripled (Amir-Arjomand 1988, 91). However, the religious societies (*heyats*), made up mostly of poor urban migrants, did not assume an overwhelmingly political and ideological character until the eve of the revolution, when they served the radical clergy as a ready-made network of revolutionary political organizations.[3]

That the Islamic discourse, shaped by such intellectual, political, and social circumstances, was indeed variegated and nuanced is amply reflected in the discourses of the three men discussed in this chapter. There is, however, a fundamental element that connects the discourses of Shariati, Khomeini, and Motahhari, an element I have referred to as "mediated subjectivity." I define *mediated subjectivity* as human subjectivity projected onto the attributes of monotheistic deity—attributes such as omnipotence, omniscience, and volition—and then partially reappropriated by humans. In this scheme, human subjectivity is contingent on God's subjectivity. Thus, although human subjectivity is not denied, it is never independent of God's subjectivity and, in this sense, it is "mediated." This situation usually leads to a core conflict between human and divine subjectivity, which in turn gives rise to other conflicts, one of the sharpest of which is the constant, schizophrenic vacillation between affirmation and negation of human subjectivity, on the one hand, and between individual subjectivity and collectivity, on the other. In the Islamic discourse, mediated subjectivity is usually expressed in the notion of the human as the vicegerent of God on earth, which in Arabic is rendered as "khalifatollah" (literally, God's caliph or successor).[4]

The main criterion for selecting Shariati, Khomeini, and Motahhari as the

3. According to Amir-Arjomand (1988, 92), by 1974, there were more than 12,000 *heyats* in Tehran alone.

4. The Quranic concept of the human as God's vicegerent on earth, which explicitly informed the discourse of Shariati and Motahhari—Khomeini did not refer to it explicitly—also constituted an important theme in the thought of other important Islamic thinkers such as Mehdi Bazargan and Ayatollah Taleqani, although an analysis of their discourses is beyond the scope of this chapter.

representatives of the Islamic revolutionary discourse in Iran was their sustained popularity among various classes and groups before and after the revolution. The words and ideas of these three men have been disseminated throughout Iran (indeed, around the world) as lectures, sermons, photocopied handouts, audio tapes, and books on a scale unprecedented in Iranian history. Shariati's appeal was the strongest among the middle- and lower-middle-class intelligentsia, who believed he could restore to them their lost selves, without altogether alienating them from their newly acquired identities as moderns.

Ali Shariati: Mediated Subjectivity and the Authenticity of the Collectivity

Born into a devout family in Mazinan, a desert village in Iran's northeastern province of Khorasan, Ali Shariati (1933–1977) moved with his family to the holy city of Mashhad, the provincial capital, soon after his birth.[5] Perhaps the greatest influence in his early childhood was his father, who, though not a cleric, was an Islamic scholar and a well-known preacher, and whose library of two thousand books must have been a great asset for Ali's intellectual development (Keddie 1981, 215; Chehabi 1990, 187).[6] Shariati received his secondary education in Mashhad, while privately learning religious science, Arabic, and some French (Chehabi 1990, 187). At age 17, he attended a normal school and, after two years, went to teach in nearby villages. At the same time, he began translating and writing on religion and Shiite topics and became active in the nationalist movement, led by Mossadeq (Keddie 1981, 215). At age 23, he entered the newly opened faculty of literature at Mashhad University and received his bachelor's degree in 1959, finishing at the top of his class. His academic success earned him a state scholarship to study abroad; after a period of delay because of his political activities, he pursued graduate studies in Paris, becoming active in the politics of 1960s France. Owing to the anticolonial movements in general and to the Algerian independence movement in particular, Paris had become a center for Third World intellectual and political activists. Shariati soon became familiar with many of them, even though, contrary

5. Shariati would later disapprove of his family's move to Mashhad because of the corrupting effects of city life, as opposed to the "purity" of desert life (Dabashi 1993, 105; Shariati 1983a, 254).

6. For a detailed discussion of Shariati's life and thought, see Rahnema 1998.

to his disciples' claims, he was not in close personal contact with famous figures such as Frantz Fanon and Jean-Paul Sartre (Chehabi 1990, 188). He received a degree in Persian philology from the Sorbonne (Chehabi 1990, 188; Keddie 1981, 215, 294; Boroujerdi 1996, 105).

Because of his political activities and involvement in the overseas branch of Bazargan's LMI, on his return to Iran in 1964, Shariati was arrested and jailed for six months. After his release, he first taught in a village in Khorasan, then in a high school in Mashhad, and finally at Mashhad University as an assistant professor of Islamic history. His very popular courses drew on his interpretation of Islam and Shiism. In 1967, at the invitation of Ayatollah Motahhari, Shariati went to Tehran, where the popularity of his lectures at the Husseinieh Ershad was to eclipse that of Motahhari himself. Until his untimely death in a London hospital in June 1977, Shariati devoted his life to the propagation of his revolutionary interpretation of Islam; he developed a large following among the religiously oriented young intelligentsia in search of an authentic, yet modern, identity.

Recovery of the Self

As the closest heir to Al-e Ahmad's legacy in broaching the crisis of Iranian identity among religious thinkers, Shariati devoted much of his discourse to this theme. Apparently much influenced by the discourse of the Western Left on alienation and reification, he identified at least fifteen different types of alienation in a series of lectures, published under the title of *Islamshenasi* (Islamology). He included superstitious religion, magic, polytheism (*shirk*), asceticism, mechanization, bureaucracy, the class system, love and faith, hero worship, scientism, money, civilization, goal seeking, society, materialism, and idealism as causes for the estrangement of humans from their authentic selves (Shariati [1972?]a, 328–66). One form of alienation not mentioned in these lectures, although a theme much discussed his other works, was "assimilation," which Shariati understood to be the effort to "distance oneself from all personal and social or national characteristics in order to identify with the other [and, in so doing,] to overcome one's [sense of] inferiority and enjoy the feeling of honor and superiority sensed in the other" (Shariati 1979a, 3).

Obviously, the result of assimilation was the "loss of self" (*khudbakhtegi*), a concept that Khomeini would often use in his rhetoric later.[7] Shariati viewed the process of "becoming modern" (*motejaded shodan*) as one of the most sinister means by which the West seduced Easterners into embracing modernity:

> The Europeans occupied themselves with the task of creating the enticement to become modern in all societies regardless of their type. They knew that if they could by some ruse create the enticement and infatuation to become modern in the Easterner, he would even cooperate with them to sever his ties to whatever was handed down to him from the past. He would sever his ties to any factor that would have made him superior to the European; with the aid of the European, the Easterner would destroy by his own hand everything that creates political character, culture, and religion. (Shariati 1979a, 19)

But in addition to the cultural dimension, imperialism as "modernization," according to Shariati, also involves a very important material dimension. Modernization comprises the transformation of both traditions and patterns of consumption. Because the old consumption patterns were based on the domestic and self-sufficient economy, the new consumption patterns, along with the European machine-made products, had to be imported and imposed (Shariati 1979a, 23–24). Here Shariati shared Al-e Ahmad's thesis that cultural imperialism was the result of the more "basic" exigency of imperialism: to find markets for its surplus products, international capitalism had to exploit the countries of the Third World; to capture their markets, it had to destroy any native traditions that got in its way.

In his book *Bazgasht be Khish* (Return to the self), Shariati, like Al-e Ahmad, referred to cultural imperialism as the "emptying" of the self (Shariati 1976a, 2). But, unlike Al-e Ahmad, for whom the category of consumerism had been but one element of this "empty" self, Shariati treated the issue of consumerism as a separate, major category in his analysis of "inauthenticity" under neocolonial conditions. As we will see later, Shariati's emphasis on consumerism was rooted in his religious ontology, which deemed the human body and anything related to it, not as items intended for consumerism, but rather as something to be tran-

---

7. One can easily see the close parallel between the "loss of self" discussed here and the "loss of authenticity." For a critical analysis of the notion of authenticity, see Adorno 1974. On the notion of authenticity in modern Islamic thought, see Lee 1997.

scended. On the other hand, Shariati complained about the loss of human volition and consciousness resulting from the process of assimilation (Shariati
1971a, 60–61).

With Al-e Ahmad, Shariati accorded a prominent role to intellectuals in
the shaping of the nation's destiny and criticized them for being alienated from
the bulk of the population. In his celebrated book *Fatemeh Fatemeh Ast* (Fatima is
Fatima), though he gave the intellectuals credit for seeking freedom (although
he did not approve of individual freedom) and equality for the masses, he
faulted them for ignoring their strong roots in religion (Shariati 1971a,
29–30). In language reminiscent of Al-e Ahmad's, Shariati fulminated against
the "modernized pseudo-intellectuals" who, wittingly or unwittingly, served as
"guides" (*rah balad*) for colonialism (Shariati 1971a, 27). In another essay, he
criticized the intellectuals in Islamic societies for imitating their European
counterparts in the struggle against religion, which, however justified in Europe, could only destroy the bulwark against imperialism in the East (Shariati
1972b, 21).[8]

Shariati observed the enormous cultural and social gap that had been created between different strata and classes in Iranian society in the twentieth century: the emergence of a "dual society," a phenomenon common in many
countries where only a relatively small segment of society becomes "modernized," at least in habits and outward appearance, was a glaring social reality in
the Iran of the sixties and seventies (see Ashraf 1981). Shariati thought that intellectuals had not only caused this problem, but also held the key to its solution. Thus he thought that the "organic" and socially committed intellectuals
were the only group of people in Iran who could bridge this gap. In his essay *Az
Koja Aghaz Konim?* (Whence do we begin?), he appealed to the intellectuals, especially the religiously oriented ones; he charged them with the task of restoring the once unified, but now lost, self of Iranians (Shariati 1975, 8). The
essential question that arises is: To what "self" did Shariati want to return? What
were the constituent elements of this utopian ipseism?

There is no doubt that the roots of this "self" were firmly established in
the Islamic past, and in Shiism in particular. Shariati did not mean to exclude
Iranian culture as such, either. Indeed, on different occasions, he alluded to

---

8. In the same essay, Shariati attacked Malkum Khan as the prototypical intellectual implanted in the East by Western imperialism (Shariati 1972b, 57–58).

the specific contributions Iranian culture had made to Islamic civilization.[9] Yet Shariati's "self," though rooted in the past, was the product of a radical reinterpretation of religion and culture. In his article "Bazgasht be Khish" (Return to the self; not to be confused with the book by the same title), Shariati used *rushanfekri* just as Al-e Ahmad had—to refer to the enlightenment of modernity (Shariati 1976a, 15). But he insisted that each society should achieve modern enlightenment (*rushanfekri*) based on its own history, culture, and language. He assailed the West for attempting to impose its own kind of enlightenment on the rest of the world: "Since the eighteenth century, the West, with the aid of its sociologists, historians, writers, artists, and even its revolutionaries and humanists, has imposed on the world the thesis that there is only one kind of civilization, and that is the Western form" (Shariati 1976a, 16–17).

Thus Shariati, like many other Third World intellectuals, had to confront the thorny conundrum of "authenticity." Although, in creating a "new" self, he would make monotheism a vehicle for achieving human moral autonomy as a universal category based on consciousness and will, he nevertheless subscribed to an essentialist view of human existence. His "new" self thus comprised particularisms such as culture, historical experience, ethnicity, and religion:

> The real or authentic existence is an existence which crystallized in the "I" in the course of centuries of building history, culture, civilization, art. It is what gives me a cultural identity vis-à-vis other cultures—the West, the East, the American and African. It is my real existence that when I am before the French, the English, the American, or the Chinese, I can say "I," as they can say "I." . . . And this is an existence that has been created in the course of history. . . . This authentic personality, my human personality, distinguishes me from the other. (Shariati 1976a, 21–22)[10]

In the same article, however, Shariati again rejected the self concocted and imposed by tradition as "neoreactionary" and "antiquarian" (*kohneh parasti*) (Shariati 1976a, 33). The "new" self that Shariati was proposing was based on a

---

9. In *Return to the Self*, for example, Shariati noted that "after fourteen centuries of companionship between Iran and Islam, a rich and expansive culture has appeared in which the two elements are indistinguishable" (1979a, 61).

10. For a good analysis of Shariati's thought and the concept of authenticity, see Lee 1997.

reading of monotheistic metaphysics, which, implicitly or explicitly, constitutes the ontological basis of what I have called "mediated subjectivity," common to all three theorists considered in this chapter.

Mediated Subjectivity as the Authentic Self

Like Khomeini and Motahhari, Shariati grounded human subjectivity in God's
subjectivity. Alluding to the Quranic conception of man as God's vicegerent, or
His successor on earth, he wrote:

> Man, before whom the angels prostrate themselves, is the successor of God in
> nature. As privy to God's secrets and as His special trustee, who possesses His
> character and shares His spirit, man has volition, freedom, responsibility, vi-
> sion, consciousness, creativity, perfection, beauty, and wisdom. He is the cre-
> ator of his destiny and responsible for his time, society, faith, culture, history,
> and future. (Shariati 1979b, 107)

As we can see, Shariati has enumerated all the elements of modern subjectivity.
He grounded humans' roundabout subjectivity in their volition: "The only superiority that man has over all other beings in the universe, lies in his will. . . .
Therefore, man is the successor of God on earth and His kin. The spirit of God
and man are nourished from the same source of excellence, that is, having volition" (Shariati [1980?], 11–12).

Yet, in Shariati's scheme (as in Khomeini's and Motahhari's), the subjective
autonomy of humans entails submission to God's will. All three theorists, implicitly or explicitly, perceive this as contradictory, and much of their philosophical efforts are devoted to dealing with this presumed contradiction, the
source of their constant vacillation between affirming human subjectivity and
then, almost immediately, negating it.

Be that as it may, all three arrived at human subjectivity through a metaphysics of monotheism that viewed human existence as a theomorphic "journey" or "movement"—one that started at the level of "matter" and that carried
and elevated humans to the level of God's spirit:

> In the language of religion, man is a divine essence, an essence superior to mat-
> ter and dominant over nature. He originates from God's Spirit, which means

he possesses God's attributes. But since the Fall [Hubut] onto the earth, nature, and society, man has forgotten his "primal self-divinity" [khud khodai nukhustin] and merely allows his material and animal inclination to develop. As a result, the sublime values invested in him die out and he considers himself merely as the highest life in the evolution of animals. He forgets that he is a spark from the divine realm, that his mission is to "divinize" the world and that his being is God-like. He reaches such a lowly status that, at the peak of civilization and scientific progress, he deems himself to be an offspring of the monkey, or the fruit of sexuality, or the product of labor. (Shariati 1977a, 19)

The journey to subjectivity thus entailed a radical flight from nature as vile materiality, to be shunned. In one of his more mystical and poetic works, Shariati defined the most important type of human estrangement in terms of alienation *in*, rather than *from*, nature. He called nature the "desolate abode" (kharab abad), in which humans as "genuine essences" were alienated from their true selves. This estrangement prevented humans from ever feeling at "home" in "unconscious" and "lowly" nature, which had engulfed them without their consent; it explained the dual mode of humans' existence, being part of nature, on the one hand, and being driven by the urge to transcend it from the very beginning, on the other, a duality reflected in the most profound philosophies (Shariati 1983a, 551).

In this stark subjectivist metaphysics, corporeal materiality and the human body were "prisons" from which the aspiring subject had to be liberated. For Shariati, religion was the effort of humans to cleanse their essence from the "pollution of existence" and to return from the "soil" to God by consecrating nature and life; mysticism, the effort to eliminate the hindrance of the material self on the journey to subjectivity (Shariati 1983a, 555–56). Even art was a manifestation of this transcendental movement away from nature, from what "is" to what "ought" to be: Shariati saw Picasso as an artist who had successfully transcended nature (Shariati 1983a, 560). Turning the admiration for the rising sun at dawn in classical Persian poetry on its head, Shariati asserted that the "unconscious" and "unwilled" break of day does not deserve the admiration of the volitive and cognitive subject: "The unconscious appearance of the dawn, without volition or sensibility, is flawed before the poet's spirit, which feels and thinks the universe. The poet seeks a dawn, which, like a wild hero, rises from behind the horizon, dagger in hand, [and] slits the black throat of the night by *intention.* . . . Nature does not offer such a dawn" (Shariati 1983a, 560; emphasis original).

Such an ontological hostility toward outer and inner nature is clearly reflected in Shariati's more sociological thoughts about the human body. To be sure, his frequent criticism of the "decadence" exhibited by Iran's Westernized middle class, especially by the women, in paying excessive attention to the body, was partially informed by his critique of the "consumerist" culture imposed by imperialism. Yet his profound contempt for the human body is also rooted in his ontological journey toward subjectivity. In *Fatima Is Fatima*, Shariati excluded sexual rights and freedoms from human rights because they merely represented the deceptions and distractions devised by cultural imperialism and capitalism to divert the attention of youth in the West and the East from the reality of their exploitation and colonization (Shariati 1971a, 62).[11]

Shariati considered Islam the perfect world religion, one that granted humans authentic subjectivity, a religion for both this world and next. It was a religion that, even as it transcended nature and elevated humans to their higher status, did not alienate them from nature because the "deification of man" took place in the "lap of nature" (Shariati 1994, 221). Islam, he believed, was the religion that gave the Bedouin Abuzar (a close companion of the Prophet, whom Shariati often praised as a model of a revolutionary socialist) a personhood and subjectivity among all the "faceless" infidels that surrounded him (Shariati 1994, 153). Most important, the authentic subjectivity provided by Islam embraced human "dignity" (*ezat*) as God's will, and rejected abjection (*zellat*). Those who were abject were so because they had acquiesced to abjection (Shariati 1994, 256). Shariati even interpreted martyrdom as a means of securing human dignity that he found in praxis and freedom of choice (Shariati 1977b, 52).

Although he grounded his notion of mediated subjectivity in consciousness, Shariati's interpretation of consciousness was quite different from that of individual subjectivity or Hegelian self-consciousness inherent in the subject's freedom. For him, consciousness was tantamount to ideology, conviction, and faith. Throughout his discourse, Shariati considered consciousness to be the ideology of the Islamic movement. "Life," he often said, "is conviction, struggle, and nothing else" (Shariati 1979a, 225).

11. It should be noted that Shariati, subscribing to Islam's traditional rejection of "asceticism," believed in the control, regulation, and disciplining of "instincts," but not in their total denial.

On the more ontological plane, however, Shariati's journey toward subjectivity arrives, not at subjectivity, but at an "annihilation" in God. Thus, in a letter to his son, using the metaphors of the sun and the ocean to represent divine origin and influence, and that of the river to represent humans' theomorphic journey toward subjectivity, he wrote that, though the river originated from the ocean, it was frozen and static without the sun's rays, which imparted consciousness to it and which made it move back toward the ocean. But, once reunited with the ocean, it took the form of "submergence" and "fusion"—"annihilation"—implying the surrender of subjectivity (Shariati 1983a, 566).

Contradictions of Mediated Subjectivity

Shariati's relation to human subjectivity, as we have noted, constantly shifted between affirmation and negation. In what amounts to an ode to human subjectivity in another poetic and mystical work, *Hubut* (The Fall), he wrote:

> Man is an animal who, just like a tree, grows toward the sky above. He is the tall statue of rebellion who has risen from the lowliness of the mundane world toward the beyond. He has been created in the image of imagination and dream to pierce all ceilings. All his organs are swords fighting whatever "is." He fights against whatever holds him, whatever imposes on him. He has a rebellious neck to stick out. He has not submitted to the corrosive effects of the elements and has not surrendered in weakness; he has not conformed to the bonds of nature. He wishes to break, tear, pierce, clutter, soar and be liberated. He is the tree of rebellion, the flower of negation. His answer to the eternal "is" is "no." By gradual negation of nature he affirms himself, creates himself, he "becomes." Nietzschean nihilism is true, the [Hegelian] return to the Absolute Idea, the Absolute I, is true. (Shariati 1983b, 144–45)

But immediately after this passage, a "voice from the depth" of his "nature" urges him not to listen to anything except revelation, which is encoded as the "pure blue color of the sky." Shariati often described his constant shifting between affirmation and negation of subjectivity as "bewilderment," as if he had suddenly realized that his ontological journey and that of the West were the same, resulting in diremption from nature and the existential angst of subjectivity. In my reading, Shariati's "desert of bewilderment" (*heyrat*) represents the core of

Shariati's ontological vacillations (Shariati 1983b, 117). Before diremption, humans were in a state of protected imprisonment, much like the fetal stage in human ontogeny, whereas, after diremption, the emerging subjects were capable of knowing nature, indeed, capable of creating both another nature and history (Shariati 1983b, 118). That being the case, Shariati bemoaned the possibility of his path leading to the "monads" of modernity and to the nihilism of the "unlimited plane of freedom" (Shariati 1983b, 119). Yet he was quite excited by the possibility of humans becoming the creators of their own selves, and astounded by the possibility of humans becoming God-like as a result of their ontological journey: " 'We all return to God.' 'Obey me so I shall make you like me.' 'I [God] wanted to create a vicegerent on earth.' 'When Man was created, I breathed *my spirit* in him!' 'God created man in His image.' All these words testify that in man God inheres" (Shariati 1983b, 135).

At the same time, however, he was alarmed and appalled by the results of a similar journey in the West, which caused him to vacillate between a subject-oriented anthropocentrism and a religious mysticism. Shariati described his ontological ambivalence in terms of the tragedy of human destiny, marked by impatience for liberation, on the one hand, and by angst over salvation from the same liberation, on the other (Shariati 1983b, 148–49). He likened the subject of modernity to the "lonely wolf," who, after challenging the Being and nature, was now horrified by the solitude of subjectivity (Shariati 1983b, 185). Not surprisingly, Shariati's solution to his bewilderment lay in submission to the Being, in annihilation of the self in God, and in finding a "new" self, who, in cooperation with God and Love, would create the universe anew in a utopia of mediated subjectivity:

> I return. I seek the paradise I left. I wash my hands of the original sin, the rebellion. I will liberate all the corners of the original paradise of my "self." [I will liberate] nature, history, society, and even myself [from my "self"]. There I, Love, and God will scheme together to create the universe anew, to create the creation again. In the new beginning, God will not be alone. In this universe, I will no longer be estranged. . . . We will bring heaven to earth, a heaven in which all trees are the forbidden tree, we will create a world whose architects are our skillful hands. (Shariati 1983b, 203–4)

In *Ma'bad* (The temple), a chronological narrative, Shariati uses the metaphors of night and day to refer to the age of "enchantment" and "disenchantment" as tandem historical processes. The "enchantment," which he presents as a time of calm and quiet, is followed by the sudden and dazzling "enlightenment," which Shariati describes as "cosmic fireworks" (Shariati 1983c, 424–27, 431). He acknowledges the "wonderful" new world that the enlightenment has brought about. But, alas, his eyes are so used to darkness that the bright new lights severely torment them. He is forced to see the lights, but it is difficult to bear their brightness. Moreover, the "soul" of the Easterner finds peace only in submission:

> My long living in the night has made my eyes so used to darkness that the bright light of these fireworks severely irritates them. . . . It is a strange spectacle; neither can I watch nor can I not watch. My heart is filled with excitement at the sight of this grand spectacle, but my soul is tormented by so many impetuous explosions, and disarrayed rebellions. . . . My soul finds peace only in submission while this spectacle tortures it. Certainty, peace, and serenity, however dark and cold and hopeless, are more consoling to my soul than the dazzling dashing and heated rebellions of restive hope. (Shariati 1983c, 433–34)

It is interesting that, for Shariati in a Marxist-positivist frame of mind, the "age of darkness" corresponds to "feudalism" (he uses the French word *féodalisme*) and the "age of enlightenment" to "science" (Shariati 1983c, 435). He yearns for the lost virtues of feudalism, such as fortitude (*hamiyat*), chivalry, and largesse, virtues that are beyond the small minds of the "petit-bourgeois hoarding and calculating mice" of enlightened modernity (Shariati 1983c, 435).

Thus, speaking for the Easterner, Shariati favors the surrender to "darkness", even though the new light might be joyous and uplifting, the burden of twenty-five centuries forces him to remain in his state of serene submission (Shariati 1983c, 437–38). Returning to the metaphors of the river, the ocean, and the sun, he sees in the river's surrender to the ocean the surrender of the aspiring subject to the Godhead, and in the "hellish" sun of the desert, which has separated the river from the ocean, the light of "enlightenment," which has separated the subject from the Godhead or Being (Shariati 1983c, 439–41). Finally, he finds in religion his "enlightenment," without the "obscurantism" (the European Enlightenment) in which the West has been engulfed. The light of faith and love turns his night into a "bright day," without costing him his cherished sanity (Shariati 1983c, 446–47).

On a less abstract level, Shariati's version of mediated subjectivity resulted in other contradictions. Even as he advocated autonomous human action, he also believed that human action must be guided by "models" for imitation and by external criteria. Thus, in *Fatima Is Fatima*, Shariati rejected the traditional concept of "saints" interceding on behalf of believers (*shafa'at*) as an instance of the negation of human autonomy. On the other hand, he thought that every human society was in need of external guidance from above in the form of "models," such as religious saints or mythical figures.[12] In *Entezar, Mazhab-e E'teraz* (Awaiting, the creed of protest), Shariati praised the early Muslims for the independence of their opinions, even vis-à-vis those of the Prophet and the attitude of God, in reasoning with the people, even as he approved of the traditional concept of imitation prevalent in Shiism (Shariati 1976b, 13; 27–28).[13]

Collectivist Subjectivity and Marxism

Shariati thus attributed a type of conditional subjectivity to human beings. In some parts of his discourse, he explicitly addressed human subjectivity in terms of agency, using the Aristotelian notion of "efficient cause," (*elliyat-e fa'eli*; literally, active cause) to refer to human agency. By "human agency," however, Shariati meant *collective*, not individual, agency:

> In the Quran, the "Messenger" is not considered as the agent [*ellat-e fa'eli*] of basic changes in history. Rather, he is introduced as the carrier of the message who has to show the true path to the people, and his mission ends at that point. It is then up to the people whether to choose or not to choose this message and truth, and there are no "accidents" possible in this religion because everything is in the hands of God. In general, the audiences of every creed and religion are the principal agents of change in their community, and, because of that, we see the Quran always addresses "the people" [*nas*]. The prophet is appointed for the people, he talks to the people, he is questioned by the people. The causes of progress, change, and decline are the people, and the people are responsible for history and society. (Shariati 1968, 13)

12. As we will see, the contradiction between human autonomy and the need for external guidance is central to Shariati's political theory.

13. Shariati ([1972?]a, 209) toyed with the idea of a "purer" type of humanism, an "Eastern humanism" derived from the Abrahamic tradition's story of Adam.

Based on this observation, Shariati concluded that Islam was the first social philosophy to consider the people, and not the elite or the "great individuals," as
the principal agents of history, directly responsible for their society (Shariati
1968, 15). Indeed, he went so far as to thematically equate "the people" with the
notion of God, although he was careful to stress that such an equation would be
blasphemous from the theological perspective. Nevertheless, in the social context, "we can always substitute the people for God" because otherwise the
Quranic injunction "to give God interest-free loans," for example, would make
no sense (Shariati 1994, 153). In equating the people with God, however,
Shariati opposed "the people" as the collectivity to the individual (Shariati
1994, 227–28; [1972?]a, 93–94).

Shariati's notion of mediated subjectivity of the collectivity is also captured
in the "Perfect Man," whom, in a reinterpretation of a similar notion among the
medieval Islamic philosophers, he defines as

> a man who has not been rendered one-dimensional, broken, defective, and
> self-estranged by life. By submitting to God, he has been liberated from all
> submissions; by surrendering to His absolute will, he has rebelled against all
> tyranny. The Perfect Man is one who has immersed his ephemeral "individual-
> ity" in "eternity of human collectivity," and by negating his "self," he has be-
> come enduring. (Shariati [1972?]a, 101–2)

Shariati's emphasis on the collectivity was undoubtedly rooted in universalistic Islamic principles, which he interpreted as vehicles for the empowerment
of the "disempowered" (*mustaza'fin*), a Quranic concept in which Shariati and
Khomeini alike would invest much political and rhetorical capital. By the "disempowered," Shariati meant the majority of the population, who had been subjected to multidimensional "marginalization," ranging from economic
exploitation and political despotism to colonization and cultural as well as religious suffocation over the course of history. It was to the "salvation" of the "disempowered" and to the elimination of "disempowerment" in this world that the
discourse of the Quran was directed, and that was why the message of the
Quran was always fresh (Shariati 1975, 1). This position reflects Shariati's clear
understanding that the dynamics of social change had to mobilize and to affect
the lives of the social universal. It led him to conclude that the defeat of the

Afghani's anti-imperialist ideology lay in Afghani's failure to ground it in the majority (Shariati [1972?]a, 250).

On the other hand, his concern with the social universal as a collective entity led Shariati to reject, in all but a few instances, the ideas of individuality and liberal democracy. Thus he attacked individual and civil freedoms on the grounds that they were merely a license to indulge in "immoral" and criminal activities, and that the only people to benefit from these freedoms were those with money and power, and not the ordinary citizens (Shariati 1979b, 157). He interpreted the Quranic concept of "altruism" (isar) as the "death of the individual" so that the "other" might simply live (Shariati [1972?]a, 61).[14]

Despite Shariati's antipathy toward the individual as the carrier of subjectivity, indeed, despite his seeming at times to wage theoretical battle against the emergence of the individual as the carrier of his mediated and inchoate subjectivity, the logic of his own metaphysics forced him to reluctantly recognize the inevitable centrality of the individual to any scheme involving human subjectivity. The most compelling reason to do so was the pivotal role he ascribed to the concept of human responsibility and its political cognate, social commitment. Shariati realized that the concept of responsibility was meaningless without the individual as the subject. This strong logic forced him to assert that, "when my 'I' is absolutely negated and my 'self' is lost, the sense of responsibility for my feelings and actions is meaningless, and when you tell the individual, you are merely a fruit of your society and have acquired all your shape, color, and even your being from your environment, naturally he will not develop a sense of being responsible for his attributes and actions" (Shariati [1972?]a, 373–74). Moreover, having elaborated on a concept of alienation of the individual by the society that he designated as "sociologism," he was forced to conclude that the Quran recognized the individual as the very foundation of the notion of responsibility (Shariati [1980?], 119; [1981?], 150–51).

One escape from the dilemma in which Shariati seems to have found himself was the possibility of two levels of "individualism," namely, a philosophical individualism, of which he approved, and a moral-practical individualism, which he disavowed (Shariati [1972?]a, 390–98). But even this did not satisfy

14. Shariati (1979b, 48) dismissed the criticisms of his antiliberal ideas as "irrelevant parliamentarianism" espoused by liberal intellectuals who did not understand and share the sufferings of the people.

him; he returned to the idea of sacrificing the individual on the altar of the collectivity, which he identified with "authenticity" (Shariati [1972?]a, 397–401).

His brief and "forced" discussion of individual subjectivity notwithstanding, Shariati developed a rather complicated relationship with Marxist theory
in his discourse. Although he rejected the Marxist reduction of subjectivity to
labor, in a close parallel to the Marxist view, he located his mediated subjectivity in the collectivity. This interesting twist allowed him to reject Marxist historical determinism based on the autonomous evolution of forces of
production, even as he returned to a teleology of the evolutionary stages of history that resembled the Marxist teleology. As we have seen, Shariati grounded
his brand of subjectivity, not in consciousness, but in the cognate concepts of
faith and conviction, components of his ideology for revolutionary praxis.
Consequently, he was unable to ground his notion of subjectivity in labor; indeed, on different occasions, he rejected this Marxist notion while holding to
the Marxist primacy of collectivity. Thus, in Shariati's philosophy of history, it
was not the labor-based evolution of the productive forces that constituted the
"base" of society; rather, it was the "form of ownership," whether collective and
communal or individual, that determined socioeconomic formation, thus also
the movement of history (Shariati 1977c, 18). This formulation enabled
Shariati to simplify socioeconomic formation to two stages. In the first stage,
society's resources, means of production, raw materials, and amenities were
available to everyone equally in the form of "primitive communism"; in the second, they were monopolized by individuals, and the public was deprived
(Shariati 1979c, 18). The obvious result of the second socioeconomic stage, according to Shariati, was class struggle; the ultimate end of history was to return
to communal ownership, but in a "higher" form.

Shariati idealized the purported "primitive communism" of the preagrarian
society, in which the individual and private ownership did not exist (Shariati
[1972?]a, 72–74). Apparently unaware of the inconsistency between this view
of historical development and his ontological flight from nature, Shariati attempted to juxtapose his stages of socioeconomic formation with parallel stages
of "socioreligious" formation.[15] Thus he viewed "totemism" as a primitive form

---

15. This inconsistency becomes of less moment if we keep in mind, as Hamid Dabashi has
repeatedly pointed out, that Shariati's primary concern was promoting an ideology for a particular social movement (see, for example, Dabashi 1993).

of monotheism (*towhid*), in which the unified identity of the tribe was represented in the collectivity as opposed to the individual (Shariati [1972?]a, 178–79). With the advent of agricultural society and the emergence of individual ownership, first of land and then of other resources, this "monotheistic" totemism was destroyed, and "polytheism" (*shirk*), in which different deities corresponded to different social classes, groups, and races, was ushered in (Shariati [1972a?], 287–88). It was at the polytheistic stage that class struggle, epitomized in the story of Cain and Abel—Cain representing the "monopolizer" and Abel representing the "disempowered" and "the people"—moved history to a higher stage of monotheism, whose pinnacle was Islam and whose goal was to launch a classless and unified society based on the worship of a single deity (Shariati [1972?]a, 287–88).

Political Theory: Committed Guidance

Shariati's political philosophy was closely related to his ontology. As we have seen, his metaphysics was informed by what I have called a "theomorphic journey," from the "lowly" level of nature and matter to the highest level of perfection, akin to that of the Godhead. For him, the "perfection" of society (*ommat*; in Arabic, *umma*; literally, community) was the embodiment of this movement. In the Islamic tradition, *ommat* referred to the larger community of believers, whose sole basis, at least in theory, was the faith of its members. Developed early in Islamic history to transcend the tribal structure of pre-Islamic Arabia, *ommat* would often be contrasted to the "modern" notion of nation-state. But in his reconceptualization of *ommat*, Shariati focused instead on what he viewed as society's "becoming," its movement toward perfection:

> *Ommat* comprises a collectivity whose members, under a great and sublime leadership, feel the responsibility for the progress and perfection of the society in their blood and life and with their convictions. They are committed to a view of life, not as "being," the comfortable stagnation of existing, but as "becoming" and moving toward absolute perfection, absolute self-consciousness, and the constant creation of sublime values. [This is the meaning of the Quaranic verse] "We are from God and to God we return." (Shariati 1979b, 50–51)

For such an ideal community to achieve its goal of transcendence, Shariati contended, "leadership" (in Arabic, *imamat*) was necessary. Traditionally, the concept of leadership (*imamat*) had been used in Shiism to designate the leadership of the Shiite community after the Prophet by his descendants through Ali and his daughter Fatima. But, claiming a semantic relationship between *ommat* and *imamat*, Shariati defined *imamat* as the leadership of the community in pursuit of his ontological goal: "*Ommat* is a community in the process of "becoming" and "moving" toward absolute transcendence. Because we now understand *ommat*, we can easily find a clear definition for *imamat* and its social role. Accordingly, *imamat* is the leadership that guides the *ommat* in this movement" (Shariati 1979b, 52).

Working from these premises, Shariati distinguished between two basic types of polity. The first type, found in the modern West, was ruled by *politique* (he used the French word); the second, found in the East, by *siyasat* (a Perso-Arabic word also meaning "politics," but with connotations of pedagogy and guidance). Under *politique*, civil society was in charge of governing and the state merely "administered" its affairs—the leadership had no responsibility to undertake any social reform, or to raise the public's consciousness so that the "youth [could] be improved in their thinking and immoral people become moral" (Shariati 1979b, 42–43). By contrast, under *siyasat*, which corresponded to Shariati's conceptualization of *ommat*, it was the responsibility of government to transform people's moral, mental, and social conditions from what they "were" to what they "ought" to be (Shariati 1979b, 42–43). This mode of thinking led Shariati to assert that the leader of *ommat*,

> unlike the president of the United States, or the host of a radio talk show, is not committed to act according to the wishes of his constituency. He is not committed to providing the maximum of happiness and gratification for members of society. Rather, he must lead the society, by the fastest, shortest, and straightest route, toward perfection, even though this perfection may cause pain for the members . . . a point that, needless to say, they have consciously accepted and that is not imposed on them. (Shariati 1979b, 66)

The pedagogic element in Shariati's conceptualization of *siyasat* led him to invoke images of children in need of "kindergarten" (*kudakestan*) to describe the citizens of Iran (Shariati 1979b, 41). Even worse, it led him to reduce citizens to "sheep" (ra'iyat) in need of leadership and therefore to deny them autonomy as subjects. Shariati's notion of "committed guidance" (rahbari moteahed), as he called his idea of leadership, thus negated the possibility of popular sovereignty, at least for a few generations to come, even though he did not totally dismiss the possibility of a democratic system:

> The principle of democratic government, in contrast to the sacrosanct exhilaration that this word carries, is opposed to the principle of revolutionary change and spiritual guidance. In a society in which political leadership is based on a particular ideology and its agenda is the transformation of corrupt and putrid traditions, the leadership [government] cannot be based on the views and wishes of the public; [it] cannot be derived from the degenerate masses. (Shariati 1979b, 153)

For a country like Iran, Shariati prescribed a combination of two leaders—one charismatic and one "selected" by the people but not responsible to them. In his book Ommat va Imamat (Community and leadership), which contains most of his thoughts on leadership, he focused on the idea of a charismatic leader as the imam who is neither appointed, elected, nor even designated by the Prophet (Shariati 1979b, 122–23). The right to be the leader, Shariati asserted, was "an innate right, inhering in the essential quality of the leader and not in external factors of 'election' or 'appointment'" (Shariati 1979b, 124). In contrast to a democratic regime, in a "regime of guidance," the people did not elect their leaders; they merely recognized them (Shariati 1979b, 125–26). In the absence of a charismatic leader, the leader would not be elected by popular vote, but "selected" by the "experts," who were trusted by the people; he would be responsible, not to the people, but to the "principles of guidance" according to which he had to move society toward its higher goals (Shariati 1976b, 14–15).

In Community and Leadership, Shariati grounded his arguments against popular sovereignty historically, in the succession following the death of the Prophet and in the emergence of Shiism. Shariati and his followers were thus able to later argue that his antidemocratic thought had merely historical significance and had nothing to do with our time. To be sure, he did not completely dismiss the possibility of a participatory democracy, although he did not elaborate on this theme. For example, in his influential book Tashayo'-e Alavi va Tashayo'-e Safavi (Alavid Shiism and Safavid Shiism), he briefly mentioned that the Islamic polity after the Prophet and the twelve Shiite imams should be grounded in popular sovereignty based on the Islamic principles of "consultation" (*shura*) and "consensus" (*ijma'*; Shariati 1971b, 258, 274). Thus Shariati's discourse contains elements both against the notions of popular sovereignty and citizenship rights and in favor of them.

It was Shariati's intention to bring forth an "Islamic Protestantism," by which he meant to use Islam itself to reform Islamic religion and culture on a large scale. To do so, Shariati introduced an elemental form of subjectivity, albeit inchoate and collectivist in nature, to a large number of Iranians hitherto not much affected by the revolution of subjectivity in modernity.

Ayatollah Khomeini: The Ascetic Revolutionary as Subject

Born into a traditionally religious family in the small town of Khomein some sixty miles southwest of Tehran, Ruhollah Khomeini (1902–1988) was the grandson of a merchant in Kashmir (hence the accusation that he was not an Iranian). His father died a few months after Khomeini's birth; he was raised by his mother and his paternal aunt, said to have been an especially strong-willed woman, until age 15, when he lost both of them (Dabashi 1993, 410). His elder brother, Ayatollah Pasandideh, then undertook his upbringing; he received a basic education in the traditional Islamic sciences. At age 19, Khomeini went to the nearby town of Arak to study under the prominent Ayatollah Haeri, later following him to the city of Qom. By 1926, Khomeini had completed his advanced study of Islamic jurisprudence and the canonical law of Shiite sources, having also studied Islamic mysticism and philosophy, a rare pursuit among the orthodox, and his primary interest when he began to teach at the age of 27 (Dabashi 1993, 410). Khomeini's major political debut came in 1944, with the publication of his book *Kashf al-Asrar* (Secrets unveiled), in which he assailed not only the "modernity" of Kasravi and his followers, but also the dictatorship of Reza Shah, who had been forced to abdicate in favor of his son in 1941. Khomeini then seems to have led a politically quiet life, under the shadow of the eminent Ayatollah Boroujerdi. He became intensely involved in his teaching and gathered a sizable following among the seminary students in Qom. Especially popular was his course on ethics, well attended by young students who found in it an unusual means of self-control (Mottahedeh 1985, 242).

In June 1963, two years after the death of Ayatollah Boroujerdi and on the anniversary of of the martyrdom of Imam Hussein in 680 A.D., the most emotionally charged day of the year in the Shiite community, Khomeini unleashed his verbal attacks on the shah's regime for having killed students in its raid on the seminary school in Qom a few weeks before. This was followed by Khomeini's arrest two days later and by widespread riots in different towns, which were bloodily suppressed by the shah's armed forces. Khomeini was released after spending a few months in prison. In the fall of 1964, the government of the United States implicitly made the granting of a large loan contingent on the granting of diplomatic immunity to its military personnel and dependents in Iran, a nonreciprocal measure, encroaching, at least symbolically, on Iran's sovereignty. When the parliament went along with this demand, Khomeini found the situation explosive. In a fiery speech, he declared, "If the Shah should run over an American dog, he would be called to account, but if an American cook should run over the Shah, no one has any claim against him" (Mottahedeh 1985, 246). He was immediately forced into exile, traveling first to Turkey and, within a year, to the Shiite holy city of Najaf in Iraq, where he had access to the vast religious, economic, and political resources of the Shiite community within and without Iran, at a safe remove from Iran. In exile, Khomeini gradually built up his revolutionary discourse against the Iranian monarchy, the West, imperialism, Zionism, and Israel, until his triumphant return to Iran in the early days of 1979, to lead the Islamic Revolution and to establish the new Islamic Republic. In 1978, Khomeini had published *Velayat-e Faqih* (Governance of the jurist), in which he had delineated his theory of a theocratic state based on a reinterpretation of Shiite doctrinal beliefs. In the last thirty-five years of his life, Khomeini's works and actions would change the lives and consciousness of millions of Iranians from all walks of life, but especially those of what he and Shariati called the "disempowered" (*mustaza'fin*).

Refinement from Above and the Move to the Spiritual Realm

In his ontological reflections, Khomeini, like Shariati, posited a move from the material to the spiritual realm, to be accomplished by both the individual and society. Although Islam provided the most effective means to accomplish this move, he argued, early in its history it had been engulfed by the Jews and their cultural intrigues and intellectual distortions (Khomeini 1978, 6–7). Islam had been attacked, first by the Crusaders and then repeatedly by the Western colonialists, who tried to neutralize Islam as a cultural force because it obstructed their economic and political aims (Khomeini 1978, 7–19). In recent history, moreover, the external enemies of Islam and Iran were greatly aided by "internal elements," that is, by secular intellectuals in Iran, who had "lost" their "selves" in the face of the cultural onslaught of the West (Khomeini 1978, 19). Using terminology that can be traced to Al-e Ahmad, Khomeini incorporated Al-e Ahmad's concept of "self loss" (*khud bakhtegi*) into his discourse to describe the Iranians' loss of their authenticity.[16]

According to Khomeini, the mechanism through which this "self" was lost and the state of "inauthenticity" ushered in was the separation of religion from politics, which began in the early stages of Islam, and which has continued in our own time through the machinations of the imperialists (Khomeini 1978, 23). The most reasonable means to fulfill the frustrated goals of Islam was thus to establish a theocratic state to enforce Islamic law. "Islam regards laws as an instrument to realize justice," Khomeini maintained (1978, 95), "an instrument for doctrinal and moral reform and refinement of man. The law exists to establish and enforce a just social order [as a necessary condition] for the development of refined [*mohazab*] men." Khomeini's interest in the moral development of "the masses" was apparent as early as 1944, when, responding to the Kasravite brand of modernity in his *Secrets Unveiled*, he declared that only religion was capable of transcending the materialist culture of modern times (Khomeini [1944?], 276).

Khomeini's views on the goal of the development of "refined men" rested on a set of metaphysical assumptions that differed little from those of either Shariati or Motahhari. Indeed, drawing on the Islamic Gnostic tradition, Khomeini often expressed what I have called the "journey toward subjectivity" in terms of agape, an attraction or love toward God:

Man has certain properties that are not present in any other being. One such property is the desire for absolute power and not limited power; absolute perfection and not limited perfection. And since absolute power and perfection are realized in none other than God, man by nature seeks God and he is not aware of it . . . [Those who seek worldly power and perfection] do not understand that in all beings the attraction to absolute perfection is the love of God, and the tragedy is that we do not understand, and mistake the one for the other. (Khomeini 1981a, 76–78)

16. According to Mottahedeh (1985, 303), Khomeini had read Al-e Ahmad's *Westoxication* and admired it.

Like Shariati, Khomeini also perceived a movement away from nature toward a higher realm. In a mystical exegesis of the first chapter of the Quran, he wrote, "Worship and prayer are also means to . . . the end of eliciting the true nature of man and making it manifest, of bringing it forth from potentially into actuality. Natural man should become divine; whatever he looks at, he will see as God. All the prophets were sent to assist man to attain this goal" (Khomeini 1981b, 415).

Just as with Shariati, Khomeini's ontological movement away from nature ends, not in the self-realization, but in the annihilation of the subject (Khomeini 1981b, 383–84). Where Shariati uses the metaphors of the river and the ocean, Khomeini (1981b, 396, 406) uses those of the "drop and the ocean" or the "wave and the ocean." His partially subjectivist ontology, expressed as movement to a higher realm, is thus at once contravened by an opposite trend rooted in the very same ontology.

In Khomeini's "creationist" worldview, beings were brought into existence by "something external to them" (Khomeini 1981b, 367–68). Although he appeared to reject any pantheistic interpretation of existence, he did not absolutely deny the possession of subjectivity by humans. Rather, he made human subjectivity contingent on the subjectivity of the Supreme Essence: "Beings that are subordinate to the Supreme Name also possess perfection, but to an inferior degree, one limited by their inherent [limited] capacity" (Khomeini 1981b, 369). This ontological paradox of positing potential human subjectivity and at once negating it represents the core of "mediated subjectivity" in Khomeini. Its full extent would be played out in his analysis of the problem of theodicy.

Mediated Subjectivity and the Problem of Theodicy

Khomeini discussed the limited, conditional, and contingent character of human subjectivity in the course of analyzing the problem of theodicy and related issues of human freedom (*ekhtiyar*) and predestination (*jabr*). Theodicy or "divine justice" has been a thorny problem for many religions. Briefly, it refers to the existence of imperfection and evil in the world in the face of omnipotent divine will that is assumed to be just (see Weber 1964, 138–39). In attempting to solve the problem of theodicy, religious thinkers have had occasion to posit a human will that is simultaneously independent of and dependent on that of the Deity. This paradox constitutes the cornerstone of what I have designated as "mediated subjectivity" in Shariati, Khomeini, and Motahhari, and accounts for their constant vacillation between the opposite poles of positing and then negating human subjectivity.

In his theology, as compared to his sociology, Khomeini was conservative. He did not invoke the notion of "God's vicegerent on earth" for ordinary human beings.[17] When the followers of Kasravi criticized his interpretation of some Quranic verses as negating human agency and volition, however, Khomeini acknowledged the existence of human agency but posited the "support" of God as having a necessary influence on human actions. Thus, even though the human mind had the capacity to choose between good and evil, human freedom lay within the framework of "divine determinations" (taqdirat-e elahi) (Khomeini [1944?], 48).[18]

Because there was evil in this world and because God was just, others had argued, the existence of evil could not have been willed by Him. This might mean that God had set into motion certain "laws" that later became independent of His original will. Within that context, both evil and human volition could take place without any detriment to the concept of God's justice. Khomeini attributed this Deistic position to the "rationalist" medieval Islamic theologians known as the Mu'tazalites (Khomeini 1983a, 59). The opposite position, that of denying human agency and volition, as well as the possibility of judging God's justice by human standards, Khomeini attributed to the Asha'rites, the orthodox opponents of the Mu'tazalites. In rejecting both positions, Khomeini opted for a third, a "position between positions" (amri bain al amrain). Humans, for Khomeini, were neither devoid of subjectivity and agency nor fully in possession of them:

> Freedom . . . implying that [human] beings may be independent in their agency . . . and necessity, implying the denial of all effects attributed to any entity other than God and claiming that God directly organizes and effects everything, are both impossible. Therefore, the true position is a position in between. This means that [humans] are "effective possibilities" [emkan-e moaser] and capable of causality [elliyat] but not immediately and independently. In all the universe there are no immediate agents [fa'el mostaqel] except the sublime

17. Indeed, unlike Shariati and Motahhari, Khomeini (1978, 54) seems to have reserved "God's vicegerency on the earth" for the Prophet alone.

18. In constructing this notion of contingent human agency, Khomeini was also responding to the Kasravi's criticisms of "apparent changes in God's will," the classical paradox of bida discussed in Islamic theology. See Khomeini [1944?], 83–89.

God. And all beings, because they are not independent in their essences, are not independent in their actions and attributes either. These [humans] have certain attributes, and effect certain actions, and achieve certain deeds, but not independently. (Khomeini 1983a, 73)

By adopting this position (which captures the essence of mediated subjectivity in his discourse), Khomeini was able to solve the problem of theodicy, while responding to modernist pressures for human agency—without encroaching on divine subjectivity.[19]

Although he often vacillated between affirming human agency and immediately negating it, because of his theological conservatism, Khomeini had a greater tendency to negate human agency. In the more abstract sections of his book *Talab va Eradeh* (Desire and will), he considered human existence "in-another" and not "in-itself," citing the verses of the Quran that denied the direct subjectivity of humans (Khomeini 1983a, 62–63, 85). But in the more concrete sections involving human volitional capacity, Khomeini attempted a reconciliation:

Man, therefore, though he is a free agent [*fa'el mokhtar*], he himself is the shadow of the Free Agent, and his agency a shadow of the Sublime God's Agency. In brief, even though God's will is applied to the [universe], it is not in conflict with man being a free agent because the Divine transcendental knowledge, which is the origin of the universe, is not in conflict with human freedom and, in reality, confirms it. (Khomeini 1983a, 129)

In subscribing to the ethics of responsibility, Khomeini was compelled to recognize human freedom and subjectivity. Because, as humans, we had to choose between good and evil, between "prosperity" and "adversity" (*sa'adat va shaqavat*) by choosing correct beliefs and practices, Khomeini rejected the notions of human "nature" (*seresht*) and predetermined character (Khomeini 1983a, 140, 142). Those born with "good" or "evil" natures were equally free to choose their deeds and equally responsible for them (Khomeini 1983a, 148–49). This line of reasoning led him to interpret Islam as a religion of action, activism, and

19. Khomeini (1983a, 80) resolved the paradox of theodicy by attributing all good to God and all evil to human actions. Adopting a "position between positions," he also claimed to have done justice to the "rights" of both God and humans at the same time (Khomeini 1983a, 77).

even militarism. Indeed, throughout his career, Khomeini stressed that Islam was a religion not only of action but of movement against oppression. Moreover, as early as 1944, he favored the promotion of martial skills in Islam, going so far as to include betting on horse racing and shooting competitions (Khomeini [1944?], 244–45). Both during and after the revolution, Khomeini made a clear connection between human "dignity" and a militarist subjectivity. In an address on the occasion of the Iranian New Year on March 21, 1980, he said,

> Beloved youth, it is in you that I place my hopes. With the Quran in one hand and a gun in the other, defend your dignity and honor so well that your adversaries will be unable even to think of conspiring against you. At the same time, be so compassionate toward your friends that you will not hesitate to sacrifice everything you possess for their sake. Know well that the world today belongs to the oppressed, and sooner or later they will triumph. They will inherit the earth and build the government of God. (Khomeini, 1981b, 287)

In line with this activist interpretation of Islam, Khomeini de-emphasized the purely devotional aspects of religion and highlighted the practical-political aspects. Again, as early as 1944, he pointed out that "the ratio of the social issues to the devotional verses in the Quran is more than one hundred to one" (Khomeini [1944?], 9). He invoked the notion of becoming a "subject" (adam; literally, human being) in the active sense used by the secularist Malkum Khan a hundred years before him. He warned against passive piety: the imperialists did not care how fastidiously Muslims observed their daily rituals. Rather, the imperialists were after mineral deposits and markets, hence their fear that Iranians might become active subjects (adams) (Khomeini [1944?], 24–25). During the revolution he went so far as to say that the political demonstrations aimed at the breaking down of despotism to advance the cause of God were a form of worship (Khomeini 1981b, 234).

All in all, however, Khomeini's notion of subjectivity, like that of Shariati and Motahhari, attempted to find liberation through submission to God. In his message to Iranian pilgrims, Khomeini exhorted his followers "to convey to all Muslims in all continents of the globe this message from God: 'Refuse all servitude except servitude to God' " (Khomeini 1981b, 276). To achieve this liberation, Khomeini had proposed training seminary students (talabehs) and politicized clergy to become "ascetic revolutionaries."

Ascetic Revolutionarism and Mediated Subjectivity

Early in his career, Khomeini sought political revolutionaries to lead the people among Islamic clerics with a penchant for political activity and especially among young seminarians. But before they could assume such a role, they had to go through "self-cleansing" (*tazkieh*) and refinement. In his 1973 book *Mobarezeh ba Nafs, ya Jahad-e Akbar* (The struggle against the self, or the greatest jihad), Khomeini urged his young seminarian followers to embark on a path of self-refinement, self-discipline, and organizational reform to check the onslaught of imperialism. This self-refinement was meant to lead to the training and development of a class of subjects (*adams*), with Khomeini again invoking Malkum Khan's concept of active subjectivity because imperialism could only be driven from Iran by such active subjects (Khomeini 1973, 89).

Becoming a subject (*adam*), in Khomeini's thought, hinged on controlling and regulating one's "natural" self and inner nature. The strengthening of the will could only be attained by the total denial of the body. In a sermon delivered during the fasting month of Ramadan, Khomeini urged the young seminary students to exert their wills on their bodily organs (Khomeini 1973, 64). Attractions toward (inner) nature, he warned, were the cause of neglecting self-refinement:

> One whose entire attention is toward the realm of nature is diverted from God and unaware of the spiritual sphere and the world beyond. He is relapsing into nature and has never embarked on self-refinement; he has failed to create a spiritual movement and vigor in himself. He has not lifted the dark veils from his heart and remains in "the lowest of the low" [*asfal al safelin*], whereas God has created man in the loftiest status. (Khomeini 1973, 1–2)

Again we can see the emphasis on distancing oneself from nature, and from inner nature specifically, as the key to becoming a subject, in this case, a revolutionary. From the earliest days of his political career, Khomeini assailed the importing of modern Western culture, with its relaxed sexual mores, as having destroyed the revolutionary and activist qualities of Iranian youth. In his *Secrets Unveiled*, he complained that European novels had displaced religious books among the masses and that the Europeans, through the dissemination of these novels, had robbed Iranian youth of the spirit of audacity, courage, and chivalry and instilled in them instead the spirit of philandering, promiscuity, and cheating (Khomeini [1944?], 121). Western music, the unveiling of women, and coed schools, he added, had had the same corrupting effects on the culture and had to be banned (Khomeini [1944?], 213–14).

It is significant that, in his early writings, Khomeini opposed the spread of this "corrupt" culture in the name of the rationality that Kasravi and his followers were advocating (Khomeini [1944?], 232). Indeed, ascetic "rationality" would become a recurrent theme in Khomeini's discourse and much effort would be expended to institutionalize it after the revolution. In one of his first major public addresses after he again set foot on Iranian soil in 1979, Khomeini returned to this theme:

> We are not opposed to the cinema, to radio, or to television, what we oppose is vice and the use of the media to keep our young people in a state of backwardness and to dissipate their energies. We have never opposed these features of modernity in themselves, but when they were brought from Europe to the East, particularly to Iran, unfortunately, they were used not to advance civilization, but to drag us into barbarism. The cinema is a modern invention that ought to be used for the sake of educating the people, but, as you know, it has been used instead to corrupt our youth. (Khomeini 1981b, 258)

Although, from the outset, he had emphasized the notion of "awakeness" (bidari) as essential to political awareness, political awareness was itself but a means to achieve what Khomeini considered to be praxis.[20] He repeatedly emphasized that the Prophet's mission was not merely to promulgate laws but to put them into practice (Khomeini 1978, 90). Moreover, on numerous occasions, Khomeini criticized the purported depoliticization of seminaries and religious establishments as an imperialist ploy to dominate Islamic lands and peoples. He urged the mullahs to be socially and politically active and, as we will see below, to take the reins of political power in their hands, for which they had to prepare themselves through self-cleansing.

Parallel to training revolutionaries, Khomeini proposed that ascetic measures be applied to "the masses" for their "refinement" on the road to subjectivity. In his discourse, the parallel notions of ascetic revolutionarism for the few and

---

20. In a speech delivered after the revolution, Khomeini (1983b, 591) grounded this notion of politicized awareness in the medieval Islamic philosophers' concept of consciousness (yaqzan; literally, awakeness), revealing his deep philosophical penchant.

ascetic refinement from above for the many converged in what he called the "governance of the jurist," which represented the very negation of universal subjectivity and popular sovereignty.

Governance of the Jurist: The Negation of Universal Subjectivity

Khomeini's ideas on the establishment of a theocratic state in which the clerics would rule on behalf of the "Hidden Imam," whose divine mandate he believed was delegated to them, came to fruition in *Velayat-e-Faqib* (Governance of the jurist), first published in a limited edition in the early 1970s; the concepts associated with the title came to constitute one of the pillars of the Islamic regime in Iran. *Velayat* (from Arabic *wilaya*) has many different meanings, chief among them "being in charge," "ruling," "running," "governing" or "governance," "managing," and "administering." It can also mean "rule," "government," "sovereign power," "sovereignty," and "mandate." *Faqib* means "Islamic jurist"; its plural, *fuqaba*, refers to a class of clerical experts in Islamic law and jurisprudence. By choosing this title, Khomeini meant to convey two messages. One was that political rule and government, in the absence of direct divine revelation or "inspiration" through the Prophet or the imams, respectively, would devolve to the Islamic jurists and, among them, to the highest juridical authority. The other message was that the people were as much in need of a caretaker as children are of a custodian to oversee their moral development and refinement.

In his 1944 book *Secrets Unveiled*, Khomeini had more or less explicitly alluded to the concept of the governance of the jurist. But it was only in the early 1970s, as a result of his resolve to oppose the Pahlavi regime and the latter's intransigence, that the idea came to its full development. In *Governance of the Jurist*, Khomeini argued that power and authority were necessary to prevent the violation of the people's rights because individuals in the pursuit of their interests and happiness would oppress others (Khomeini 1978, 46–48). Khomeini did not consider it necessary to establish the reasons for a theocratic government, probably because he had done so in *Secrets Unveiled*. There he had argued that "reason" dictated that government belong only to "Him who owns everything" and "who has the absolute right of disposal of His property," which is to say, God, and only God, might establish a government, the obedience to which was incumbent on every human being (Khomeini [1944?], 181–82). The era of the Prophet's revelations and the authority of the imams having come to an end, the Islamic jurists had to be in charge not only of juridical affairs but also of political affairs, and the one among them with the highest qualification of "justice" and knowledge of the Islamic law had to assume the highest position of leadership. Khomeini argued that the political authority of this supreme jurist, though not his spiritual authority, was equal to that of the Prophet (Khomeini 1978, 63).

The most important implications of Khomeini's discourse on the concept of the governance of the jurist pertain to the sphere of positive law. In *Secrets Unveiled*, Khomeini had railed against the purported vacuity of positive law, saying that it could not compete with divine law (Khomeini [1944?], 312–13). He had argued that, unlike positive law, divine law was truly universal in at least two senses. First, being far above humans, divine transcended all particular interests, whether those of the rich in the capitalist countries or those of the elite in Communist countries (Khomeini [1944?], 290–91). Second, in contrast to positive law, divine law transcended the artificial geographic boundaries of nation-states and applied to all of humanity (Khomeini [1944?], 267). Throughout his discourse, Khomeini rejected the idea of human legislation, and therefore also of legislatures, on the grounds that, because true consciousness and justice were not within the province of humans, they had no right to "forge" legislation. "In Islamic government, instead of a legislative assembly . . . there is a programming assembly, which draws up programs for different ministers . . . in the light of laws of Islam" (Khomeini 1978, 53).[21]

> The Islamic government is neither absolutist nor despotic but conditional. . . . It is conditional in the sense that . . . the rulers are bound by a set of conditions specified by the Quran and tradition of the Prophet. . . . Herein lies the fundamental difference between constitutional monarchs and republics, on the one hand, and Islamic government, on the other: whereas, in those regimes, the people's representatives or the king engage in legislation, in Islam, legislation and the power to pass laws belong exclusively to God. (Khomeini 1978, 52–53)

In Khomeini's theoretical schema of the state, the government had the duty to provide justice and order from above, so that members of the community

---

21. Khomeini called for such a programming assembly despite the de jure provision for a parliament in the constitution of the Islamic Republic and the de facto existence of a very active parliament since the revolution of 1979.

could go about their business with peace of mind. The government had also to be a trustee of the people, who would entrust their destiny to it, assured by its protection and its law (Khomeini 1978, 192). The implication that citizens under such a government should remain passive and not participate in the social and political affairs of the community is unavoidable. Indeed, Khomeini had equated the governance of the jurist with appointing a custodian for minors (Khomeini 1978, 65). Owing to the contradictory nature of mediated subjectivity, however, Khomeini's discourse could also "accommodate" the type of citizenship, based on mass mobilization and participation, called for by the logic of revolution and the eight-year war against Iraq.

Mass Mobilization in Revolution and War:
Participation and Citizenship

Although most of Khomeini's thoughts on mass mobilization and participation were conveyed in his political writings or speeches rather than in his philosophical or formal political treatises, in *Governance of the Jurist*, he urged the mullahs to mobilize the people to overthrow the shah's regime, "to fight for Islam" (Khomeini 1978, 181). Khomeini's political success was in large part due to his ability to use the strong universalistic principles of Islam to create a sense of subjectivity, however limited and inchoate, among the social universal. In the course of the 1970s and especially during the revolution, he invested much political and intellectual capital in the notion of the "disempowered" (*mustaz'afin*), as had Shariati. Khomeini would return, again and again, to the theme of empowering the oppressed and disempowered: "You [the disempowered] are in the right: the hand of God Almighty is with you, and it is His will that those who have been oppressed should assume leadership and become heirs to their own destiny and resources" (Khomeini 1981b, 240).

Again and again, Khomeini would also return to the related theme of mass participation in politics, encoded in the phrase "the permanent presence of the people on the scene" (*huzur-e hamishe-ye mardom dar sahneh-ha*). In his speeches and addresses during the revolution, Khomeini often praised those demonstrating against the Pahlavi regime and encouraged them to remain "on the scene." He argued that, if there were only one benefit deriving from the establishment of the Islamic Republic, it would be the presence of the people on the social and political scene, which was tantamount to a miracle not realized elsewhere

(Khomeini 1985, 79). He even extended the right of participation to women, without whom, he admitted, the revolution would not have succeeded (Khomeini 1985, 99). At times, he even sounded as though the people, by participating in the revolution, had earned the right to participate in the affairs of their own country. In his famous speech to a large crowd gathered in Tehran's central cemetery on his return from exile on February 2, 1979, Khomeini coupled the notion of revolutionary activism with the right of participation: "I ask God Almighty that he grant success to all of you, and I proclaim to all of you that it is our duty to continue this movement until all elements of the Shah's regime have been eliminated and we have established a Constituent Assembly based on the votes of the people and the first permanent government of the Islamic Republic" (1981b, 259).

Indeed, the mass participation of the people in the revolution and in the war with Iraq compelled the Islamic state to recognize its responsibility to the people. Although, to be sure, this responsibility did not include all spheres of social life, in the area of politics the new state felt it was responsible to popular demands. Thus, for example, even though one could not claim certain personal freedoms, such as those pertaining to the dress code, especially for women, members of the populace could express their political opinions more freely than before. Moreover, Khomeini invited the people to hold him accountable: "If I set a foot wrong, the nation has the duty to say that you have set your foot wrong, be watchful and restrain yourself. All the nation has the duty to oversee the affairs of Islam" (Khomeini 1981a, 149). He congratulated the people for demanding to participate in the affairs of the country. As a result of the revolution, "owing to the new consciousness the people are no longer afraid of tanks and artillery . . . there is a spiritual revolution all over Iran; [those] who would not think about the affairs of the country, the youth, the children, women and men, now discuss current affairs in their circles; before this was not so" (Khomeini 1985, 61). Women, Khomeini asserted, had also to take part in the essential affairs of the country:

The laws of Islam are in the interests of women and men. Women must participate in the principal decisions of the country. As you played an essential role in the movement, now again you must share in the victory, and do not forget that, whenever necessary, rise up and revolt. The country belongs to you. God willing, you must build the country. Women in early Islam participated with men in battles. We see that women side by side with men and even ahead of them are lined up in battle . . . women must participate in their own destiny. (Khomeini 1985, 139)[22]

The exigencies of the eight-year war against Iraq, which resulted in hundreds of thousands of deaths on the Iranian side alone, also served to manifest the militarist side of subjectivity in Khomeini's discourse:

When there is a war, man overcomes his languor and laxity and becomes active, as the human essence, which is to be moving and active, manifests itself. In rest and comfort, man becomes languid and feeble, particularly those who are used to debauchery and gratification; but when there is war . . . man abandons feebleness and lethargy . . . war is a blessing because it releases the courage inherent in man. (Khomeini 1981a, 178–79)

In an ironic twist of the dialectics of his discourse, Khomeini grounded acquiring rights in martyrdom, or near-martyrdom: being killed or severely wounded at the war front was a "certification" of rights for the martyrs or veterans or their survivors in this world and the world to come (Khomeini 1982, 27–28).

There is no doubt that Khomeini's discourse at this stage can be described as "populist" in several obvious and not so obvious respects.[23] Most obviously, it entailed the mobilization of the people against the intellectuals and the more affluent classes (Khomeini 1981b, 265, 270, 304). It also entailed a xenophobic campaign against foreign imperialism, as well as demagoguery designed to create the illusion of power in the people. In Khomeini's discourse and the political regime built upon it, we find a limited and indirect empowerment of the social universal—an empowerment whose philosophical underpinnings I have called

---

22. The Islamic theorists' position on women's participation in the essential affairs of the country has been mostly, though not entirely, lip service. Khomeini's discourse on women in the early 1960s started from such an unfavorable position that some of his later pronouncements may seem progressive by comparison. In 1963, he explicitly declared his opposition to the shah's proposed reform of "voting rights" for women. Also in the 1960s, he opposed women working in modern jobs. During the uprising in Kurdestan soon after the revolution, when some of his women supporters asked permission to go to battle, to join the male forces to suppress the uprising, Khomeini replied, "No, it is not advisable, the nation itself [the men], the army will accomplish the task" (1985, 119).

23. For an analysis of Khomeini's discourse and the Islamic movement in Iran from the populist perspective, see Abrahamian 1993.

"mediated subjectivity." Significantly, however, and consistent with the populist nature of Islamic discourse and regime alike, this empowerment affects the people as a collectivity and not as individual citizens. Khomeini did not explicitly address the issues of individuality and the collectivity in his writings, finding the concept of full-fledged modern individual rights unacceptable. On the other hand, whereas Shariati's discourse, by emphasizing the priority of the collectivity, served to hinder the emergence of individual subjectivity, Khomeini's, by not discussing the issue, allowed it more space, at least potentially.[24] Khomeini's discourse also did not reject private property, at least not in principle. Indeed, throughout his career, Khomeini upheld the right to individual ownership, which may in the long run prove to be the key to unlock his version of mediated subjectivity, to release and realize the potential for subjectivity in his discourse. In the treatment of mediated subjectivity, however, it was Motahhari, of the three Islamic thinkers discussed in this chapter, who paid greatest attention to the issue of the individual.

Ayatollah Motahhari: The Metaphysics of Individual Subjectivity

Born into a clerical family in the small village of Fariman near Mashhad, the religiously significant provincial capital of Khorasan, Morteza Motahhari (1920–1979) was the son of a religious scholar who had studied in the Shiite holy city of Najaf, Iraq, and who had spent some years in Egypt and Arabia before returning to Iran (Motahhari 1985a, 9). In 1936, after a short period of study in Mashhad, Motahhari's interest in Islamic philosophy drew him to Qom, where philosophy was at least tolerated; there, in 1945, he began his advanced philosophical studies under Khomeini, becoming one of the most prominent protégés and eventually a fast friend of Khomeini (Dabashi 1993, 148). While in Qom, Motahhari also studied with Mohammed Hossein Tabatabai, who taught a course on "materialist philosophy" and Avicennan philosophy (Dabashi, 1993, 149). Beginning in the mid-1940s, when the power of the Tudeh Party was at its zenith and Marxist thought was receiving much attention in Iran, Motahhari took upon himself the task of challenging Marxist

24. Essential for realizing such a potentiality, of course, is overcoming the "governance of the jurist."

ideology from an Islamic perspective, a task he would pursue until his death. He began studying Marxist literature, all in Persian or Arabic translations, mostly of secondary sources, produced in Iran and Egypt. Even though his primary concern was with Marxism in Western thought, as we will see, he was also reacting to non-Marxist Western thought and inevitably engaged in a dialogue with it.

In 1952, Motahhari settled in Tehran; within two years, in a rare instance of connecting university and seminary before the revolution of 1979, he began to teach Islamic philosophy in the faculty of theology at Tehran University. In the 1960s, he took part in the activities of religious associations devoted to the propagation of politicized Islam. He became a central figure in the Monthly Religious Association (Anjoman-e Mahane-ye Dini), which sponsored monthly lectures on religious and sociopolitical themes; these were published in *Goftar-e Mah* (The Discourse of the Month), the journal of the association by the same name, which was banned by the government in 1963. In an attempt to attract the attention of educated young Iranians to political religion, Motahhari became one of the founders of Husseinieh Ershad in 1965. His involvement in the center, however, would soon be overshadowed by the magnetic personality and discourse of Shariati, who was becoming increasingly popular among Iran's religiously oriented educated youth. Although the controversy over the relationship between Motahhari and Shariati and their personal and doctrinal differences is beyond the scope of this chapter, as we will see below, their doctrinal differences are quite evident, even though their discourses were formed in the same matrix.

In the 1960s, and 1970s, Motahhari was quite active in propagating his brand of religious ideology and in writing many books. Although secretly in touch with his exiled mentor, Khomeini, he did not come into direct confrontation with the Pahlavi regime until the June 1963 uprising instigated by Khomeini and his followers, after which he was briefly imprisoned. During the Islamic Revolution, however, he assumed a particularly important role as Khomeini's representative and as a member of the Revolutionary Council, the shadow government of the revolutionary movement. On May 1, 1979, less than three months after the establishment of the new Islamic state, Motahhari was assassinated by Furqan, an esoteric political organization opposed to his views. Weeping in public at Motahhari's funeral, Khomeini called him the "fruit of my life" (Motahhari 1985a, 19).

From the Physical to the Meta-Physical:
The Theomorphic Journey to Subjectivity

Just like that of Shariati and Khomeini, but perhaps more articulately and explicitly, the ontological cornerstone of Motahhari's discourse is based on a
movement away from nature to beyond nature, to meta-physics. As we have
seen, early in his career, Motahhari had committed himself to challenge Marxist thought and what he considered Western materialist thought. In challenging
the philosophical tenets of Marxism, Motahhari relied on an interpretation of
monotheistic ontology, positing an animal, material, and corporeal side to
human existence, on the one hand, and a cultural and spiritual side, on the
other. Marxism, he argued, denied our true humanity by emphasizing the animal and material side to human existence. It was through a flight from the material side to the spiritual side that the journey toward subjectivity would be
realized.

> The truth is that the course of man's evolution begins with animality and finds
> its culmination in humanity. This principle holds true for individual and soci-
> ety alike: Man at the outset of his existence is in a material body; through an
> essential evolutionary movement, he is transformed into spirit or a spiritual
> substance. What is called the human spirit is born in the lap of the body; it is
> there that it evolves and attains independence. Man's animality amounts to a
> nest in which man's humanity grows and evolves. It is a property of evolution
> that the more the organism evolves, the more independent, self-subsistent,
> and governing of its own environment it becomes. The more man's humanity
> evolves, in the individual or in society, the more it steps toward independence
> and governance over the other aspects of his being. An evolved human indi-
> vidual has gained a relative ascendancy over his inner and outer environments.
> (Motahhari 1985a, 29)

Although this unmistakable metaphysics of subjectivity led Motahhari, just
as it did Khomeini and Shariati, to the realm of consciousness as a high point in
the ontological movement, it ultimately arrived, not at Hegelian self-
consciousness, but at religious belief and faith. As Motahhari went on to say,

> the evolved individual is the one who has been freed of dominance by the
> inner and outer environments, but depends upon belief and faith . . . The

more evolved human society becomes, the greater the autonomy of its cultural life and the sovereignty of that life over its material life. Man of the future is the cultural animal; he is the man of belief, faith, and method, not the man of stomach and waistline. (Motahhari 1985a, 29–30)

Even though Motahhari ultimately collapsed self-consciousness into faith and belief, on occasion, he would allude to the importance of the emergence of self-consciousness. Thus, in a treatise on ethics in which he struggled with modern European philosophy, he argued that the prophets had come to transform human consciousness to self-consciousness, the achievement of which was tantamount to the achievement of ethics (Motahhari 1987, 132).[25]

To ground his subjectivist approach, Motahhari invoked the Quranic concept of the "vicegerency of man" as God's successor on earth:

In the Quranic perspective, man is a being chosen by God, his successor [khalifa] and vicegerent on earth, half spiritual and half material, with a self-conscious nature, free, independent, a trustee of God, and responsible for himself and the world. He is in control of nature and earth and heavens, knows of good and evil. His being starts from weakness and impotence and evolves toward power and perfection, but he does not find solace except in God's presence and by his memory. (Motahhari [1979?]a, 252)

For Motahhari the existentialist à la Sartre, humans were architects and painters of their existence, the only beings endowed with the ability to build their own nature and to "paint" their own "visage" in whatever manner they chose (Motahhari [1979?]a, 253, 268). For Motahhari the subjectivist, as for Khomeini and Shariati, the Quranic notions of dignity and magnanimity (karamat va ezat-e nafs) constituted an ethical pivot (Motahhari [1978?]a, 44; 147).

In Motahhari's view, even though they could not completely sever their ties

---

25. Motahhari also argued that, whereas the notion of human consciousness is suppressed in the Judeo-Christian tradition, as evidenced in the story of Adam and Eve in Genesis, it is encouraged in the Islamic tradition. According to the Quran, God teaches Adam all the names (realities) and then commands the angels to prostrate themselves before him (Motahhari 1985a, 32). Based on this ontology, Motahhari also arrived at a subjectivist epistemology. Drawing on the seventeenth-century Iranian philosopher Mulla Sadra, he argued for a subjectivist epistemology in which consciousness and intellect are the primary faculties involved in processing of sense data and therefore also in representation. See Motahhari and Tabatabai [1978?], 63–72.

to heredity, nature, society, and history, humans should rebel against their limitations and liberate themselves from these sources of alienation, to realize their subjectivity through the power of their reason and faith (Motahhari [1979?]a, 272). He saw history as a process of "dis-alienation," in which subjects overcame their alienation (*maskh*) and self-estrangement to achieve their authentic selves by virtue of consciousness and intellect—a far cry from Shariati's Heideggerian view of authenticity (Motahhari 1980, 35–36).

True to the duality of mediated subjectivity, Motahhari's discourse had another, opposing side, fraught with the negation of human subjectivity. He argued that the Kantian notion of moral autonomy "is both true and untrue. It is true in the sense that in reality man's heart inspires these [moral duties] to him. But it is not true in the sense that [it assumes] that human conscience is independent of theism." The problem with Kant was that he portrayed the "conscience" as the only source of duty, without reference to the ultimate, divine source (Motahhari and Tabatabai [1978?], 128–29). Just as in that of Shariati and Khomeini, so in Motahhari's discourse, the ultimate stage of the movement from nature to beyond nature ultimately ends in the annihilation of the potential subject in the universal; indeed, for Motahhari, the reunification of the drop of water with the ocean represented the highest stage of "self-consciousness" (Motahhari [1979?]a, 299–302).

After describing humans as the architects and painters of their existence, Motahhari immediately added that religious institutions were necessary to show humans how to build and shape their future (Motahhari [1979?]a, 269). And, having attributed independence and freedom to humans in one essay, he denied the possibility of human agency in another, arguing that it would be in conflict with the "Universal Subject" (Motahhari 1979b, 53). Motahhari also addressed the issue of vacuity in human reason. Although humans might be able to apply their instrumental rationality to achieve certain ends, the ends were either set by their instinctual inclination, which was not acceptable, or by some external source transcending human reason (Motahhari [1978?]a, 26). Revelation, he concluded, had determined the major contours of the ends of human action, and our vacuous reason could only move within these contours (Motahhari [1978?]a, 43–46).

Of the three thinkers discussed in this chapter, Motahhari was the only one who was interested in the individual. As we will see, however, this interest was not so much intrinsic to his discourse as it was "forced" upon it by Motahhari's total opposition to Marxism. Thus he often associated the "corporeal materiality," from which humans had to distance themselves in the journey to the higher level existence, with individuality: "The elevated and ideal aptitudes of humanity are born of its faith, belief and attachment to certain realities in the universe that are both extraindividual, or general and inclusive, and extramaterial, or unrelated to advantage or profit" (Motahhari 1985a, 27).

In brief, Motahhari's discourse belonged to the paradigm of mediated subjectivity, in which the constant vacillation between affirming human subjectivity and denying it was a central characteristic. In his discourse, as in Khomeini's, the conflict between the two poles of mediated subjectivity took place in the context of his discussion of theodicy and predestination (*qaza va qadar*).

Theodicy and Predestination

Motahhari wrestled with these two issues all his life. He recognized the central importance of the problem of theodicy and its secularizing implications for a religious nation encountering the revolution of subjectivity. In *Adl-e Ellahi* (Divine justice), Motahhari pointed out that, unlike other theological questions, theodicy was something that occupied the minds of "illiterate countryman" and philosopher alike (Motahhari 1974, 22). In *Ensan va Sarnevesht* (Man and destiny), he explained his own lifelong preoccupation with theodicy and related issues. There he resolved to find out the reasons for the decline of the Islamic civilization, a civilization that was once a "brilliant phenomenon" and a "resplendent light," but was now in a pitiful state. Among the reasons cited by the Westerners for the decline of the Muslims were belief in predestination, belief in the next world coupled with contempt for this world, belief in intercession by the saints, dissimulation (concealment of one's beliefs in face of the enemy), and the expectation of deliverance (*entezar-e faraj*). As a seminary student in Qom, Motahhari identified the issue of predestination as the most significant:

> I was reading the second volume of Muhammad's biography by Mohammed Hussein Heikal. . . . In the second chapter there was a [quotation] by Washington Irving [to the effect] that the belief in "necessity" [namely, that] being killed or defeating the enemy were both [considered] victory . . . made the Islamic troops so fearless and powerful that no army could be a match for them. But at the same time the belief contained such a poison that it destroyed the impact of Islam. Ever since the successors to the Prophet ceased being warriors

and ceased conquering the world . . . the belief in "necessitarianism" [*jabr*] revealed its devastating character. (Motahhari 1979c, xiii-xiv)

Motahhari took these reasons, which he found to be "false accusations," as a challenge; he set out to prove them wrong, thus engaging in a lifetime dialogue with different aspects of modernity. There is no doubt that in his challenging the juggernaut of modernity he was as much affected by it as he wished to affect it. As a result, one of the major tasks he undertook was to reconcile human with divine volition. In doing so, he, like his mentor Khomeini, discussed the issue of free will and providence in the historical context of the debate between the early Islamic "rationalists," the Mu'tazalites, and their opponents, the Asha'rites. Motahhari agreed with the Mu'tazalites that the criteria set by humans to judge good and evil could also serve as measures for divine actions (Motahhari 1974, 9). Because evil could not be attributed either to God or to Satan, it followed that humans had to be free to choose their courses of action, which might result in good or evil. But, as the Asha'rites pointed out, and as Motahhari reminded his readers, granting agency to humans meant denying God's agency and subjectivity (Motahhari 1974, xxiv). Like Khomeini, Motahhari attempted to reconcile this perceived contradiction by adopting a "position between positions," at times seeming much bolder than Khomeini in positing human subjectivity: "In the Shiite philosophy and theology, man's freedom is posited without man being portrayed as a partner in 'God's property,' and without God's volition being subjugated and subordinated to human will. Divine providence [*qaza va qadar-e elahi*] has been established in the entire universe without implying man's compulsion by God's will" (Motahhari 1974, xxx).

Motahhari opposed the necessitarianism of the Asha'rites because of the social evils it generated. He argued that the belief in humans' unfreedom left the oppressors free to act, even as it restricted the ability of the oppressed to fight back: those who had usurped a position of power or plundered the public wealth always talked about God's grace toward them, and those who were their victims did not protest because it would be considered a rebellion against the divine decree (Motahhari 1979c, 19). Motahhari therefore came down on the side of human and individual responsibility and against necessitarian views (Motahhari 1979b, 133).

But, true to the logic of mediated subjectivity and as though pressured by his own emphasis on human subjectivity, Motahhari attempted to resolve the putative contradiction between human freedom and providence from a slightly different perspective. He postulated that human agency was on the level of "action" and compulsive action at that, whereas divine subjectivity was on the level of creativity (Motahhari 1979b, 127). According to this view, human subjectivity is a category *subsumed* under "Universal Subjectivity." As Motahhari put it, "the borderline between theoretical belief and disbelief is 'subsumption' [*az Ou-ii*; literally, "from-Himness"]. Believing in a being whose existence is not subsumed under Him is disbelief [*sherk*]. Believing in a being whose 'action' is not subsumed under Him is also disbelief" (Motahhari 1979b, 102). Thus Motahhari grounded human volition in divine volition or providence rather than in human volition itself, the "will to will," of modern subjectivity.

In Motahhari's discourse, however, the vacillation characteristic of mediated subjectivity sometimes strongly swings in the direction of positing human agency. Immediately after subsuming human agency and volition under "Providence," Motahhari postulated the possibility of "change in the Providence because of providence," through human agency (Motahhari 1979c, 48). He came to an "intriguing" conclusion that even God's knowledge is subject to change:

> Is God's knowledge subject to change? Are God's decrees subject to revolution? Can the lower influence the higher? . . . Yes, God's knowledge can be changed, that is, some of God's knowledge is subject to change; God's decrees can be changed. Yes, the lower can influence the higher. The "lower order" [*nezam-e sufli*] particularly man's will and action may shake the "higher order" [*nezam-e ulvi*] and cause changes in it. This is the highest form of man's control over destiny. I confess this is bewildering, but it is true. These are sublime and exalted issues of the change in an earlier divine decree [*bida*] discussed in the Quran for the first time in the history of human culture. (Motahhari 1979c, 49–50)

To be sure, after such bold remarks, Motahhari immediately negated the possibility of independent human subjectivity. Nevertheless, he was forced to postulate the idea of independent "essences" with "wills of their own" to explain the existence of evil: "Evil exists because beings are different in their own essences and not because of the deficiencies in the transcendental emanation" (Motahhari 1974, 126). Such a tendency on the part of Motahhari inclined him to be relatively more receptive to the idea of individual subjectivity, of course within the limits of mediated subjectivity. Motahhari's interest in the individual, as we have noted, was not intrinsic to his paradigm. Yet, because of the peculiarity of his slightly different paradigm, he was able to accommodate the individual more openly than either Shariati or Khomeini was. In a book apparently written to refute Marxist philosophy, *Jame'-e va Tarikh* (Society and history), Motahhari often assumed a philosophical instead of a theological approach to issues. He postulated that in the "lower" echelons of existence, in inanimate objects, the individual and the universal were enmeshed in one another, that is, the individual was submerged in the universal (*kol*). As they climbed up the ladder of existence, beings acquired more individual independence from the universal and there was a combination of plurality within the unity. In humans, this condition was most advanced, and, though there was constant conflict between the individual and the universal, in human society the autonomy of the constituent individuals was most developed (Motahhari [1978?]b, 331–32). In the range from the absolute priority of the individual to the absolute priority of the collectivity, Motahhari chose the middle ground, advocating a type of society in which neither the collectivity nor the individual would dominate the other. In such an ideal society, which was approved by the Quran, the organic character of the collectivity was maintained, even as the "relative autonomy of the individual [was also] preserved" (Motahhari [1978?]b, 326).

Insofar as he posited the element of subjectivity in his system of mediated subjectivity, Motahhari realized that subjectivity and freedom must be located in the individual, without denying the importance of the collectivity. In his view, although the Quran accords subjectivity, power, and viability to the society, it "considers the individual capable of disobeying the society" (Motahhari [1978?]b, 320). Motahhari took the concept of "responsibility" to its logical conclusion and located it in the individual:

> The teachings of the Quran are entirely based on responsibility, responsibility for the self and for society. The command to do good and refrain from evil is the injunction for the individual to rebel against corruption and depravity in society. The stories and parables of the Quran often contain the rebellion and revolt of the individual against social corruption. The story of Noah, Abraham, Moses, Jesus, the most noble Prophet . . . they all contain this element. (Motahhari [1978?]b, 331)

In giving credence to the individual in his discourse, Motahhari's sociological views obviously came into conflict with Shariati's. For Motahhari, the ideal

"Islamic classless society" meant a society without discrimination or deprivation, but not without differentiation (Motahhari 1979b, 69). Indeed, he saw society as an "arena for competition toward progress and perfection," in which "the barriers that confine[d] the individual on the way toward perfection" had to be eliminated (Motahhari 1979a, 76). It is significant that even in his attempts to achieve a synthesis between the individual and collectivity, at least on some occasions, he was more on the side of the individual:

> Islam is certainly a social religion and believes in the importance of society. It believes in the priority of the interests of the collectivity over the individual and has canceled class privileges. At the same time, the Islamic social system does not ignore the real rights and privileges of individuals; it does not devalue the individual before the society. Unlike some world thinkers [i.e., Marx,] it does not claim that the individual is nobody and society is everything; that all rights belong to the society, and not to the individual; that the society is the owner, not the individual, or that society is authentic, but not the individual. Islam definitely believes in private rights, private ownership, and the authority of the individual. (Motahhari 1979d, 115–16)

Motahhari's interest in the individual, though partly a response to the modernist discourse, was motivated as much by his opposition to Marxist determinism, or more so.

Critique of Marxist Determinism

Motahhari found the Marxist emphasis on human labor, production, productive forces, means of production, and matter to be a reversion to nature; as such, he opposed it: "Does human nobility lie in labor or in thought? Is the human an offspring of labor or of thought?" (Motahhari [1978?]b, 372). Against the Marxist reduction of human "essence" to labor, and of consciousness to mere epiphenomenon, Motahhari proposed a "realist" approach that privileged consciousness over labor, while recognizing the "mutual influence of labor and thought" (Motahhari [1978?]b, 372–73).[26]

Based on these premises, Motahhari criticized Marxism for attributing sub

26. Referring to the medieval Islamic philosophers' position that human speech (*nafs-e nate-qeh*) constituted the distinguishing characteristic of the human species, Motahhari ([1978]b, 376) criticized the Marxist treatment of human consciousness as a mere epiphenomenon.

jectivity to the collectivity instead of to the individual (Motahhari [1978?]b, 383). Characterizing the Marxist "philosophy of labor" as a type of alienation worse than the original alienation it sought to remedy, he accused Marx of forgetting that real people actually thought and made decisions (Motahhari [1978?]b, 385). With regard to the concept of historical materialism, Motahhari pointed out that the means of production did not develop spontaneously and without humans: they were developed only by thinking human agents willing to explore and investigate nature (Motahhari [1978?]b, 418–19). Significantly, it was the determinism implicit in historical materialism that negated human subjectivity:

> According to the deterministic theory of historical materialism, material social conditions determine man, give him direction, and construct his character, will, and choice. He is but a mere empty vessel and raw material vis-à-vis the social conditions. Man is made by the social conditions instead of social conditions being made by him. Prior conditions determine the future direction of man; man does not determine the future direction. Therefore, freedom cannot have any meaning whatsoever. (Motahhari [1978?]b, 362–63)

Motahhari criticized Islamic radicals who had embraced Marxism's historical materialism, even though they might have rejected philosophical materialism (Motahhari [1978?]b, 367). At the zenith of Islamic populism, he even criticized them for their populism, again based on his critique of Marxism, although his own discourse could also be considered populist, at least in part.

Primarily intended to refute the tenets and determinism of Marxism, *Jame'-e va Tarikh* (Society and history) emphasized the freedom of subjectivity and even that of the individual subject. Yet, at the very end of this book, Motahhari, true to the paradigm of mediated subjectivity, declared the freedom of subjectivity and the potentiality to change history as the unfolding of divine providence, reconfirming his subsumption of human subjective will under the universal.[27] As a result, it is not surprising that the contradictions inherent in the

---

27. Although the synthesis between the subject and the universal has been the at the very core of the modern quest for harmony ever since Hegel, it must be remembered that, in "subsumption," subjectivity is in a rudimentary stage and not fully developed, whereas "synthesis" presupposes a fully developed subject, seeking harmony with the universal while maintaining its full-fledged subjectivity.

paradigm of mediated subjectivity manifested themselves in the more sociopolitical aspects of Motahhari's thought.

Contradictions in Motahhari's Sociopolitical Thought

Motahhari's writings on political issues are relatively scant, perhaps because of his more cautious stance toward the Pahlavi regime, perhaps because he was assassinated so soon after the Islamic Revolution. Shortly before his death, Motahhari wrote a few essays, some unfinished, on revolutionary politics; they were collected in *Piramun-e Jomhuri Islami* (Regarding the Islamic Revolution), published posthumously. In an interview included with the essays, he expressed his forebodings about the trampling of freedom by the revolution and the strong populist trend within it, although he acknowledged the necessity of social justice (Motahhari 1985b, 22–23). In another essay in the same book, though he advocated "freedom of thought" (*azadi fekr*), Motahhari opposed what he called "freedom of opinion" (*azadi aqideh*). He defined thought in terms of "reason" (*aql*), as opposed to "faith" (*iman*), arguing that, in contrast to Christianity, which had suppressed reason and stressed faith, Islam had emphasized reason (Motahhari 1985b, 92–95). On the other hand, he rejected "opinion" (*aqideh*), which he defined in terms of "convictions" (*e'teqad*) and "attachments" (*delbastegi-ha*), because these were grounded in "emotions" (Motahhari 1985b, 97).[28] This line of reasoning led Motahhari also to espouse guidance from above and thus to deny the freedom of citizenship:

> What is required to respect man? Is it to guide him on the path to progress and perfection? Or is it to claim that because he is man and possesses human dignity, he is free to choose whatever he wishes for himself and we should respect it because he has chosen it for himself, even though we know . . . it is false with myriad consequences? What man chooses for himself might be chains. How can we respect these chains? (Motahhari 1985b, 100)

28. Thus Motahhari (1985b, 97–98) judged monotheism to be sound because it was grounded in reason, whereas he judged nonmonotheistic religions to be unsound because they were grounded in "opinion." Accordingly, he criticized the British government for granting religious freedom to all forms of "idol worship" as an abuse of both freedom of thought and the Declaration of Human Rights (Motahhari 1985b, 99–100).

Yet in still another essay in the same book, he asserted that the people should have enough political freedom to develop their political consciousness, to learn, for example, how to elect a representative to the Parliament. Even in regard to religion, he thought the people should have a certain freedom to develop their consciousness. He used the analogy of someone who needs to be left alone, despite discomfort, to learn something by trial and error (Motahhari 1985b, 123).

These contradictions, rooted in Motahhari's mediated subjectivity, also found expression in his writings on women. Before the revolution, he had written articles on the "safe" issue of women for the secular and mainstream women's magazine *Zan-e Ruz* (Modern Woman). In his book on the subject of the veil for women, for example, he had argued that the traditional head-to-toe wrapping of women was not the proper Islamic "covering" (*pushesh*), which was intended neither to isolate women socially nor to confine them to the private sphere. Although he had nothing against women driving, Motahhari considered women's demand for equal rights "selfish lust," likely to "create scandal" (Motahhari 1991, 226–27). Here his deep-seated prejudice toward women came to the fore. Because he considered the human lineage to be the exclusive property of men, Motahhari offered the partial rights of his mediated subjectivity to men only. His discourse thus failed to universalize even these incomplete rights.[29]

The extreme vacillation of Islamic revolutionary political thought in Iran can thus be traced to the mediated subjectivity of its major architects, Shariati, Khomeini, and Motahhari. It is my contention that the contradictions inherent in this paradigm manifested themselves in the institutions, practices, and, to a large extent, constitution of revolutionary Iran. Indeed, the constitution of the Islamic Republic, most of whose more progressive principles have been grossly violated, has been the object of much attention and contention.

Although many different groups with different political and religious agendas competed for the right to draft provisions of the new constitution, the final document bears the clear imprint of the Islamic religious establishment,

29. Indeed, Motahhari (1991, 61) argued that the reason why men so jealously kept their wives from contact with other men was that "Creation" had entrusted men and only men with preserving their lineage.

and of the revolutionary clerics and Khomeini in particular. Reflecting the strong universalist and populist tendencies of the Islamic discourse, the constitution establishes certain social and economic rights as universal, for example, the rights to social security, health services, education, and a dwelling (Articles 29–31).

True to the contradictory duality of mediated subjectivity, however, the constitution of the Islamic Republic grants only "half rights" to individual citizens. Sovereignty does not belong to the people, even though they are assumed to be in charge of their own destiny (Articles 2 and 6). Although legislation is approved by a parliament whose members are the elected representatives of the people, the right to legislate belongs exclusively to God (Articles 2 and 58). Indeed, the constitution institutionalizes the antidemocratic notion of the "governance of the jurist": according to Article 107, the highest Islamic jurist in the land is appointed as the "Supreme Leader" of the country. But he is "selected" by an "Assembly of Experts," in turn, elected by the people. Once appointed, the Supreme Leader is responsible only to God, yet can be dismissed by the same Assembly of Experts if he no longer fits the criteria for qualification. Moreover, even though the constitution confers vast powers on the Supreme Leader, it also provides for a "President," who is elected by popular vote and responsible to the people (Article 24). Article 4 grants much power to run the affairs of the country to the "Guardian Council," composed of twelve men, six appointed by the Supreme Leader and six elected by the Parliament from among Muslim jurists nominated by the head of the Judiciary, himself appointed by the Supreme Leader. At the same time, Article 6 recognizes the people's right to participate in the affairs of the country. The constitution guarantees freedom of the press and freedom of peaceable assembly—provided the exercise of these rights is not "detrimental to fundamental principles of Islam" (Articles 24 and 27).

∽

Because of its inherent contradictions, mediated subjectivity now plays only a transitory role in Iran's evolving discourse, albeit with a potential for transforming itself, society, and history. Whether this transformation will take place, and a full-blown universal subjectivity emerge, will depend to a large extent on which elements take the upper hand—those supporting universalizable subjectivity or those opposing it. Notwithstanding the prevalent belief that monotheistic religion and modernity are mutually exclusive, we can see the dialectical contributions of monotheism to the emergence of modernity in Iran. Modernity developed out of monotheism once before, in Europe; it can do so once again, in Iran and the Middle East. Chapter 5 will examine such a possibility in the context of religious discourse and postrevolutionary developments in Iran.

5

Postrevolutionary Discourses

The Contraction and Expansion of Subjectivity

Contrary to what might be expected after the triumph of a revolution and the establishment of a strongly ideological regime, in Iran the development of sociopolitical thought did not end in 1979. Indeed, the postrevolutionary period has witnessed a proliferation of sociopolitical discourses articulated by groups and individuals inside and outside the country, despite all attempts by the clerical regime to censor and control the flow of information.

Several factors may explain this turn of events. Soon after the clerical establishment consolidated its political and cultural control of the country at the successful conclusion of its "mini civil war" against the internal opposition in the early 1980s, a large number of lay intellectuals withdrew their stock in the Islamic discourse. Even though this phenomenon did not have an immediate impact on the populace caught up in the zeal of revolutionary activities, it prepared the way for the emergence of different discourses and for the evolution of religious discourse.

The total mobilization of the populace during the war with Iraq (1980–88) had contradictory effects on the development of sociopolitical discourses. On the one hand, the clerical establishment was able to realize and reinforce its revolutionary ideology in mobilizing the populace, but, on the other, this mobilization required that the populace participate in the social and political affairs of the country. This participation fueled the popular demand for, and expectation of, greater and more democratic participation, both of which would be recognized and articulated in the postrevolutionary discourses.

The factional division among clerical rulers and nonpolitical clerics alike helped create a political atmosphere conducive to competing theoretical discourses and to the expression of different views, otherwise not possible given the oppressive nature of the new Islamic regime.

The devastating human and material costs of the war with Iraq, the drastic reduction in oil revenues due to the changing geopolitical balance, and the new regime's pursuit of strict nonalignment and isolationism, especially during the first few years after the revolution, combined with economic sanctions imposed on Iran by certain Western countries and with economic mismanagement by the ruling elite, brought Iran to dire economic straits, with important sociopolitical consequences. The most obvious of these consequences has been the desire for economic development expressed by most classes and strata of Iranian society; this desire has in turn given rise to a national discussion over the issue of modern technology in a society mobilized by religious ideology. The issues of economic development and modern technology have necessitated the broaching of the larger cultural context of modernity, especially democracy and freedom and their affinity with religion and religious institutions.

Two additional factors have served to make social life in postrevolutionary Iran more complex. As a result of unregulated rural migration into cities crowded with war refugees, Iran's major urban areas have experienced manifold population growth. The difficulties of life in the city, with its impersonal relations, money orientation, and fast pace, have been exacerbated by economic hardship; the changing cultural ethos demands adjustment to the realities of modern urban life. A second factor increasing the complexity of social life in Iran has been the rapid population growth among the young. During the first years of the revolution, the clerics encouraged a higher birthrate, partly as a means of countering Iraq's technological advantage in the war and partly on religious grounds. The result has been a vast increase in the proportion of young people in increasingly crowded urban settings; these young men and women now challenge the archaic and atavistic cultural policies of the Islamic regime.

The effects of globalization on Iranian culture, the Islamic regime's principal battlefront in its war against the "corrupting influence" of the West, have also been considerable. From the first days of the Islamic Republic, the state and its various apparatuses have focused their efforts on curbing the penetration of Western culture. Yet, from the very start of the new regime's cultural crackdown, Iran has been inundated by shortwave signals from abroad. To these, in the 1990s, were added television signals, despite the regime's attempts to ban satellite reception, and Internet computer signals flowing back and forth across international telephone links. The black market distribution of banned foreign videos has also served as a major conduit for outside cultural influences.

As a consequence of these factors, both secular discourses and a variety of religiously oriented discourses have emerged in postrevolutionary Iran. Because of their limited following among the populace, we will not concern ourselves with the secular discourses (although they show promise of eventual wide-spread social acceptance and convergence with some of the religiously oriented discourses). Among the postrevolutionary religiously oriented discourses, however, two distinct discourses clearly merit our attention.

Judged against the basic criterion of modernity discussed in this work, namely, universalizable subjectivity, the first of these discourses, foremost represented by the philosopher Hussein Hajfaraj Dabagh, known by his pen name Abdolkarim Sorush, consciously seeks accommodation with modernity, to an extent unsurpassed by previous religious discourses in Iran, especially with regard to its gradual espousal of modern democratic principles. Although this discourse can trace its intellectual lineage to the paradigm of mediated subjectivity discussed in chapter 4, it has gradually emerged from that paradigm and, as a result, exhibits fewer of its contradictions. This is not to say it avoids the vacillations of mediated subjectivity altogether; only that, compared to those exhibited by its intellectual parents, its own vacillations are much more subdued.

Having served in the highest echelons of the state cultural apparatus of the Islamic Republic and having actively participated in the revolution, Sorush began his intellectual career in close affinity with the intellectual heritage of the Islamic revolutionary discourse examined in chapter 4. But as years have passed, he has elaborated and expanded the element of subjectivity in Shariati, Motahhari, Khomeini, and other Islamic thinkers, arriving at what seems to be the threshold of modern democratic principles. I will elaborate on the works of Sorush in the latter part of this chapter.

Although Sorush is only one of a range of thinkers to contribute to this first religiously oriented postrevolutionary discourse, there is only space to briefly consider two others. Mohammad Mojtahed-Shabestari (b. 1936), a cleric who served as the director of the Islamic Center in Hamburg for a number of years before the revolution, is currently a professor of theology at Tehran University (Boroujerdi 1996, 168). Using the principles of Western hermeneutics to analyze Islam, and arguing that the changes and fluctuations in the history of knowledge apply equally to religious and secular knowledge, Mojtahed-Shabestari has concluded that knowledge about God and the prophets is only possible in light of overall human knowledge in each historical period (Mojtahed-Shabestari 1996, 33). He has also applied his theoretical insights to the abject social conditions in Iran by discussing the absence of a philosophy of civil rights in the country's sociopolitical discourse (Boroujerdi 1996, 168). Another cleric, Ne'matollah Salehi-Najafabadi, whose book *Shahid-e Javid* (The eternal martyr) created quite a stir in seminary intellectual circles in the 1970s by casting doubt on the predestined character of Imam Hussein's martyrdom and his decision to fight against the enemies of Shiism, no matter the odds, during the first century of Islam, has also contributed to the discourse associated principally with Sorush (Moussavi 1992, 107). In his new book, *Velayat-e Faqih: Hukumat-e Salehan* (Governance of the jurist: Government of the righteous), written after the revolution, Salehi-Najafabadi (1984) has reinterpreted Khomeini's concept of the governance of the jurist in a direction more compatible with the democratic principles of popular sovereignty, focusing on the pronouncements of Khomeini that encourage the populace to participate in political and social affairs of the country.

The second postrevolutionary religiously oriented discourse, the radical religious antimodernist discourse, can trace its lineage more to secular than to religious sources. It has strong adherents among clerics and lay religious intellectuals alike, and owes most of its intellectual parentage to the "secular" Iranian philosopher Ahmad Fardid, whose antimodern interpretation of Heidegger, as we saw in chapter 3, was very popular among some lay intellectuals in the 1970s. Despite its "secular" roots, however, this discourse has adopted a strict religious rhetoric against modernity and human subjectivity. Its central figure, whose thought we will examine in the following section, is Reza Davari-Ardakani, a professor of philosophy in Tehran University with seminary training and formal training in Western philosophy at Tehran University. Although Davari-Ardakani is the most profound and original figure in the development of this discourse, numerous conservative clerical and lay religious intellectuals from diverse intellectual backgrounds have made significant contributions as well. What brings them together is Davari-Ardakani's use of Western counter-Enlightenment metaphysical assumptions to promote a traditional religious view of society and politics. Most of the intellectuals and journalists adhering to this second discourse have been involved in a polemical debate with the adherents of the first discourse, severely attacking their ideas, especially those of Sorush, for allegedly undermining the Islamic ethos.[1]

Even though the two discourses are in many ways intertwined, I will discuss

---

1. For the views of some of the other individuals contributing to the discourse associated with Davari-Ardakani, see, for example, Karimi 1990 and Larijani 1993.

the views of Davari-Ardakani first because his radical ontological assumptions seem to have provided Sorush with grounds for adjusting his own assumptions. Sorush has gradually changed his positions, partly in response to the social implications of the conservatives' theoretical positions, partly for other reasons.

Davari-Ardakani: The Leap from Being into Truth

Born in 1933 in the provincial town of Ardakan, between Yazd and Esfahan, Reza Davari-Ardakani studied there until the ninth grade. At age 18, he became a teacher, being laid off after the CIA-sponsored coup against Mossadeq in 1953, probably because of his sympathies for the liberal nationalist movement. He attended the seminary in Esfahan, then enrolled at the faculty of letters at Tehran University, where he became interested in philosophy (Davari-Ardakani 1996, 7). He received his doctorate in philosophy from Tehran University in 1967 and has been teaching there ever since. In an interview with the journal *Kayhan Farhangi*, he described the philosopher Ahmad Fardid as having had an important influence on him, and as having "saved" him from "Durkheimian positivism and sociologism" (Davari-Ardakani 1995, 8). Davari-Ardakani's doctoral dissertation was on political thought in Greek and Islamic philosophy; he published two treatises on Islamic philosophy based on it. He has also translated Camus's *Letter to a German Friend* into Persian. During the revolution, he published *Falsafe Chist?* (What is philosophy?), in which he laid out his major theoretical premises. After the revolution, he published several books and numerous articles elaborating his theoretical views on sociopolitical issues. He served as a researcher at the Islamic Republic's Academy of Philosophy and the Iranian Academy of Science and as the editor of the journal *Nameh Farhang*, published by the Ministry of Culture and Islamic Guidance (Boroujerdi 1996, 158).

As it did many other Iranian intellectuals in the second half of the twentieth century, the concept of Westoxication (*gharbzadegi*) provided Davari-Ardakani a point of departure, although, as we will see, his interpretation of this concept is very different from that of Al-e Ahmad, who first promoted the concept, and whose name has become almost synonymous with it.

Subjectivity and Reason as Westoxication

Though first coined by the "secular" philosopher Ahmad Fardid, the concept of Westoxication was later adopted and promoted by Jalal Al-e Ahmad to designate Iranians' loss of their subjectivity by surrendering their identity to the West. In his ground-laying work *What Is Philosophy?* Davari-Ardakani dismissed Al-e Ahmad's notion of Westoxication as a disease incidental to science, industry, and modern culture, viewing modern science and technology as inseparable from modern culture (Davari-Ardakani 1980, xix). "Modern *technique*" (he used the French word to designate "technology") had imposed its dominion over everything, including humans, and if there was going to be any change, it should start in the manner humans view the universe, themselves, and the origins of both (Davari-Ardakani 1980, xix). Thus Davari-Ardakani returned to Fardid's original conception of Westoxication as the preponderance of "egotistic" and "narcissistic" over all other aspects of human existence. In the rise of the West, he maintained, a world had been created in which humans considered themselves the center and axiom of everything. The rise of subjectivity in the West had brought about the rise of modern science and the fall of the Truth (*Haq*), which had become occluded ever since Western humans had advanced their hubristic claims of theomorphism (Davari-Ardakani 1980, xix).

Davari-Ardakani contended that, in failing to realize that the "realm of power" (by which Davari-Ardakani meant "subjectivity") underlay it, Al-e Ahmad had never penetrated to the bottom of Westoxication. Nor had Al-e Ahmad ever understood that the Western tradition of "humanism" constituted the core element of Westoxication; as such, Westoxication was an affliction, first and foremost, of Westerners, which had come to engulf all of humanity (Davari-Ardakani 1980, 59).

One of the words Davari-Ardakani has chosen to render "subjectivity" is "selfness" (*nafsaniyat*), which has historically carried negative connotations in Iran (Davari-Ardakani 1980, xii). Elsewhere, he has made use of the French word *subjectivité* as the foundation of the modern world (Davari-Ardakani 1994, 369); on many occasions, he has advanced "self-foundationism" (*khod-bonyadi*) as the basic principle of modernity. Another key notion in Davari-Ardakani's discourse is the concept of "the Truth" (*Haq*). The Perso-Arabic word *haq* has many meanings, including "rightness," "authenticity," "fairness," "correctness," "reasonableness," and, often, "God." With the emergence of subjectivity (*nafsaniyat*), Davari-Ardakani has claimed, the Truth (*Haq*) was eclipsed; indeed, "Westoxication began when man arrogantly claimed the status of the Truth [*Haq*] for himself and in the West this claim, knowingly and unknowingly, became the foundation of all ideologies, views, rules, institutions, and norms" (Davari-Ardakani 1980, xviii).

In a different essay, Davari-Ardakani observed that, because it had traditionally connoted appetites (*hava*), *nafsaniyat* might not be an apt translation for "subjectivity" as the ontological basis of modernity. He suggested instead the cognate *nafsiyat* to translate "subjectivity," apparently wishing not to evoke the perennial opposition between reason (*aql*) and appetites (*hava*) in Islamic tradition (Davari-Ardakani 1994, 65). Indeed, having suggested that "Western reason," as manifested in subjectivity, constituted the core of modernity, he proceeded to demonstrate a strong affinity between "Western reason" and appetites (*hava*) in modernity (Davari-Ardakani 1994, 65, 67).

Davari-Ardakani has held philosophy, as such, responsible for the emergence of human subjectivity and modernity. In his view, modern philosophy, in particular, is nothing more than the positing of subjectivity (*enaniyat*), humanism, and anthropocentrism (Davari-Ardakani 1980, 49). According to Davari-Ardakani, at the beginning of history, the philosopher was a lover of knowledge itself. With Hegel, however, philosophy was no longer love of knowledge, but knowledge itself, and humans claimed to have reached absolute knowledge. Whether one called this phenomenon "nihilism" or "Westoxication," the reality was that it represented a manifestation of humans as the Truth [*Haq*], from which many of the strengths and weaknesses of contemporary humans have emanated (Davari-Ardakani 1980, xxi). Although pre-Renaissance philosophy set our feet on the path, it was modern philosophy that led us away from the Truth:

> Notwithstanding the roots of Westoxication in Greek philosophy and its 2,500 years of history, its specific and predominant form has emerged with the Renaissance. With the appearance of Westoxication, the old form of history is abolished and a new man is born, who is no longer submissive to the Truth [*Haq*]. He forgets the Truth, so that he can replace Him and expropriate the earth and the sky. (Davari-Ardakani 1982, 58)

In Davari-Ardakani's analysis, modern epistemology, especially that of Kant, is responsible for the creation of the modern benighted neglect of the Truth. Kant reduced "existence" (*vojud*) to the object of knowledge. As a result, two types of knowledge have become possible in modernity: scientific knowledge of objects and "knowledge of the conditions of the possibility and realization of such science," called "critical philosophy" (Davari-Ardakani 1980, 96). "That Kant put aside the category of existence and emphasized knowledge, reducing philosophy to epistemology, was not merely an accident resulting from personal observations; rather it was necessitated by the unfolding of the history of metaphysics" (Davari-Ardakani 1980, 96).

Indeed, in Davari-Ardakani's Heideggerian interpretation, modern science is a moment of metaphysics, which has realized its absolute form in science and technology (Davari-Ardakani 1980, 83). As we saw in chapter 4, the notion of metaphysics in Islamic culture has been very close to "Western metaphysics," a flight from nature (*physis*) toward subjectivity, despite distortions in its religious form. Davari-Ardakani's views on metaphysics thus have the potential to run contrary to traditional views on this topic in Iran; as we will see, he has grappled with this issue in his discussion of classical Islamic philosophy. Given the importance of modern science and technology for a country like Iran, Davari-Ardakani's pronouncements on their metaphysical origins have had far-reaching implications and created much debate on the issue.

As the link between subjectivity and modern science, Davari-Ardakani (1980, 129) proposed the notion of "representation" (*tamasol*):

> In the view of the classics, reason is the faculty of the ego with which it perceives and gains knowledge of the beings. But modern reason is the faculty of representation [*tamasol*] and an aspect of subjectivity, in which whatever exists is mainly an object for the subject of knowledge. With this representation and reason, which is the representing faculty, modern science is born.

One of the central themes in Davari-Ardakani's discourse has been the question of imperialism and its ontological foundations, a question that has come into prominence in Iran with the anti-imperialist campaigns of the past two decades. Davari-Ardakani has maintained that domination is an inherent part of the culture of modernity. Placed at the center of the universe, the subjects of knowledge, by their very nature, have sought domination (Davari-Ardakani 1980, 153). Imperialism is the logical expression of the preponderant spirit of domination in modernity. Rejecting the Leninist view of imperialism as the highest stage of capitalism, Davari-Ardakani has seen imperialism as the realization of the core element of modern culture, philosophy, art, and literature (Davari-Ardakani 1982, 28). Accordingly, he has maintained a qualitative difference between modern imperialism and premodern conquests (Davari-Ardakani 1982, 149–51). Furthermore, he has suggested that, just as imperialism is an inevitable expression of modernity, so the reality in which some peoples dominate others is also inevitable because every subject needs an object of domination (Davari-Ardakani 1982, 165). This pessimistic reading of the notion of "master and slave" has prompted him to conclude that, because it is impossible for all to be dominant, universalization of subjectivity is impossible in any form (Davari-Ardakani 1982, 165). Thus the peoples of the Third World, by emulating the modern nations of the West, will at best become imperialists themselves (Davari-Ardakani 1982, 171). This conclusion applies not only to international relations but equally to intersubjective relations, where it is impossible to delimit the subjectivity of the "self" with that of the "other" (Davari-Ardakani 1985, 95).

Davari-Ardakani was thus led to seek solutions to the ontological problems of modernity, not in some form of intersubjectivity, but in the eradication of subjectivity altogether. And, in this ontological quest, he was chiefly guided, not by Islamic sources, but by European counter-Enlightenment philosophers. Despite his hostility toward them, Davari-Ardakani has demonstrated a remarkably accurate understanding of the primary philosophers of modernity. Paraphrasing Heinrich Heine, he drew a direct line from Kant to Robespierre, portraying Kant as the designer and teacher and Robespierre as the journeyman who put Kant's designs into practice (Davari-Ardakani 1982, 110). On many occasions, Davari-Ardakani has also referred to Hegel and the enormous but unrecognized influence of his ideas on modernity (see, for example, Davari-Ardakani 1980, xxi). But he has found even Hegel's philosophy of no use in overcoming the ontological problems of modernity, representing as it does the ultimate, perfected expression of the revolution of subjectivity that had been in the works since the classical Greeks.[2]

For Davari-Ardakani, Nietzsche is the transitional figure in the quest to overcome modernity. Whereas, in Hegel, humans are self-conscious first and belong to nature, to which they must be reconciled, only second, in Nietzsche, humans are animals first and conscious second (Davari-Ardakani 1980, 206). He credits Heidegger with reversing "metaphysics" altogether. What the philosophies of Plato, Aristotle, Plotinus, Augustine, Aquinas, Descartes,

---

2. Although his reading of Hegel's philosophy is relatively sophisticated, Davari-Ardakani makes no mention of Hegel's efforts to overcome the ontological problems of subjectivity and modernity. See Davari-Ardakani 1980, 165–94.

Hegel, Marx, and even Nietzsche have in common is that all represent a variation of metaphysics (Davari-Ardakani 1980, 225). The plight of modern humans, reflected in their inauthentic existence, is rooted in the fact that they are
alienated from the Being (*Vujud*) and cannot hear its summons (Davari-
Ardakani 1980, 153–4). It was Heidegger who demonstrated that the proper
station of humans is to be attentive and heedful toward the Being (Davari-
Ardakani 1980, 232). Indeed, by plumbing the depths of Western philosophy,
Heidegger revealed the inner truth of the West, which can help liberate Iranians from the prison of Westoxication (Davari-Ardakani 1994, 56–7).

Because his views of metaphysics might lead him into conflict with traditional Islamic metaphysics, Davari-Ardakani has attempted to reconcile his
and Islamic notions of reason, accommodating the latter in his attack on metaphysics as the unfolding of human reason (see, for example, Davari-Ardakani
1982, chap. 2; 1994, 53–65). Accommodation notwithstanding, however, he
has spared neither Islamic philosophy nor even the rational theology of
Kalam, charging that some texts of Kalam have been so profoundly influenced
by philosophy as to be virtually indistinguishable from it (Davari-Ardakani
1980, 245–46). Moreover, he has held that the truth of Islamic religion does
not need the rationalistic arguments of Kalam to stand (Davari-Ardakani 1980,
254). Yet Davari-Ardakani has been more sympathetic toward Kalam than toward Islamic philosophy because it recognizes human poverty and inability,
whereas Islamic philosophy is based on human power and reason (Davari-
Ardakani 1980, 270). Indeed, according to him, Islamic philosophy is in
essence Greek and, as such, Islam has no need for it (Davari-Ardakani 1980,
289–90).

By contrast, Islamic mysticism (*tasawwuf*) is, for Davari-Ardakani, the complete antithesis of humanism (Davari-Ardakani 1980, 298). In the mystical tradition of the Sufis, human essence lies in " 'nobodyness' and nothingness. [Man]
has no real existence and essence. His essence lies in annihilation" (Davari-
Ardakani 1980, 299). Davari-Ardakani's adoption of the "philosophy of Being"
thus led him to embrace the Sufi notion of annihilation of the subject, a process
that has involved a leap from the Heideggerian conceptualization of the Being,
which arose from the Europeans' experience of modernity, to the Sufi notion of
submersion in the Truth (*Haq*). For Davari-Ardakani, however, the reversal of
metaphysics and annihilation in the Truth were not mere theoretical constructs:
they would be embodied in the Islamic Revolution.

The Islamic Revolution: The Antidote to Westoxication

In the introduction to *What Is Philosophy?* Davari-Ardakani described the Islamic Revolution as a reaction to Westoxication that portended the end of domination of the West and the beginning of a new era in which religion would douse the fires of the "holocaust of Westoxication" (Davari-Ardakani 1980, xxii-xxiii). He described the revolution in terms of the renewal of the covenant with God, a covenant broken by modernity:

> The Islamic Revolution must . . . summon a return to the beginnings and a renewal of the Covenant. This renewal . . . requires that we [Iranians] break the covenant to which we acquiesced in Westoxication. . . . [W]e take refuge in God and ask Him for assistance in our renewed Covenant, a covenant that is the future of mankind. (Davari-Ardakani 1980, xxiii)

With Kierkegaard, Davari-Ardakani invoked Abraham's willingness to sacrifice his son as the price for renewal of the covenant, suggesting that, to achieve it, Iranians had to sacrifice all worldly attachments and submit to God (Davari-Ardakani 1982, 122)

In the manner of proponents of the great world revolutions, Davari-Ardakani gave his imagination free rein, viewing Iran's revolution as the one that would end all modern revolutions inspired by the revolution of subjectivity. By undermining the current world politics, the people

> would be at the threshold of a revolution that is in essence different from the revolutions of modernity. The French Revolution and anti-imperialist revolutions of the subjugated nations, have all been [waged] in order to establish and realize the truth of the West. But there is another [type of] revolution that undermines the West and, when expanded, it will overthrow the West. With this revolution, mankind may renew the forgotten Covenant of the past and in a way a new era will be established. This revolution would no longer be the realization of philosophy because a new horizon would open in which mankind would be encouraged to . . . question the [regime of] *"technique."* . . . [T]he experiment of the Islamic revolution will shed light on many things. (Davari-Ardakani 1982, 131)

Davari-Ardakani's radical interpretation of anti-imperialist strategy is reflected in his thoughts on the impossibility of reconciling modernity and what he considers to be Islam. For Davari-Ardakani, such a reconciliation would entail becoming accomplices with imperialists of the East and the West, who have expropriated and dominated everything in the world. The purpose of the Islamic Revolution is not to compete with these imperialists nor to surpass them in domination (Davari-Ardakani 1982, 210–11). In recognizing the enormous power of modernity that surrounds the Islamic Revolution in Iran, Davari-Ardakani does not accept that modernity must stay and the Islamic Revolution must adapt itself to its demands. On the contrary, with the expansion of the Islamic Revolution, law, politics, science, and technology should conform to Islam because Islam cannot conform to them and remain Islam (Davari-Ardakani 1982, 263). Apparently sensitive to social forces demanding modern science and technology, however, especially as a result of the war and economic difficulties after the revolution, Davari-Ardakani seems to have gradually adjusted his positions on this issue (Davari-Ardakani 1995, 142–43). In *What Is Philosophy?* he viewed technology as the very essence of modernity. In his later and less theoretical writings, however, he has reluctantly accepted the necessity of modern science and technology (Davari-Ardakani 1982, 211). As long as the "sovereignty of *technique*," that is, the domination of modernity and the West, exists, the need for technology in a country like Iran remains: "The purpose of our revolution has not been to achieve ideal perfection in modern civilization, but until the West starts to crumble from within, we will not shun technology and technological sciences and [will] earnestly seek modern science" (Davari-Ardakani 1982, 237). Thus Davari-Ardakani's attitude toward technology is merely utilitarian: Iran needs modern positivist technology to survive, but it must confine its use of it to the achievement of evil but necessary worldly ends, otherwise technology's dominance would be established again (Davari-Ardakani 1994, 99). Because his acknowledgment of the indispensability of technology for Iran goes against his earlier and, it would seem, strongly felt position, Davari-Ardakani has advanced a mitigating distinction between the "founding" and the "adopting" of technology. Iranians may avoid the founding of technology and its cultural parent, subjectivity, by *adopting* and appropriating this illegitimate but attractive child of European civilization:

> Modern *technique* has already been founded, but other nations, who have not been involved in its creation, can use Europe's experience and appropriate and borrow science and modern technology. In other words, a distinction must be made between the founding of technology and its borrowing. . . . [Persian]

Gnostic thought does not deprive mankind from the amenities that technology has provided, rather it liberates mankind from bondage to technology and to objects. (Davari-Ardakani 1994, 141–42)

Davari-Ardakani has contended that merely "adopting" technology would not result in the renewed dependence of Iran on the West (Davari-Ardakani 1994, 137). Assuming he is correct, one might ask whether this approach would not again lead to the ascendance of positivist subjectivity without the cultural aspects of subjectivity to ensure democratic institutions to check positivism. Davari-Ardakani would say no because in the West itself, where all aspects of subjectivity have existed more or less together, profound changes are taking place. The collapse of the Soviet Union (intellectually part of the West) and the lack of enthusiasm in Western thought for modernity portend the collapse of the rest of modern civilization:

Today the conditions of the West have changed. That means there is nothing in Western thought to advance the power of the West and modernity any longer. The Soviet Union, with all its territory, population, and God-given natural resources, is abolished. The West also, like the Soviet Union, has lost its endurance and longevity. The West has no more hope in the future, and its thinkers view philosophy as finished off and talk of the end of modernity. They have called the contemporary period the "limbo" of postmodernity, which is the shaking of the foundations of modernity before the start of a new era. (Davari-Ardakani 1994, 18)

Politics of the Leap into Truth

If Davari-Ardakani has been somewhat receptive toward the science and technology of modernity, he has been much less sympathetic toward other aspects of modernity, such as political institutions and norms. Belonging and subordinated to the Truth (*Haq*), our human polity is determined by God, he has argued. As was the case in the Golden Age of early Islam, the Islamic government is neither democracy nor despotism; its rulers execute divine law (Davari-Ardakani 1982, 100). By contrast, notions such as modern politics and political rights are grounded in "Western reason," which in turn is grounded in the accursed humanism and subjectivity (Davari-Ardakani 1982, 84). This antiliberal position has led Davari-Ardakani to criticize Iran's Constitutional Revolution as the realization of the ideas of Westoxicated Iranian intellectuals (Davari-Ardakani 1982, 94). Indeed, he has referred to it as a "foreign sapling" that never took root in Iran and that withered "until [it] had to be pulled up and thrown away" (Davari-Ardakani 1982, 96). Moreover, the popular uprising at the time of the Constitutional Revolution was not for democracy, but merely against the despotism of the Qajar shahs, implying the irrelevance of democratic institutions in a religious society (Davari-Ardakani 1982, 99).

Davari-Ardakani's antidemocratic sentiments are not confined to Iran:

> The freedom of religious beliefs in the Declaration of Human Rights means alienation from religion; it means leaving the individuals to their own devices so that they may do whatever they want with religion in their private lives and have any religion they want. . . . [M]odern man sees his own image in the mirror of the Truth [Haq] and instead of entering into a Covenant with the Truth, he has entered into a covenant with himself. Therefore it is inevitable and natural that such a man would turn his back on religion and cover up his acts with claims of nationalism, internationalism, liberalism, collectivism, and individualism. (Davari-Ardakani 1982, 52)

Faithful to the antisubjectivist ontology of his discourse, Davari-Ardakani has articulated thinly disguised sentiments against literacy projects in a country like Iran, where until recently a large proportion of the population could not read or write: "Assuming that literacy programs and other similar projects are practical and simple, it does not mean that illiterate people in the world cause wars. . . . Beware of the abuse of the knowledge and the practice that results in the eclipse of the Truth [Haq]" (Davari-Ardakani 1982, 139–40).

As we have noted, Davari-Ardakani's ontology led him to dismiss the antiimperialist struggles of other nations as futile, which, being also grounded in human subjectivity and modernity, would at best result in the assimilation of the oppressed to the oppressors (Davari-Ardakani 1982, 172–74). For Davari-Ardakani, the only true and effective anti-imperialist struggle is the one the Islamic movement in Iran has embarked on, which aims at eradicating the notion and practice of human autonomy (Davari-Ardakani 1982, 175).

Fully in agreement with his ontology of the Truth (Haq), Davari-Ardakani believes that there should be no separation between religion and politics (Davari-Ardakani 1982, 225–26). This position has led him to support the doctrine of "governance of the jurist," the ideological mainstay of the clerical rule and the antidemocratic institutions of the Islamic government in the postrevo-lutionary era. He has been careful, however, to distinguish between despotic clerical rule and what he considers to be the execution of the divine mandate:

> Islamic polity is the exercise of divine sovereignty, and this can be accom-plished by those who are not only experts in the knowledge and practice of re-ligious laws, but whose eyes, ears, tongues, and hands, in their closeness to the Truth [*Haq*], have become His eyes, ears, tongue, and hands. The Islamic gov-ernment is the government of the "confidants" [*olya*] of God, whereas the prevalent meaning of politics is the management of social and economic af-fairs in which man is viewed as a being whose existence is the aggregation of material and mundane needs and abilities. (Davari-Ardakani 1982, 254)

In a different essay in the same book, Davari-Ardakani distinguished between the regime of the governance of the jurist and despotism. More generally, he differentiated between two types of rule, one exercised by humans over humans and the other—the sovereignty of God (Haq)—exercised by God over hu-mans. In the first case, if the rule was that of one or a few individuals over the collectivity, it was despotism, and if that of the majority over the collectivity, democracy. In both instances, what mattered, however, was the rule of human desires, appetites (*ahva*), and the "sovereignty of *technique*," in which in the world was engulfed. In the second case, that of divine sovereignty, its human embod-iment, namely, the theocratic state, being obedient to God, had guardianship over the people, on the one hand, and was their servant, on the other. Mindful of the close affinity between a theocratic state and despotism, Davari-Ardakani warned that "it is possible that some individuals or groups, in the name of reli-gious government, take to despotism and oppression, in which case the govern-ment is despotic and it is one of the worst forms of despotism." But, he was quick to point out, "the truth of the 'governance of the jurist' is not despotism, nor can it be compared with democracy either" (Davari-Ardakani 1982, 175–76).[3]

Shortly after the revolution of 1979, the issues of nation-state versus larger Islamic state and of divine versus national/popular sovereignty became major

---

3. Other proponents of the antisubjectivist discourse have expressed views on the doctrine of the "governance of jurist" that are much less sophisticated than those of Davari-Ardakani. Shahriyar Zarshenas (1992, 51–52), for example, has unequivocally supported the notion of po-litical rule by the clerics without discussing the possibility of despotism in his discourse.

subjects of political debate in Iran. Davari-Ardakani (1985) addressed them in the essays of *Nasionalism, Hakemiyat-e Melli va Esteqlal* (Nationalism, national sovereignty, and independence). In "The Essence and Forms of Nationalism," he attacked the notion of civic nationalism—based on the idea of universalizable subjectivity—because of its subjectivist element:

> From its very beginning [in Europe,] nationalism meant that the populace should be independent of any force in their exercise of power, creation of laws and norms and the control of social relations and transactions. And because in that period the established power was the Church and its rule, nationalism was instituted in opposition to the Church. But what was the source of this spirit of independence, and how did man find the courage and the strength to rebel against the Church, which he considered the shadow of the heavens? We might say that this spirit of independence emerged shortly after man considered himself the center of the universe and the source of knowledge, power, and will; when a revolution took place in the political, social, economic, and intellectual sphere. (Davari-Ardakani 1985, 22)

In the same essay, he assailed the right of individuals as individuals, or even as a collectivity, to participate in government and the process of governing themselves as an "innovation," brought about by the anthropocentrism of modernity and closely tied to the notions of national sovereignty and nationalism (Davari-Ardakani 1985, 20).

In another essay in the same book, Davari-Ardakani explicitly rejected national and popular sovereignty and constitutions, which "in their origin and essence are incompatible with religion because the chief principle of all constitutions is based on a [notion] that sovereignty derives from the people's will and that the people must legislate, whereas in religion sovereignty belongs to God and the rulers [merely] execute divine ordinances" (Davari-Ardakani 1985, 163). He even warned that Khomeini's pronouncements on social participation against oppression must not be interpreted as encouraging national sovereignty (Davari-Ardakani 1985, 42). However, he also rejected the "ipseism" of nationalistic movements and sentiments because it might result in chauvinism (Davari-Ardakani 1985, 23).

As we have seen, Davari-Ardakani has retreated from some of his earlier radical positions on modern science and technology, apparently as a result of social pressure. Although he has made some concessions on other issues as well, these concessions seem to be mostly rhetorical in nature and represent no substantive change in his persistently antisubjectivist discourse. Thus, having recently stated that freedom and equality have their "roots in human nature," he almost immediately dismissed them for being rooted in the anthropocentrism of the Renaissance (Davari-Ardakani, 1994, 53–54).

The persistent antisubjectivism of Davari-Ardakani's discourse is nowhere more apparent than in his polemics, especially those against Abdolkarim Sorush, whom Davari-Ardakani has criticized and opposed on a range of topics in numerous magazine articles and collected essays. Whereas Davari-Ardakani's discourse moves toward a contraction of subjectivity, Sorush's moves toward its expansion, indeed, its liberation from the confines of mediated subjectivity.

Sorush: The Expansion of Mediated Subjectivity

Known chiefly by his pen name Abdolkarim Sorush, Hussein Hajfaraj Dabagh was born in a lower-middle-class family in south Tehran in 1945. He attended Alavai High School, newly established by pious Bazari merchants to provide instruction in modern science as well as religious studies. After receiving his degree in pharmacology from Tehran University, he spent two years in the army and was then sent to Bushehr to render part of his medical service.

He soon departed for England, where he first studied analytical chemistry at the University of London, later developing an interest in philosophy and history of science and matriculating in the Department of Philosophy of Science (Sorush 2000, 8).[4] At the outbreak of the revolution, Sorush returned to Iran and published his first sociopolitical works. After the revolution, he was appointed to the High Council of the Cultural Revolution, which was charged with the task of revamping and Islamicizing the entire educational system in Iran. He has also taught philosophy and philosophy of science at Tehran University and conducted research at the Institute for Cultural Research and Studies (Boroujerdi 1996, 158–59). Since 1995, however, Sorush has come under severe attack, at times physical, by the conservative forces of the Islamic Republic.

---

4. I am thankful to Mehrzad Boroujerdi for the information that Sorush never completed his doctoral dissertation in London.

Eschewing the Metaphysical Path to Subjectivity

In his first book, *Naqdi va Daramadi bar Tazad-e Dialikitik* (A critique and introduction to dialectics), published in 1978, just before the triumph of Islamic Revolution, and reprinted several times, Sorush criticized the "dialectical method" and the cosmologies associated with it for being rigid and for not lending themselves to critique or revision. He went even further, charging that, because it was grounded in the metaphysical approach, the dialectical method was inappropriate for a valid understanding of the world and social events.

In the same book, Sorush criticized a version of the "journey to subjectivity" articulated by Abolhasan Banisadr, the ill-fated first president of the Islamic Republic (Sorush [1978], 140). Indeed, Sorush would fault the notion of a theomorphic journey in his other works. As we saw in chapter 4, such a journey constituted an important ontological basis for the Islamic revolutionary discourses of the prerevolutionary sixties and seventies. In an article originally published in the magazine *Kayhan Farhangi* in 1985 and later reprinted in his book *Tafarroj-e Son'* (Promenading creation), Sorush criticized the notion of humans as a "becoming toward perfection" (Sorush 1987, 263). Obliquely criticizing the expectation that citizens would become morally perfect, Sorush blamed the Islamic government for setting unrealistically high moral standards for Iranians. He advised government officials that the first lesson they needed to learn in managing a polity was tolerance of human imperfection (Sorush 1987, 265–66). In another essay, he denied that the mission of the prophets was to elevate humans to perfection: "The prophets were not sent to angels, nor did they view humans as imperfect angels [to be transformed into] perfect angels. Man is man and he is not to be transformed into an angel" (Sorush 1984, 62). Indeed, in yet another essay, Sorush warned that the desire to achieve the status of divinity was the first step toward corruption and evil (Sorush 1984, 158). He also warned that applying the notions of human perfectibility and theomorphism to the political sphere could result in certain individuals according themselves special rights and privileges as the vicegerents of God on earth (Sorush 1984, 171).

Thus Sorush's eschewing the path to metaphysics and theomorphism, an essential aspect of the discourses of Shariati, Motahhari, and even Khomeini, was motivated, at least in part, by the Islamic regime's intolerance of human imperfection, which was manifested in rigid moral requirements and the monopolization of political power by the clerics. But it was chiefly motivated by the clear realization on the part of Sorush that the theomorphic "journey toward subjectivity," however firmly grounded in Islamic metaphysics, could proceed no further in a religious society such as Iran's. To avoid the otherwise inevitable dead end of such a journey, Sorush had to take a detour.

Epistemological Detour: Knowledge of Religion as the Object of Subjectivity

In his 1992 article "Paradoks-e Modernizm" (The paradox of modernism), Sorush identified the "essence" of modernity as the emergence of certain, altogether new types of knowledge, such as modern ethics, sociology of religion, philology, and the study of tradition and ideology, that had created an unbridgeable gap between modern humans, on the one hand, and the ancients and the world of "objects," on the other (Sorush 1992, 12). By emphasizing the epistemological dimensions of the knowing subject, Sorush detoured around the direct metaphysical discussion of subjectivity. In doing so, he added a hermeneutic element, likening the external world to a text in need of interpretation:

> No text reveals its meaning [on its own]. It is the mind of the philologist that reads the meaning in the text. Phrases are "hungry" for meanings. . . . Accordingly, the meanings of phenomena are not written on them and are not obtained by simple looking. The observer must know the "language" of the world to read and understand. Science and philosophy teach us this language (or languages). And these languages are neither stagnant nor perfect, but in constant transformation. (Sorush 1991, 192).

In a related vein, Sorush argued that our understanding of the world was necessarily historical: social and human institutions, "instead of being fixed by nature [were] fluid," and we could only truly observe them when we "[sat] by their ontological stream and watch[ed] their flow" (1991, 198).

In what is probably his most important book, *Qabz va Bast-e Teoriki-e Shariat* (The theoretical contraction and expansion of the Sharia), Sorush applied this subjectivist approach to knowledge, to our understanding of religion and sacred knowledge:

> [Just] as no understanding of nature is ever complete, and always enriched by newer scientific works and the arrival of competing views and historical devel-

opments, so are understandings of religion. This applies both to jurispruden-
tial [*feqhi*] views as well as convictions and beliefs [*nazariyat-e e'teqadi va usuli*].
Muslims' understanding of God, resurrection, and providence [*qaza va qadar*]
reveal some of their meanings in theory and practice [gradually]. Similarly, ju-
risprudential views such as the "governance of the jurist" and the [Quranic pre-
cept of] the "injunction to do good and avoid evil," and so on, reveal their
exact meanings in the historical process. (1991, 214–15)

In his interpretive approach to religion, Sorush repeatedly pointed out that our
knowledge of religion was contingent on other branches of knowledge that
emerged historically. He argued that religious knowledge derived from the
Quran, Islamic tradition, and the lives of religious leaders was a "consumerist"
type of knowledge and, as such, directly influenced by "productive" forms of
knowledge (the physical and social sciences, philosophy, and the humanities).
Because all types of religious knowledge were contingent on these "external"
branches of knowledge, which were always in flux, they, too, would change
(Sorush 1991, 79–80). Furthermore, Sorush argued, there was a close relationship between our modern view of humans (modern philosophical anthropology), our knowledge of nature, epistemology, and our religious knowledge
because they constituted "parts of a circle" (Sorush 1991, 88). As a result, the
style of religion was different in each epoch, and religious knowledge was subject to "contraction and expansion" in different individuals and at different peri-
ods depending on changes in the external branches of knowledge of the time
(Sorush 1991, 89). The contingency of the religious knowledge on other
knowledge, in Sorush's view, applied even to the words of God: "The discovery
of the innermost [meanings] of the words of God . . . is directly contingent on
the development of human knowledge [*ma'aref-e bashari*], including the mystical,
philosophical, and scientific forms of knowledge" (Sorush 1991, 203).

Sorush made a crucial distinction between "religion in itself" and our
"knowledge of religion." The essence of "religion in itself," as a divine creation,
was constant and not subject to change, whereas our understanding or comprehension of religion that led to religious knowledge was a human phenomenon
and, as such, subject to change and interpretation (Sorush 1992, 42). Indeed, in
Sorush's distinction between the two categories, which seemed to parallel
Kant's distinction between noumena and phenomena, "religion is sacred and
heavenly, but knowledge of religion is mundane and human. What remains
fixed is religion, but what changes is religious knowledge" (Sorush 1991, xi).

This distinction, Sorush argued, would allow Muslims to reconcile the eternal and sacred, on the one hand, and the changing and profane, on the other, which would result in the revival of Islam and in harmony between Islam and the modern age (Sorush 1991, x). Indeed, Sorush claimed that his theory of "contraction and expansion" of the Sharia would reconcile tradition and change, "earth" and "sky," "reason" and "revolution" (Sorush 1991, ix). He repeatedly described "religion in itself" as "silent" (*samet*) and in need of human interpretation, which constituted our knowledge of religion. He even went so far as to claim that what Imam Ali understood of God could be different from our contemporary understanding of the "Divine Essence" (Sorush 1991, 45).

Based on those theoretical constructs, Sorush advocated a "dynamic jurisprudence" (*fiqh puya*), as opposed to the traditional jurisprudence of the conservatives. In his view, only this dynamic jurisprudence could provide solutions to some of the practical problems that the Islamic regime faced in its encounter with modernity, problems rooted in the clerical regime's conflict with the modern juridical sphere, economics, culture, the arts, the media, and so on (Sorush 1988, 51). Based on his epistemology, Sorush attempted a reconciliation between religion and modern enlightenment (*rushanfekri*). In his view, religious modern enlightenment—an oxymoron from the viewpoint of conservative Muslims—was possible, considering the epistemological dichotomy yet dialogue between the inner essence of religion and human understanding of it.[5]

It is my contention here that what Sorush has been striving for in his theoretical efforts is nothing less than an epistemological subjectivity in which the human subject treats "religious knowledge" as the object of subjectivity. In eschewing metaphysics, for the reasons explained above, Sorush has, for the most part, avoided direct references to the concept of human vicegerency or to the Islamic concept of the human as God's successor on earth. Instead of such a direct approach to human subjectivity, Sorush has emphasized the Quranic grounding of human vicegerency in "knowledge" (Sorush 1984, 48). Not only

5. *Rushanfekri* can be translated as "intellectualism," a sense that Al-e Ahmad, Shariati, and Sorush certainly intend to convey in some of their writings. Yet, in their elaborate discussions of this concept, one can find, as I have argued in this book, another sense of this term that stands for a core concept in modernity, which I have translated as "modern enlightenment." See "Return to the Self" in chapter 3 and "Recovery of the Self" in chapter 4. In his 1988 book *Rushanfekri va Dindari* (Modern enlightenment and religion), Sorush attempted to reconcile the two sides of perhaps the widest cultural rift in Iran in the second half of the twentieth century.

has he treated "religious knowledge"as an object of interpretation by active human agency; he also suggested a similar approach to historical data (Sorush 1991, 162).

Just because Sorush has not pursued the "metaphysical" path to subjectivity taken by his predecessors, Shariati, Motahhari, and even Khomeini, does not mean he has avoided the notion of human subjectivity altogether. To be sure, he has rarely referred to Quranic verses for this purpose, invoking instead the Islamic mystical tradition, especially the poetry of Rumi (d.1273) (Sorush 1987, 146–48). Indeed, in some of his writings, Sorush has vacillated between positing and negating human subjectivity, much as had Motahhari, Shariati, and Khomeini in the mediated subjectivity of their revolutionary discourses. Suffice it to say that Sorush's ambivalence and vacillations are much more subdued than those of his predecessors; indeed, in arguing against Davari-Ardakani's type of discourse, he posits an ontology of human subjectivity that is more or less unequivocal.[6]

Sorush's methodology and discourse, by his own admission, owe much to Karl Popper. Sorush has found Popper's flexible and fluid approach to "probabilistic" modern science much more compatible with the principles of a democratic society and polity than the "absolutist philosophy" of the ancients (Sorush 1995, 14). Given Sorush's training in the philosophy of history and science, it was only natural that his detour to subjectivity would pass through the realm of modern science.

Social Construction of Probabilistic Science

Treating Popper's contingent notion of falsifiability as the validating cornerstone of modern science, Sorush has advanced a view of science that is much more "probabilistic" than positivistic and absolute. Indeed, he has criticized Iranian Marxists for rigidly basing their thinking on dialectical materialism, proposing that they adopt an epistemology grounded in the Popperian notion of falsifiability (Sorush [1978], 132). To the charges that Popper's methodology was itself positivist, Sorush has replied that what constitutes positivism in traditional scientific methodology is its insistence on verifiability and induction,

---

6. See, for example, Sorush (1987, 295), which rejects Davari-Ardakani's "philosophy of Being" and discusses different aspects of human agency and subjectivity with regard to nature.

both of which Popper's methodology has disavowed and overcome (Sorush [1978], 177).

Sorush seems to have found scientific methodology useful as a means to resist the fanaticism and obscurantism of some of the conservative religious forces that gained power after the Islamic revolution. He has warned Iranians against repeating the European experience with religious fanaticism: "We do not want what happened to Galileo to take place in this country and under the aegis of the Islamic Republic. That means we do not want religion to be an impediment to science" (Sorush 1987, 196). In the name of the struggle against "cultural imperialism," Sorush maintains, these conservative forces have tried to stamp out humanistic culture in Iran by closing the universities and by waging war against all modern cultural products and services, whether foreign or domestic. Sorush cautioned Iranians not to deprive themselves of "the achievements of others . . . [the fruits] of humanity's thought are valuable and needed by all of humanity, unless through critique some of these [thoughts] may be falsified. Therefore, the rule should be not to close the doors upon ourselves [by refusing to use] other's thoughts" (Sorush 1987, 195). Nor should even the "human sciences" be divided into Eastern or Western and accepted or dismissed because of their origins (Sorush 1987, 191).

Sorush has used the scientific method in his efforts to reduce the ideologizing of social life in Iran after the revolution. Maintaining an unbridgeable gap between science and valuation, a position he developed on the eve of the revolution (Sorush [1978], 173), he has promoted the purported neutrality of science as a remedy for the heavy-handed reliance on ideology in postrevolutionary social sciences in Iran.[7] Aware, on the one hand, of the heightened sensitivity of the religious to the secular culture of modernity and, on the other, of the indispensability of modern branches of human knowledge, Sorush took refuge in the putative neutrality of natural sciences (Sorush [1978], 197).

Given his educational background and the positivistic cultural milieu of the Pahlavi era, it is not surprising that at times Sorush has displayed strong positivist tendencies.[8] Nevertheless, he has generally distanced himself from positivism,

7. In a major departure from Shariati, Sorush has taken an increasingly critical view of Shariati's efforts to ideologize Islam.

8. For example, Sorush (1991, 233) maintained that the strongest impetus for social change emanated from the natural sciences, which influenced the humanities and the other "human sciences," including religion.

while maintaining a strong confidence in natural sciences.[9] To do so, he has not only incorporated Popper's notion of falsifiability into his scientific methodology; he has also subscribed to a conception of science as social construction. Thus, in *Promenading Creation*, Sorush (1987) favorably cited Peter Winch's view of the intersubjective construction of social norms and institutions:

> Peter Winch believes that man's life consists entirely of conventions and agreements that he creates, consents to, and practices, or that he cancels and replaces with other norms. Social institutions are nothing but social conventions . . . such as marriage, ownership, "superintendence" [*riyasat*], honor, insult, voting, punishment, reward, and so on. One of the most obvious and most visible conventions is language itself . . . if people have private languages . . . social life becomes impossible. Language is a convention that is a social construct. . . . Language is a paradigm and a model for Mr. Winch[, who] believes that understanding in society and social behavior is similar to understanding in a language. [Thus] the model for social sciences must be language.(45)[10]

Sorush extended these observations to the natural sciences: "The objectivity of science depends on its being public" (1987, 51). Referring to the discursive nature and "social identity" of the construction of science, he declared: "What exists only in the mind of an isolated thinker is not science. . . . Science must lift the veil from its face and expose itself to the judgment and critique of others. What constitutes science is the product of public critique and understanding as well as the meanings given to terms by the scientific community" (Sorush 1987, 177). Based on these premises, Sorush has advocated the free exchange of different viewpoints and ideas for attaining "truth"—a proposition quite different from "the Truth" (*Haq*) of Davari-Ardakani and his cohorts—with significant social and political implications (Sorush 1987, 184–85).

The Secular Ramifications of Sorush's Thought

In his book *Rushanfekri va Dindari* (Modern enlightenment and religion), Sorush discussed the effect of Ali Shariati's work on the secularization of religion. How

---

9. One indication of Sorush's dissociation from positivism is his critique of behaviorism and the "stimulus-response" paradigms in the social sciences. See Sorush 1987, 68.

10. Sorush (1987, 301) went on to cite Wittgenstein on the impossibility of a private language and the dialogical, social, and participatory nature of language.

could Shariati not be positively affected by the ideas of Voltaire, Descartes, and Sartre? (Sorush 1988, 79). Given Sorush's familiarity with the obscurantism of the Church in medieval Europe, his rhetorical question might as easily have been addressed to himself and his own writings. Believing religious knowledge to be contingent on other knowledge available in a given period, he has seemed to endorse the secular cosmology embodied in modern philosophical anthropology and sociology as the standard by which to evaluate religious cosmologies and the search for religion that is "attentive" to human needs (Sorush 1991, 109). Indeed, he has gone so far as to claim that "values and responsibilities (good and evil) . . . and conventions (language, customs, etc.) are characterized [by the fact that] they do not inhere in truth, and change by human decision. They are not universal or eternal . . . they are not true or false" (Sorush [1978], 185).

In a similar vein, Sorush has viewed the notion of divine providence in terms of human subjectivity:

> History is not dependent on an "external sphere." No hand from outside diverts it and there is no [external] force over history. This is true even with regard to a divine view of history . . . God's actions are realized through the agency of the natural dispositions of beings, or [in the case of humans,] their wills. Men have lived in history as their humanness has necessitated and what has occurred in history has been natural and no cause except men's humanness has given rise to historical events. (1987, 261)

In his later articles, Sorush has cast a shadow of doubt on hitherto absolute and determined categories such as ethics. In "Akhlaq-e Khodayan" (Ethics of the gods), Sorush has claimed that absolute ethics belonged only to the gods and not to the human sphere. Ethics was not an exact and systematic science and would never reach an ideal precision and rigor (Sorush 1994a, 23). Even if we assumed that good and evil were absolute, we could not determine what course of action the subject had to take in difficult ethical situations (Sorush 1994a, 23). Furthermore, because ethics was as much subject to temporal and spatial considerations as the other categories of knowledge he discussed, its injunctions were neither absolute nor eternal (Sorush 1994a, 23). "Ethics," he concluded, "is contingent on life and must befit it, not vice versa" (Sorush 1994a, 25). Assailing the "transcendental," absolutist ethics of the revolutionary period, with its tragic consequences, Sorush has proposed an ethics based on "exceptive" and fluid principles (1994a, 26–30).

One of the most important and most often discussed themes in Sorush's discourse is that of "temporalizing religion" (*asri kardan-e din*). Based on his earlier notion that religious knowledge is contingent on the secular knowledge of a given period, Sorush has advocated not only that life and the "age" become religious, but also that religion become temporal and humanized, an idea that seems only inevitable in the aftermath of the revolution of subjectivity (Sorush 1991, 215).

Expansion of Political Philosophy

Although there is no doubt that, despite his minor ontological vacillations, Sorush has been a key and consistent contributor to expanding the horizons of political philosophy in postrevolutionary Iran, he has been even more consistent in his support for political democracy. Sorush has exposed and criticized the totalitarian tendencies in the discourse of his religious opponents and the moral sclerosis that seized Iran after the revolution. He has railed against the populist rhetoric of religious philosophers such as Davari-Ardakani and championed the cause of "critical reason" against what he sees as the demagoguery of "mass society" (Sorush 1996a, 67).

Central to Sorush's political discourse is the concept of "faith," a concept that was elaborated on by Shariati, as we saw in chapter 4. But in Sorush's case, faith belongs to the individual. In his article "Modara va Modiriyat-e Mo'menan: Sokhani dar Nesbat-e Din va Demokrasi" (Conciliation and administration of the faithful: A discourse on the relation between religion and democracy), Sorush argued that the faith of individuals was possible only if they were free to choose. Consequently, faith and freedom, the foundations of a religious democracy, were inseparable:

> The faith of each individual is the exclusive experience and the "private property" of that individual. Each of us finds faith as an individual, [just] as we die as an individual. There may be collective rituals but there is no collective faith. . . . The realm of faith is the realm of resurrection, and in resurrection people come as individuals. . . . True faith is based on individuality and freedom. . . . [Moreover], not only can faith not be forced, it cannot be homogenized

either, and to the extent that people have different personalities, faith is also variegated and nuanced. (Sorush 1994b, 7)

Sorush distinguished between a liberal democracy with a secular society, on the one hand, and a "religious democracy" with pluralistic principles, on the other. In a liberal democracy, the freedom of "inclinations" (amyal) and desires was the foundation of pluralism and secular society, whereas a "religious democracy" might be built on the basis of freedom of faith (Sorush 1994b, 8). In his article "Tahlil-e Mafhum-e Hukumat-e Dini" (An analysis of the concept of religious government), Sorush identified protection of the freedom of faith and creation of social conditions conducive to such freedom as the main tasks of a democratic religious state (Sorush 1996b, 39).[11]

Sorush has placed special emphasis on the idea of human freedom in the more overtly political aspect of this discourse: "Freedom is prior to everything. I have recently come across some speakers in our society who, by way of criticism and reproach, have said, 'For some, freedom is a foundation.' Yes, why shouldn't freedom be a foundation? Even if we accept religion, submissiveness, and obedience, we do so because we have freely chosen them" (Sorush 1996c, 253).[12] He has grounded his notion of human freedom in thought and reason, arguing that "emotionally" based action leads to the surrender of the individuality of the individual to the "other." Reason might engender antagonism and conflict, but its principle outcome is independence and that prevents the surrender of one's subjectivity to the other (Sorush 1996c, 254).[13] This position has led Sorush to criticize the power of ideology in postrevolutionary Iran and to advocate freedom of convictions and beliefs:

11. In his more theoretical and abstract writings, Sorush has considered only the individual as "real," viewing the collectivity as a theoretical construct, whose reality is merely hypothetical. This ontological priority of the individual over the collectivity seems to ground his later political writings, in which the individual is central. See Sorush [1978], 79.

12. In emphasizing this idea of freedom, Sorush was careful not to neglect the concept of social justice: "The conflict some have projected between freedom and justice (under the rubric of the conflict between democracy and socialism), that if we choose freedom, justice is destroyed and if we choose justice, freedom is sacrificed, is a spurious conflict" (1996c, 254).

13. In this respect, Sorush's analysis approaches that of totalitarianism by some of the Frankfurt School; indeed, he has explicitly referred to Erich Fromm's notion of "escape from freedom" (Sorush 1996c, 247).

Freedom of beliefs is the legitimate offspring of epistemological falsifiability, which has encircled the prevalent dogmatic thinking of bygone times. The difference between the modern and the old world is the difference between certainty and uncertainty, and this difference led to humans' transcending ideology in the modern world, whereas, in the old world, convictions were always prior to humans. Humans both killed and were killed for their convictions, but today people are not victims of intolerance because of their convictions, which is considered [a violation of] human rights. (1996d, 273)[14]

From early in his career, Sorush has criticized the concept of the "governance of the jurist," at first obliquely, but later more and more openly and directly. In recent articles, he has pointed out that, because the "Supreme Jurist" (Vali-e Faqih) derives his right to rule from God, little is left for the people in the arena of governing. Indeed, the people's role is "at most to discover who has this [God-given] right" (Sorush 1996b, 5). He has argued, however, that because the Assembly of Experts is elected by popular vote and because the "Supreme Jurist," as the highest power in the Islamic Republic, derives his legitimacy from this assembly, the sovereignty of the Iranian people is guaranteed, if not directly, then at least indirectly by the constitution. And once the people's sovereignty is recognized, it cannot be partial. Thus full sovereignty, even over the position of the "Supreme Jurist," belongs to the people:

> If you have the right to oversee the government, it can easily be demonstrated that you also have the right to govern. . . . As soon as the right is released, it will occupy all the space. Without a doubt, the foundation of democratic government is that people constitute the "principle" in it. That means people are the creator, the critic, and the observer of the government. (Sorush 1996b, 5)

Central to his schema of the religious democratic state is the concept of mutual rights and responsibilities. Sorush has observed that, in contrast to traditional society, which emphasized responsibilities instead of rights, democratic society emphasizes mutual rights instead of responsibilities. Further, as

14. Although a strong supporter of freedom of individual subjectivity, Sorush has upheld the necessity of the veil (hejab) for women—a vestige of the vacillations of the mediated subjectivity from which Sorush's discourse originates. See, for example, Sorush 1982, 101.

Imam Ali demonstrated, mutual rights are most significant in the relations between the citizens and the state (Sorush 1984, 209–13).

As we have seen, Sorush distinguishes between a religious and a liberal democracy, a distinction grounded in freedom of faith and freedom of inclination, respectively. Although both kinds of democracy are founded on respect for individual freedom, in a religious democracy, freedom derives from the free choice of faith; in a liberal democracy, from free choice in inclination and desire.[15] Accordingly, Sorush has associated "liberalism" with lack of faith and with a society where religion is deliberately put under siege, and where, to establish human rights, the "rights of God" are abandoned.

In a religious democratic society, on the other hand, both human rights and the rights of God would be respected (Sorush 1996d, 273–74). Significantly, and in sharp contrast to other Islamic political theorists, Sorush does not ground his theory of religious democracy in an Islamic principle, such as consultation (*shura*), consensus (*ijma*), or contract (*bey'a*), but in secular principles, such as human rights, justice, and limited power (Sorush 1994b, 3). Moreover, his religious democracy is to be founded on "reason," which is socially grounded and therefore fluid:

> The foundation of justice is the fulfillment of the needs of the people . . . the realization of their rights, and the elimination of discrimination and oppression. Thus there is a stable connection between justice and human rights. . . . [B]ecause justice is an extrareligious category . . . the discovering of just methods of government, the distribution and limitation of power, and the areas of human rights will have their roots primarily in reason and not in religion. . . . [T]he emergence of reason, that is, "fluid social reason" [*aql Jami'i sayal*] will pave the road for the appearance of an epistemological pluralism, which is the very foundation of democracy. (Sorush 1994b, 4)

In a religious democratic society based on these principles, there is no need for revolution and violence to limit the powers of the rulers, correct their policies, and to elect or dismiss them. To achieve these ends, such a society relies on universal education, empowerment and demonopolization of the media, freedom of speech, freedom of association, freedom of political expression, public elections, a parliament, and separation of powers, as well as checks and balances.

---

15. Sorush provides no example of a liberal democracy.

Under these principles, Sorush has declared, democracy is not incompatible with religion:

> The faithful abandoning their faiths . . . the total laicization of religion, and the undermining of its divine foundation are not necessitated by democracy. . . . What is incompatible with democracy is forced religion or punishment of "irreligion," and if these are, in some people's opinion, permissible in the "theocratic" [feqhi] government, in a democratic religious state, they are impossible and undesirable. (1994b, 4)

Sorush's insistence on the distinction between liberal democracy and religious democracy notwithstanding, there seems to be little difference between a religious and any other democratic polity. Sorush himself seems to have recognized this when he noted that "because people are religious, the state is religious, and not because the state is religious, the people must become religious" (1996b, 10). Indeed, he has suggested that the only difference between religious and other democratic societies is that, in a religious society, "the state machinery would be in the service of the faithful" (1996b, 11). In a reference that may be surprising to some, Sorush proposed as a possible model for a religious democratic society de Tocqueville's America, where, even though religion and politics were separate, religion guided the American society and polity and where the ethics of universality in religion had a bearing on the harmony between the freedom of subjectivity and democracy (Sorush 1994b, 12).

Sorush's political thought continues to evolve. Yet his discourse seems to have set the stage for achieving subjectivity at a universal level without, one must hope, falling into the positivist trap.

Conclusion

The path to modernity in the West has been long and tortuous, with the goal of balancing subjectivity and universality still to be achieved. Yet some of the boons and banes of this evolving modernity—popular sovereignty, civil and personal freedoms and rights, higher material standards of living, on the one hand, and alienation, the threat of mass destruction, environmental damage, on the other—are evident and well established. The revolution of subjectivity, the underlying ontological foundation of modernity, has left almost no part of the world untouched. Through colonization, economic exploitation, and cultural objectification, and through the introduction of new ideas, norms, and institutions, the modern West has reshaped the destiny of all societies on the globe. Third World countries have responded with denial, emulation, infatuation, confrontation, resentment, or a combination of these. Iran has been no exception. Over the century and a half of its belated encounter with modernity, these responses have constituted the major elements of its history.

What makes Iran unique, however, is its preoccupation with the metaphysical foundations of modernity—a preoccupation whose origins lie in a deeply entrenched tradition of monotheism going back to pre-Islamic religions and in an equally ancient sense of cultural identity, and one that has had important ramifications for Iran's institutions. It can be seen in the protomodernist religious movements of Babism and the Bahai faith in the nineteenth century, in the liberal democratic movement that culminated in the Constitutional Revolution at the beginning of the twentieth century, and in the establishment of the Islamic Republic in the closing decades of the twentieth century. One of the most important consequences of this preoccupation may be that modernity sinks deeper and more extensive roots in Iran than elsewhere in the Third World, although at the cost of strife, pain, and blood, and of reinventing modernity and establishing democratic principles under highly adverse circumstances. Thus Iran's encounter with modernity has gone far beyond its reaction to imperialism in the mid–nineteenth century—Iran has examined and grappled with the metaphysical foundations of Western modernity. Here, perhaps, lie the reasons for the profound and sometimes troubled way modernity has unfolded in Iran.

Many of the works on Iran characterize the eclipse of the democratic achievements of the Constitutional Revolution, the advent (and reinstallation) of the Pahlavi Dynasty, the defeat of the democratic nationalist movement led by Mossadeq in the early 1950s, and the takeover of the 1979 revolution by conservative Islamic forces merely as failures of modernity to establish democracy in Iran. To be certain, these were great setbacks for modernity in Iran. Yet the development of modernity has nowhere proceeded along a straight path. As we saw in chapters 2 and 3, the Constitutional Revolution largely reflected the contradictory nature of Iran's appropriation of modernity, in which elements of both positivist and universalizable subjectivity were present. That universalizable subjectivity, as manifested in the democratic institutions and universal citizen participation envisioned by the Constitutional Revolution, failed to take root was not the end of Iran's experiment with modernity. Even as the Pahlavi regime directed its energies at appropriating the positivist aspects of subjectivity, opposition forces, the leftists, the liberal democrats, and certain Islamic groups concerned themselves with expanding and deepening universality.

Although the Iranian Left set for itself the broad goals of universalizing and deepening subjectivity, and although it significantly broadened awareness of modern rights, its ultimate shortcoming lay in its collectivist approach to achieving those goals. Indeed, Iran's backwardness in applying universalistic principles accounts in large part for the persistent appeal of the populist ideals of the Left throughout the reigns of the Pahlavi monarchs.

With the defeat of liberal democracy and the Left in the aftermath of the CIA-sponsored coup d'état of 1953, expansion and deepening of universality fell to the Islamic groups; the Islamic discourse of the sixties and seventies carried forward the cause of populist and collectivist universality that the Left and the liberal democratic forces had been forced to abandon. Which is not to say that it discarded the category of subjectivity. Rather, as we saw in chapter 4, it incorporated the subjectivist element in the peculiar configuration I have called "mediated subjectivity," characterized by a constant vacillation between affirming and negating human subjectivity. This vacillation, in my view, constitutes the ontological foundation of the political philosophy and institutions of the Islamic Republic, which exhibit a similar vacillation between allowing and denying citizenship rights. Yet mediated subjectivity is also characterized by two other features. The first is its enormous potential for universalizing inchoate subjectivity to the whole of society. Because of it, the Islamic discourse has succeeded in mobilizing the Iranian population to sustained and thoroughgoing participation in the life and history of the country. The second is its highly dynamic tendency for transformation from within, a tendency that springs from its contradictory nature. In revealing the complex and dialectical relationship between the forces of modernity and the metaphysics of monotheism in Iran, this contradictory nature has shown that monotheism and modernity—God and the Juggernaut—are not totally antithetical entities, indeed, that monotheism may be reincarnated in modern forms. The implications of this point for the study of categories often depicted as mutually exclusive and totally discontinuous, such as modernity and premodernity, religion and democracy, tradition and change, are quite significant.

The internal dynamism of mediated subjectivity in Iran has given rise to two postrevolutionary discourses, which have adopted opposite tendencies in the revolutionary Islamic discourse articulated by Shariati, Motahhari, and Khomeini and taken these tendencies to their logical conclusions. The discourse chiefly associated with Abdolkarim Sorush represents the affirmative moment of mediated subjectivity and strives to posit human subjectivity. The discourse associated with Reza Davari-Ardakani represents the negative moment and strives to eliminate the humanist element from contemporary Iran. Both theoretical discourses have engendered practical, sociopolitical discourses of their own, adopting diametrically opposed positions on democratization in postrevolutionary Iran. Because of its broad base in the populace and its respect for individual subjectivity, the doctrine of a religious democratic polity, if implemented, could usher in a new era of democracy in Iran and the Middle East. On the other hand, the antagonism among conservative Islamic forces toward the cultural aspects of modernity and the strong and widespread desire for technology among the populace in Iran could result in the selective borrowing of modern technology without its cultural accompaniments, giving rise to a regime of positivist modernity in which a doctrine of "morality of the East and technology of the West" would be reincarnated in a religious body.

Whatever the short-term manifestations of unfolding modernity in Iran, the nature and expression of religion there will inevitably be changed. As Louis Dupré has observed about the evolution of religion in the West, the revolution of subjectivity has shifted religion's center of gravity "from the objective insti-tution to the subjective individual" (1982, 24). The subjectivization of religion, the sine qua non for its pluralistic expression, seems to be taking place in Iran today.

Being principally concerned with the theoretical and ontological founda-tions—the ideational factors—of the emergence of civil society in Iran, this study has paid little attention to the structural factors. However, the interac-tion between ideational and structural factors appears to have set the stage for the emergence of civil society and the attitudes of citizenship. As we saw in chapter 5, fragmentation among the ruling clerics and economic hardship in the postrevolutionary period have combined to encourage the expectation of democratic reforms and economic development. The mobilization of the pop-ulace during the revolution and the war with Iraq has aroused a widespread de-sire to participate in the sociopolitical affairs of the country. Moreover, economic contraction and the consequent cutbacks in government spending have led to

a frenzy of activity and entrepreneurship in the small-scale private sector of the economy—the small farmers, cultivators of produce, bazaar merchants and traders, proprietors and workers in small urban workshops and service es-tablishments, and those in the so-called informal sector—which accounts for whatever dynamism is left in the national economy. (Banuazizi 1995, 564)

Interacting with ideational factors, these structural factors have laid the groundwork for the emergence of a popularly based civil society quite apart from, and antagonistic toward, the official theocratic state in postrevolutionary Iran. This antagonism is expressed in a variety of ways, from occasional out-breaks of spontaneous rioting to more prevalent and quieter forms of resistance on the part of various groups and strata. Women, in particular, have shown re-sourcefulness and ingenuity in their resistance to the repressive policies of the theocratic state in recent years (Banuazizi 1995, 577). The election in the spring of 1997 of a president whose theoretical positions were close to those ar-ticulated by Sorush and his colleagues—much to the surprise of many observers of Iranian politics—was achieved by Iranians from all walks of life, but espe-cially by the young and by women, who displayed a clear sense of having the right to participate in determining their own destinies and the affairs of their country.[1]

In the absence of reliable information, we cannot accurately assess the development of attitudes of citizenship in a country such as Iran. Yet there are indications that empowerment and demarginalization among the lower classes, even among the historically abject tribal groups and the peasantry, have begun to occur. Field researchers in Iran have recently reported a growing feeling of subjectivity—the basis for attitudes of citizenship— among the lower classes of urban and rural populations alike.[2]

These observations raise questions as to the nature of the Islamic Republic. There is no doubt that the rule of the Islamic clerics has been one of the most oppressive experiences of the Iranian people in recent history. The pain and suffering imposed on the populace and on different groups in particular since the victory of the Islamic Revolution are well documented and do not need to be reexamined here. Yet the unintended consequences of the Islamic revolutionary process may be another matter altogether. This study, by analyzing the theoretical discourses that have informed Iran's sociopolitical thinking in its encounter with modernity, has shed light on the potential for an unlikely candidate, the Shiite clergy, to bring modernity to Iran as a result of the unfolding of the contradictions of the Islamic discourse. Should this potential become a reality, such an outcome would owe much to the historically significant emphasis

---

1. Since the election of Muhammad Khatami as the president of the republic, the sense among the people that they are entitled to political and social participation and citizenship rights has sharply increased, making itself known in a grassroots social movement for democracy in the country that has won two important elections: one for local governments and the other for an overwhelmingly reformist parliament.

2. On the social changes that have occurred in Iran since the revolution and the war with Iraq, see, for example, Ehsani 1995. As a result of their participation in the revolution and the war, traditionally submissive groups have developed a sense of subjectivity that manifests itself in the defiance of the state and its officials. "This was demonstrated vividly," Ehsani writes, "when [I] accompanied an official of the Ministry of Agriculture, who had to collect data from peasant workers in the fields. In one case after another, we drove to the edge of the field where the official would call over to a busy peasant who, invariably ignoring us, continued with his work. As we waded through the mud, dressed in our city shoes and clothes, my companion sounded decidedly nostalgic when he mused over the old days when the peasants would 'drop their shovels and whatever they were doing, and submissively run over the moment an official Jeep turned the corner of the village' " (1995, 49).

on the social universal and the encouragement of mass sociopolitical activity by Islamic forces.

For modernity to be fully realized in Iran, however, the mediated subjectivity of the Islamic discourse and movement must eventually be replaced by a more direct form of subjectivity. This would entail the inevitable problems associated with the monadic subjectivity experienced in the modern West, problems that can be remedied only by maintaining a balance between subjectivity and universality.

Appendix

Works Cited

Index

Appendix

Dialogues with Modernity

At the outset of this study, I delineated the essential framework of Critical Theory needed to understand the foundations of modernity by drawing on the philosophies of Kant and Hegel. Because, as was only to be expected, both the phenomenon and the discourses of modernity have continued to develop, I have provided this appendix to help readers who wish to pursue further the theoretical discussion of modernity, especially as it bears on the conditions of modernity and the Iranian experience of them.

Modernity and Capitalism

We are so often told that capitalism and modernity are closely related we might well imagine the two to be but mirror images of one another. The main contention of this section is that capitalism has promoted subjectivity and universality as the principles of modernity, even as it has hampered and circumscribed them. The dialectic of capitalism and modernity is most evident in the connection between free market and freedom of contract. On the one hand, the idea of subjectivity, working through the mechanism of the free market, would appear to have eliminated all the historical and "natural" restraints imposed on participants in contracts, making them free agents. On the other hand, as Marx has shown, the freedom of contract, when applied to class relations, turns out to be little more than an illusion.

As mentioned in chapter 1, subjectivity cannot simply be reduced to freedom of the individual; it also involves acting on the world. In this sense, the bourgeois entrepreneur is the best embodiment of subjectivity. Not that the entrepreneur consciously promotes emancipation. Rather, as Marshal Berman (1988, 72) has put it, "with his eye for the main chance, his celebration of selfishness and his genial lack of scruple, the capitalist entrepreneur very much conforms to Goethe's Mephisto rather than Faust's utopian dreams about human potentials."

But what these bourgeois entrepreneurs, as subjects, have achieved is quite revolutionary in the history of modernity. First, they have shattered most of the religious and medieval restrictions on subjectivity. Second, they have developed the productive forces beyond what could be imagined in the premodern era, in ways that help overcome the natural restrictions on emancipation. Third, they have changed the mechanism of social domination from one of caste and semicaste to one of class. And fourth, they have at once expanded and restricted universality.

In the relationship between modernity and capitalism, Protestantism has played a pivotal role as the historical matrix of modern capitalism, a role that exemplifies what Hegel called the "cunning of history," whose ultimate results and consequences are often unforeseen (see also Weber 1958, 90).

The Protestant emphasis on labor—whatever its origins might be—conforms well with the acting on the world that characterizes subjectivity. Indeed, the worldly activity of labor is an indispensable prerequisite for the emergence of the autonomous subject. Related to this essential activity is the empowering of the subject through the discipline and methodical rationalization of the Protestant reformers:

> Protestant asceticism contested the values of "traditional" society by replacing one form of discipline with another, more "modern" form. In accepting as its model the ideal of the self-made man who is the product of his labor and responsive to his "calling" and who is likewise free from any internal dependence on tradition or community, the call to labor became a moral imperative. . . .
> Through labor, the authority of norms is internalized; the self-made man is the precursor of Kant's autonomous subject, and may be identified by the virtue of the fact that he is able to give himself the law. (Cascardi 1992, 170–71)

Perhaps the most important contribution of Protestantism to modernity is the form of individuality it gave to subjectivity. Indeed, according to Weber (1958, 104), the Calvinist doctrine of predestination brought an unprecedented feeling of inner loneliness to the individual. Moreover, by eliminating the priestly hierocracy as a mediator, Protestantism removed a significant obstacle from the road to the subjectivity of the individual.[1]

Weber emphasized the economic dimension of Protestantism at the expense of its "political" dimension—the centrality of the individual. Thus he paid scant attention to the Protestant rebellion against the priestly hierarchy, symbolized in the defiant act of Luther nailing his theses on the church door, which paved the road for the emergence of the autonomous subject. Nevertheless, embedded in his analysis are the core mecha-

---

1. Protestantism neither intended nor, during the lifetime of its founders, would it have been able, even if it had, to create anything close to an individual subject, which, as we saw in chapter 2, can exist only in an inchoate state under traditional monotheism.

nisms for expanding not only modern subjectivity but also universality. The universalistic tendency among Protestant capitalists had its origins in their social background:

> At the beginning of modern times it was by no means the capitalistic entre-
> preneurs of the commercial aristocracy who were either the sole or the pre-
> dominant bearers of the attitude we have here called the spirit of capitalism. It
> was much more the rising strata of the lower industrial middle classes. Even in
> the nineteenth century its classical representatives were not the elegant gen-
> tlemen of Liverpool and Hamburg with their commercial fortunes handed
> down for generations, but the self-made parvenus of Manchester and West-
> phalia, who often rose from very modest circumstances. As early as the six-
> teenth century the situation was similar, the industries which arose at that time
> were mostly created by parvenus. (Weber 1958, 65)

That the humble social origins of the emerging class of parvenu entrepreneurs inclined
them to expand universality on their way up, however, did not prevent them from restricting that very universality once they became the ruling class (consider the suppression of universal suffrage in most Western countries until quite recently). Thus the
ethical puritanism and the harsh and repressive discipline of Protestantism promoted
modernity as subjectivity through commercial activity, even as it promoted suppression
of that subjectivity through the very negation of individual subjects.

But the relationship between modernity and capitalism can and should be explored
beyond Protestantism. With regard to the principle of universality, for example, the exchange relations found in full-fledged capitalism are at once supportive and repressive
of universality. Hegel acknowledged the tendency of capitalism to expand universality
when he observed that

> in civil society each member is his own end, everything else is nothing to him.
> But except in contract with others he cannot attain the whole compass of his
> ends, and therefore these others are means to the end of the particular mem-
> ber. A particular end, however, assumes the form of universality through this
> relation to other people and it is attained in the simultaneous attainment of the
> welfare of others. (Habermas 1987a, 37–38)

What Hegel did not address in this analysis was the countervailing tendency of capitalism to restrict its universality, in large part because of its drive to maximize gain in a
world with finite resources.

Consequences of Modernity

As I noted in the introduction to this work, the most visible and perhaps most important effect of the emergence of self-defining, autonomous subjects has been its transformation of primary relationships of domination and subordination, chief among them the relationships between the transcendental God of monotheism and human worshippers. Indeed, at the bottom of the secularization of the modern era, the rise of human subjectivity in the West since the Renaissance has severely weakened the sovereign-subordinate relationship between God and humans.

This weakening has had a ripple effect on all other primary relationships, although, to be sure, the changes from this effect have come about gradually and in varying degrees at different times. The relationship between priest and parishioners has been transformed, as best exemplified in the diminished power and importance of the clergy in Protestantism; monarchy has been abolished or relegated to a largely symbolic role throughout the Western world (and much of the Eastern world, as well).

Most recently, relationships between parents and children, and intrafamilial relationships generally, have also been transformed by the ascendancy of the autonomous subjects of modernity. Thus the neuroses Freud encountered at the turn of the century were very much a result of the changes that modern subjectivity was bringing to intrafamilial relationships and the anxiety associated with the disruption of these relationships. The anomie described by Durkheim refers to a similar, but more widespread disruption of norms associated with old primary relationships (not just those within the family), which were undercut without being replaced by norms based on new primary relationships.

What, then, are the new relationships of domination and subordination? The medieval castelike relationships have been, from one perspective, transformed into modern class relationships or, from another, replaced by contractual relationships.[2]

Michel Foucault has examined evolution of domination, focusing on crime and punishment in their premodern and modern contexts. He noticed that, in the premodern era, punishment of the criminal constituted the embodiment of the power of sovereign over "subjects" (subordinates)—hence its physical, personal, and torturous form (Foucault 1979, 57). In modernity, on the other hand, the power exercised in criminal punishment has become much more subtle, impersonal, and thereby more insidious. It operates through what Foucault calls "discipline," which he defines as "methods which make possible the meticulous control of the operations of the body, which assumed the constant subjection of its forces and imposed upon them a relation of docility-utility" (Foucault 1979, 137). In the same vein, Foucault notes the Church's morally charged in-

2. The more recent extension of this trend can be found in Foucault's analysis (1979) of the disciplinary type of domination.

tervention in marital relations decreased as "medicine made a forceful [but morally neutral] entry into the pleasure of the couple" (Foucault 1980, 41). Thus the objectifying subject is now the administrator, the doctor, the expert. In other words, now the *citizens* objectify *other citizens* through abstract and impersonal disciplinary power mechanisms. There are two principal implications to Foucault's analysis of power in the modern era. First, power has been decentralized; there are no longer one or two centers of power such as the monarchy and the Church (Foucault 1980, 49). Second, because the subject and object of power are both citizens (subjects) the unidirectionality and absoluteness of power has decreased.

Perhaps the most elaborate and articulate analysis of contractual domination and subordination is to be found in the work of Jürgen Habermas (see "Habermas: Language Mediating Subjectivity and Universality" below). According to Habermas, modern subjectivity has separated the three spheres of the "lifeworld"—objective (related to cognitive and scientific propositional truths), social (related to normative, moral, and legal truths), and subjective (related to aesthetic and expressive truths)—from their religious and metaphysical grounding (Habermas 1984, 71–72).[3] Again, as I noted in the introduction, in the premodern era, these three component spheres of the lifeworld were mediated through the sacred and were part and parcel of the religious establishment, whereas, with the coming of modernity, they have been separated out, and the truths of each sphere subjected to criticism and left open to revision, which in the social sphere may lead to the undermining of the modern relations of domination and subordination (Habermas 1984, 52).

Modernity and Discontent

The early thinkers of the Enlightenment were overly optimistic about the emancipation that the emergence of human subjects would bring. The benefits of material progress, liberation, and equality have been accompanied and significantly offset by a discontent peculiar to the modern era.

As I explained in the introduction, discontent that the subject imposes on the "other," through colonialism, domination, and exploitation, has profoundly affected the overwhelming majority of the world's people and changed the course of history—and will continue to do so for a long time to come. But, at the same time, it has made the col-

3. The notion of *Lebenswelt*, translated as "lifeworld," was first elaborated on in the later philosophy of Edmund Husserl and subsequently given a social dimension by his more sociologically oriented student, Alfred Schutz. As the phenomenological or experiential dimension of intersubjectivity—the intersubjectively constituted social world— lifeworld is now a key concept in Habermas's thought. For a good discussion of lifeworld and its treatment by different thinkers, see Dallmayr 1989.

onized, dominated, and exploited increasingly aware of the need to universalize, an awareness evident in national struggles for independence, as well as in women's, civil rights, and international human rights movements.[4]

Discontent in which the subject suffers more directly can be traced back to the separation of reason from nature, brought about by the emergent subjects as they attempted to impose their will on nature. This discontent can, in turn, be subdivided into (1) discontent rooted in what Habermas calls the "cognitive sphere" and the expansion of instrumental rationality; and (2) discontent arising more directly from the loss of the "firm grounding" of traditional society.

Discontent of the first subtype can be broadly characterized as what Weber calls "loss of freedom," manifested in the impersonal, formal, and mass social settings and organizations to which Weber applies the metaphor of the "iron cage." In their attempt to achieve subjectivity, the "free" agents of modernity have increasingly objectified nature and, through rationalization, bureaucratization, and reification, have expanded instrumental rationality; in so doing, they have lost the very freedom they sought to attain.

Discontent of the second subtype has to do with what Weber calls "loss of meaning" and what Hegel refers to as "vacuity." In Hegel's analysis, separating ethics from its suprahuman source, as do Kant and his followers, renders it "vacuous." For Weber, disenchantment with and disbelief in a transcendental and substantive source of culture have resulted in the rejection of all particular beliefs and a resultant sense of meaninglessness (cited in Habermas 1981a, 44–47).

It seems that meaning has to come to us from outside; left to ourselves, we are incapable of satisfying our own existential needs.[5] Nevertheless, different theorists have responded to this and related issues in different ways. Marx and Engels (1872, 476), for example, celebrated the destruction of what they deemed to be the superstitions and prejudices of the premodern era in the process of capitalist modernization on the pages of the *Communist Manifesto:* "All fixed, fast-frozen relationships within their train of ancient and venerable prejudices and opinions are swept away, all new-formed ones become antiquated before they can ossify. All that is solid melts into air, all that is holy is profaned, and man is at last compelled to face, with sober senses, his real conditions of life and his relationships with his kind."

Seeing both the opportunity to achieve "human history" (as opposed to "prehistory" thitherto) and the loss brought about by the enormous force of capitalist moder-

---

4. Although the labor movement in the West was perhaps the earliest sociopolitical movement, its awareness of the need to universalize subjectivity is less acute today, in part because the Western working class has attained some of the power it has historically struggled for.

5. By contrast, Habermas (1984) implicitly suggests throughout the two volumes of *Theory of Communicative Action* that we are indeed capable of satisfying our own existential needs for meaning.

nity, Marx thought that Communist society would integrate elements of premodern "stability" with the modern excitement of creating a new human history. But other, more conservative thinkers, such as Edmund Burke, Daniel Bell, and, to a certain extent, Peter Berger, have looked at the same phenomenon with pessimism, seeing in capitalist modernity its overriding cultural destructiveness, even as they have championed its economic cause.

In *Cultural Contradictions of Capitalism*, Daniel Bell (1978) has demonstrated this "destructive" tendency of capitalism most forcefully. According to him, most social structures and cultures have shown some sort of unity and consistency through history. Christendom exhibited ordered social hierarchies with regard both to the Church and to heaven and hell in the human quest for salvation. Similarly, in early modernity, "bourgeois culture and bourgeois social structure fused a distinct unity with a specific character structure around the theme of order and work" (Bell 1978, 36). Today, however, the social structure— the "techno-economic order"—and the cultural sphere are radically disjunct. The social structure is organized around the economic principle of "efficiency and functional rationality, the organization of production through the ordering of things, including [humans] as things," whereas the cultural sphere is "prodigal" and "promiscuous":

> The character structure inherited from the nineteenth century, with its emphasis on self-discipline, delayed gratification, and restraint, is still relevant to the demands of the techno-economic structure, but it clashes sharply with the culture, where such bourgeois values have been completely rejected—in part, paradoxically, because of the workings of the capitalist economic system itself. (Bell 1978, 37)

Bell implicitly acknowledges the principle of subjectivity when, on the one hand, he identifies "a restlessness to search out the new, to rework nature and to refashion consciousness" as the impulse driving both the entrepreneur and the artist, and, on the other, he characterizes the modern human as the "self-infinitizing creature who is impelled to search for the beyond" (Bell 1978, 16, 47). But these two aspects of subjectivity became antithetical to each other when "the bourgeois economic impulse was organized into a highly restrictive character structure whose energies were channeled into the production of goods and into a set of attitudes toward work that feared instinct, spontaneity and vagrant impulse," while the cultural impulse "turned into rage against bourgeois values" (Bell 1978, 17). Thus, when the cultural "nihilism" of capitalism stemming from the principle of modern subjectivity was perceived as a threat, it was checked by a conservatism that channeled the creative impulses released by subjectivity into an aggressive, commercial activity, while cultural activity was made to revolve around the conservative institutions of the Church, and especially the family.

Peter Berger, among others, has pointed out another type of the discontent brought about by modernity: the individual's loss of a sense of community, a loss that jeopardizes social cohesion and solidarity. In *Facing up to Modernity*, Berger (1977, 70–80) identifies five "dilemmas" of modernity: (1) living in an abstract social setting; (2) futurity (a profound concern with temporality and future); (3) individualization; (4) liberation; and (5) secularization. Running through most of these dilemmas is the loss of a sense of belonging to a community. Modern subjectivity in the form of individual rights and liberties has driven a wedge between the individual and community, making them antithetical. As Berger points out, however, this antithesis has historically been mitigated by patriotism toward one's nation-state (also a product of modernity and sometimes combined with or replaced by patriotism toward one's ethnic group), which seems to have functioned as a substitute (albeit not always a successful substitute) for the loss of a strong sense of community.

Marx: Overcoming Modernity

For Marx, labor, the means by which humans create and re-create themselves, is the key to human subjectivity. Humans create themselves by appropriating nature and producing the conditions of their existence; they re-create themselves, first, through labor, and then, through reproducing their species. Thus they are created by themselves and not by an "alien" being who has control over them, such as God or gods. And because humans owe their existence to themselves alone, through their labor, they are, or rather should be, the masters of themselves and their conditions—a position of subjectivity.

This is not the actual state of affairs, however. Through alienation, the majority of humans have lost their mastery over themselves and nature. Private property, the material expression of human labor, and its agent, the bourgeoisie, have become the masters of humans and have forced them into servitude.

In describing alienation, Marx also revealed the negative aspect of human labor as the vehicle of subjectivity. Not only is labor a means by which humans create themselves, it can also become an external force that has power over them. The commodity, which is objectified human labor, assumes a life of its own and gains control over human life. Yet it was the bourgeoisie that brought about the reversal of subjectivity (alienation) for the majority and indirectly for itself. The problem of modernity for Marx thus had two aspects: subjectivity had been reversed, on the one hand, and the majority had been deprived of it (negation of universality), on the other. And because subjectivity and its universalization were closely intertwined, negation of the one entailed negation of the other, at least for the proletariat in the capitalist era.

The key to overcoming alienation, in Marx's analysis, lay in universalizing subjectivity by abolishing private property, thus restoring subjectivity to humans in general.

But because Marx viewed the subject not as an individual but as a class and as a collectivity—the proletariat—his universalization excluded individual subjectivity. This exclusion was to have far-reaching consequences for Communism. Indeed, it is very much
the source of Communist totalitarianism, for, with the dismissal of the individual as the
agent of subjectivity, it was all but inevitable that the party or the state would become
the subject and everyone else its object.

Adorno: The Dialectic of Modernity

Although closely linked to Marx's critique of capitalism as alienation, Adorno's analysis
is directly informed by the category of subjectivity. Indeed, Adorno views the history of
modernity as the evolution of subjectivity. The thrust of his argument is that modern
subjectivity, in "enthroning" itself, has objectified itself and thus annulled its own subjectivity. In the *Dialectic of Enlightenment*, he and Max Horkheimer argue that

> in class history, the enmity of the self to sacrifice implied a sacrifice of the self,
> inasmuch as it was paid for by a denial of nature in man for the sake of domi-
> nation over non-human nature and over other men. This very denial, the nu-
> cleus of all civilizing rationality, is the germ cell of all proliferating mythic
> irrationality: with the denial of nature in man not merely the Telos of the out-
> ward control of nature but also the Telos of man's own life is distorted and be-
> fogged. As soon as man discards his awareness that he himself is nature, all the
> aims for which he keeps himself alive—social progress, the intensification of
> all his material and spiritual powers, even consciousness itself—are nullified
> and [indeed] the enthronement of the means as an end, which under late cap-
> italism is tantamount to open insanity, is already perceptible in the prehistory
> of subjectivity. *Man's domination over himself, which grounds his selfhood, is almost al-*
> *ways the destruction of the subject in whose service it is undertaken.* (Adorno and
> Horkheimer 1972, 54; emphasis added)

Thus, in their account, the development of subjectivity, in its moment of instrumental
rationality, has landed the evolution of the Enlightenment in Fascism, where any notion
of subjectivity, except for that of the Führer, is abandoned.

However, Adorno has a somewhat different account of what happens to subjectivity under Fascism in a different context. Analyzing Fascism in terms of mass psychology, Adorno employs a Freudian approach: with Freud, he views the mass phenomenon
as the fusion of individual subjects into the collectivity through the specific mechanism
of "identification." The family serves as the cell in which the individual, as a young
child, surrenders his individual subjectivity and "identifies" with father; this identifica-

tion prepares the way for the fusion of the individual, as an adult, into the collectivity, "transform[ing] libido into the bond between leader and follower and between the followers themselves" (Freud 1965, chap. 7; Adorno 1978, 125).

Adorno viewed Fascism, which he once called "psychoanalysis in reverse," as the abandonment of subjectivity, on the one hand, and as a revolt against subjectivity, on the other. He saw modernity, at least in *Dialectic of the Enlightenment*, strictly in terms of instrumental rationality, whose development inevitably led to Auschwitz (Habermas 1981a, 350). Adorno did not take into account the evolution in liberal democracies of secular law and morality, which have served to counter the abandonment of or revolt against subjectivity, and whose evolution has paralleled that of instrumental rationality. Because Adorno did not consider the separation of the cognitive-instrumental, moral-practical, and evaluative-expressive spheres of the lifeworld, as had Habermas, he could not envision the evolution of the last two spheres in parallel to that of the first (cognitive-instrumental) and the system of checks and balances these evolved spheres might provide.

Adorno's critique of mass culture in advanced capitalist societies with a claim to liberal democracy, however, has placed the exaggerated claims about individual subjectivity by its apologists in a proper perspective. In this critique, the "culture industry," as the creature of world capitalism embodied in consumerism, is a negation of subjectivity:

> Mass culture discloses the fictitious character of the "individual" in the bourgeois era and is merely unjust in boasting on account of this dreary harmony of general and particular. The principle of individuality was always full of contradiction. Individuation has never really been achieved. Self-preservation in the shape of class has kept everyone at the stage of a mere species being. . . . The individual who supported society bore its disfiguring mark; seemingly free, he was actually, the product of its economic apparatus and social apparatus. (Adorno and Horkheimer 1972, 155)

Nietzsche: Radical Intoxicated Subjectivity at the Expense of Social Universality

Viewing the individual as absolute sovereign, Nietzsche took the Enlightenment notion of human subjectivity to its most extreme limit:

> If we place ourselves at the end of this tremendous process where the tree at last brings forth fruit, where society and the morality of custom at last reveal *what* they have simply been the means to; then we discover that the ripest fruit is the *sovereign individual*, like only to himself, liberated again from morality of

custom, autonomous and supramoral (for "autonomous" and "moral" are mutually exclusive). (Nietzsche 1967, 59; emphases original)[6]

Nietzsche considered traditional society as the primary obstacle—albeit historically instrumental—to the development of modern subjectivity (Nietzsche 1967, 59).

The "will to power" expresses Nietzsche's view of human subjectivity in all its radicalness.[7] This notion, of course, has been a source of the controversy surrounding much of his thought. Although, in one passage, Nietzsche (1967, 79) describes the will to power as the "essence of life . . . the spontaneous, aggressive, expansive, form-giving forces that give new interpretations and direction," in others, he equates it with domination by one elite or one dictator or one race.[8]

It should not therefore be surprising that subjectivity also becomes domination in Nietzsche's scheme. He believed that subjectivity could not be universalized; indeed, that, to exist, it had to be confined to the few, the strong, the elite, a belief amply demonstrated in his remarks against "democratic" reforms and measures, or what he called the "impulses of the masses," demanded by the progressive forces of his time.

Nietzsche's thought is as replete with contradictions as it is rich with insights. Thus, although the few subjects who gain mastery over the majority of humanity engender "resentment" among their "slaves," in the hands of the clergy, the slaves' "resentment" is transformed into what Nietzsche calls *"ressentiment,"* resignation and the ethos of existing as "objects"—into good that engenders the moral (Nietzsche 1967, 128). Yet the two notions implicitly contradict one another: if the desire for subjectivity cannot be universalized, its objects, the "slaves," should not develop "resentment" against the domination imposed on them, much less "resentment" so strong the clergy has to emasculate it by transforming it into *ressentiment.* Nevertheless, on rare occasions Nietzsche exhibits sparks of understanding with regard to the universality of subjectivity. Thus he

6. To be certain, Nietzsche's conception of subjectivity is a peculiar one. Mediated by the aesthetic dimension of the Dionysian, and surrendering itself to madness and intoxication, it pits the aesthetic dimension against reason, instead of trying to bridge the gap between them. See Habermas 1987, 92–97.

7. Nietzsche rejected the Enlightenment idea of science and reason as the "vehicles" of modern subjectivity, considering them instead obstacles on the way to subjectivity. Only art, the Dionysian dimension, could lead to emancipation. He thus anticipated some of the ideas later developed by Frankfurt School figures such as Herbert Marcuse.

8. On the historical aspects of subjectivity, Nietzsche observed: "What does the Renaissance prove? That the reign of the individual has to be brief. . . . In the Reformation we possess a wild and vulgar counterpart to the Italian Renaissance, born of related impulses; only in the retarded north, which had remained coarse, they had to don a religious disguise. . . . Through the Reformation, too, the individual sought freedom; 'Everybody his own priest' is . . . a mere formula of libertinage" (1968, 57).

traces the genealogy of justice to primitive exchange relations: "justice on the elementary level is the good will among parties of approximately equal power to come to terms with one another, to reach an 'understanding' by means of a settlement" (Nietzsche 1967, 70).

For Nietzsche, the major consequence of modernity was the loss of meaning, or what he called "nihilism," which he both feared and celebrated as the destiny of Europe for the two hundred years to come (Nietzsche 1967, 161). On the one hand, he considered nihilism to be the opposite of the will to power—the quest for subjectivity (1967, 157). On the other, he saw in nihilism the loss of belief in an ultimate end, in unity, and in truth (1968, 12–13). These losses meant a departure from belief in essences, utopias, and overarching and totalizing systems of truth. In this respect, Nietzsche paved the way for the postmodernist critics.

Althusser: Ambiguity of the Subject

Does individual subjectivity actually exist in the West? After all the historical processes that have transpired—the Renaissance, the Reformation, the scientific and industrial revolutions, the democratic revolutions—have autonomous, self-willing, and self-defining individual subjects emerged in all their universality? These are the questions to which Althusser has responded in his important essay "Ideology and the State" (Althusser 1971, 127–83).

A part of his answer lies in his concept of "interpellation," by which Althusser means something very close to Gramsci's notion of hegemony, in which individuals are, without the use of force, brought to a "make a statement" or to believe that a certain state of affairs is true and that they are the "authors" of such a "statement." In Althusser's fourfold system of interpellation (1971, 180–81), individuals are accomplices in the fabrication of the illusion that they are subjects; because they believe they are in a position of subjectivity, the modern social system operates without much friction. But the key to understanding modern subjectivity lies

> in the ambiguity of the term *subject*. In the ordinary use of the term, subject in fact means (1) a free subjectivity, a center of initiatives, author of and responsible for its actions [and] (2) a subjected being who submits to a higher authority, and is therefore stripped of all freedom except that of freely accepting his submission. This last note gives us the meaning of this ambiguity, which is merely a reflection of the effect which produces it: the individual *is interpellated as a (free)* subject in order that he shall submit freely to the commandments of the Subject, i.e., in order that he shall make the gestures and actions of his subjection "all by himself!" There are no subjects except by and for their subjec-

tion. That is why they "work all by themselves." (Althusser 1971, 181–82; emphasis original)

These are sobering insights into the actual state of subjectivity in the modern world, yet they are only a partial representation of modernity and its potentials.

Modernity and Postmodernity

Leaving aside whether postmodernity represents an abrupt break from modernity or merely a phase of it, this section schematically discusses aspects of the work of Fredric Jameson and Jean-François Lyotard on postmodernity, as they bear on the analysis of modernity presented in this book.

For Jameson, postmodernity has three principal characteristics. First, it is characterized by the consumerism of late capitalism in its multinational and global phase (Jameson 1984, 79–88). Second, it is characterized by the transformation of modern solid "representation" (what Lyotard calls "metanarratives" such as science, reason, etc.) into postmodern simulacrum—vague representation (Jameson 1984, 66). Thus, just as the solidity of religious tradition and its understanding of the world have been shattered by modernity, so the solidity of science and reason and their understanding of the world have been shattered by postmodernity. And third (not unrelated to the second), it is characterized by the disintegration and fragmentation of modernity's putatively comprehensive, totalizing, temporally unified, and cohesive processes of meaning, or, in Jameson's words (1984, 71), "the breakdown of the signifying chain"—much like schizophrenic disjunction as described by Jacques Lacan.

According to Jameson (1984, 63), in the shift from modernity to postmodernity, "alienation of the subject is displaced by the fragmentation of the subject." The logical extension of this position is that, when schizophrenic disjunction replaces "alienation" as the "cultural style," it "ceases to entertain a necessary relationship to the morbid content we associate with terms like schizophrenia, and becomes available for more joyous intensities, for precisely that euphoria which we saw displacing the older affects of anxiety and alienation" (Jameson 1984, 74).

The schizophrenic disjunction of postmodernity brings with it another consequence: the effort to transcend the given is abandoned. Architecture no longer strives for "protopolitical utopian transformation," while political philosophy forgoes the "luxury of the old-fashioned ideological critique" (Jameson 1984, 81, 86).

Perhaps the most far-reaching consequence of postmodernity in Jameson's analysis is the death of the subject as rebel: the isolated, eccentric rebel has become the bag person—homeless, harmless, and manageable (Jameson 1991, 322). Does this mean the death of the subject as such? Jameson does not provide a direct answer, but, judging from the structure of his thinking on postmodernity, he does not believe the extinction of great men as subjects means the end of subjectivity as such. Rather, he seems to view subjectivity as something already accomplished, therefore able to be fragmented. Thus the modern alienated individual deprived of subjectivity and the postmodern individual as fragmented subject, even though they seem mutually exclusive, can exist side by side in contemporary society.

Concurring with Jameson, Lyotard finds that the "metanarratives" of reason, science, nation-states, and so on, having displaced religion, are in the process of disintegrating. However, he disagrees with Jameson's claim that this disintegration is a result of the consumerism and globalization of capitalism; rather, he finds the metanarratives to be inherently illegitimate (Lyotard 1984, 37–39). Scientific knowledge, for example, "cannot know and make known that it is the true knowledge without resorting to the other, narrative, kind of knowledge, which from its point of view is no knowledge at all" (Lyotard 1984, 29).

Lyotard does not address the origins of the metanarratives of modernity, and thus also not their function as a response to the diremptions accompanying the emergence of modern subjectivity. What interests him is the totalizing effect these metanarratives have had in the creation of the unitary subject. Like Jameson, Lyotard diagnoses the postmodern emergence of fragmented subjectivity and the loss of credulity toward the metanarratives. But, unlike Jameson, who approaches postmodernity dialectically, Lyotard wholeheartedly embraces it, declaring war on totality and the unitary subject. Unlike either Jameson or Lyotard, Habermas, with his theory of communicative rationality, attempts to maintain a wholesome notion of the subject, while embedding the unbridled subjectivity of modern times in a notion of universality.

Habermas: Language Mediating Subjectivity and Universality

Much of the first volume of Habermas's *Theory of Communicative Action: Reason and the Rationalization of Society* is devoted to the effects of the revolution of subjectivity on the modern "lifeworld," with the concept of "rationality" effectively standing in for that of subjectivity. *The Philosophical Discourse of Modernity* (Habermas 1988, 16) quotes Hegel to the effect that the modern age is marked by a structure of self-relation, which Hegel calls "subjectivity." Indeed, Habermas himself recognizes the principle of subjectivity as the core constituent of modernity: "An unprecedented modernity, open to the future, anxious for novelty, can only fashion its criteria out of itself. The only source of normativity that presents itself is the principle of subjectivity from which the very time-consciousness of modernity arose" (1987, 41).

Habermas contends that, in traditional society, value was not yet differentiated:

the validity aspects of the true, the good, and the perfect were integrated in the knowledge of God, whereas, in modern society, as a result of the emergence of subjectivity, the three "value spheres" of culture have been separated from their religious-mythical grounding, thus also from one another, and the sacred has become "linguistified":

> From Durkheim to Lévi-Strauss, anthropologist have repeatedly pointed out the peculiar *confusion between nature and culture*. We can understand this phenomenon to begin with as the mixing of two object domains, physical nature and sociocultural environment. Myths do not permit a clear, basic, conceptual differentiation between things and persons, between objects that can be manipulated and agents—subjects capable of speaking and acting, to whom we attribute linguistic utterances. (Habermas 1981a, 48; emphasis original)[9]

Building on Weber's characterization of cultural modernity as the separation of the "substantive reason" expressed in religion and metaphysics into three autonomous spheres of science, morality, and art, Habermas (1981b, 8) constructs a three-sphere conception of culture—objective (science), social (morality), and subjective (art)—that is central to his theory of modernity. In the dimension of validity claims, for example, the categories of truth, normative rightness, and authenticity-beauty correspond, respectively, to his objective, social, and subjective spheres, whereas, in the dimension of attitude, the categories of knowledge, justice and morality, and taste correspond, respectively, to these spheres (Habermas 1981a, 71; 1981b, 8) (see table 1). Habermas claims that, as a result of modernity, two sets of related things happen to these three spheres. First, they are extricated from their sacred matrix and, as reflected in table 1, differentiated from one another.[10] Second, they are progressively uncoupled from what Habermas calls the "steering media" (system integration) of money (capitalist economy) and power (administrative power), even as they are made dependent on these very same steering media (Habermas 1984, 305).

9. One should be careful to differentiate the various stages of "premodernity"; Habermas seems here to collapse the mythical and religious stages together.

10. With regard to the objective, social, and subjective spheres, Habermas points to "the humanism of the Renaissance [that] made the Roman-Greek heritage accessible to the science, jurisprudence, and art that were emancipating [Europeans] from the Church" (Habermas 1984, 286).

TABLE 1

Dimensional Correlates of Habermas's Three Spheres

	Objective	*Social*	*Subjective*
Validity claim dimension	Truth	Normative righteousness (good)	Authenticity, beauty
Action orientation dimension	Cognitive-instrumental	Moral-practical	Aesthetic-expressive
Attitude dimension	Knowledge	Justice, morality	Taste
Institutional dimension	Science	Morality, law	Art

Before proceeding to this second point—what Habermas calls the "colonization of the lifeworld"—let us briefly consider Habermas's critique of premodernity in its role as foil for his theory of modernity. At the core of his critique is the idea that validity claims pertaining to the three spheres in traditional settings are not open to criticism and revision: "Mythical worldviews are not understood by members [of premodern society] as interpretive systems that are attached to cultural traditions, instituted by internal inter-relations of meaning, symbolically related to reality and connected with validity claims—and thus exposed to criticism and open to revision" (Habermas 1981a, 52–53). Consequently, the abstraction of the validity claims and their elevation over and above the members of traditional society create "alienation" and severely handicap any process of social change. This situation is best illustrated with regard to "traditional law," where "norms are taken as given, as conventions that are passed on" (Habermas 1981a, 258).

In contrast, Habermas believes it is only in modern society that criticism and revision of legal norms are allowed (Habermas 1981a, 258–60). Such allowances are conducive to a just society because, in modernity, "the model for justifying legal norms is an uncoerced agreement, arrived at by those affected, in the role of contractual partners who are in principle free and equal" (Habermas 1981a, 261). Indeed, Habermas emphasizes that civil and democratic rights can exist only in the cultural milieu of modern society: "The interest in the protection and extensive use of civil rights and democratic self-determination are two equal, mutually complementary components, which are equally rooted in cultural modernity" (1983, 7).

Like his predecessor Hegel, however, Habermas clearly recognizes the problems created by the "unchecked" subjectivity of the modern age as well as the associated problems of domination. And like Hegel, acknowledging the diremptions that resulted from the expansion of the principle of modern subjectivity, he tries to overcome them through a theory of intersubjectivity, as opposed to mere subjectivity (see Habermas 1987, esp. lectures 1 and 2). But he criticizes Hegel for attempting to develop intersubjectivity based on the principle of modern subjectivity itself, and for failing to ground it in a communicative action theory, as he himself has done (Habermas 1987, 30–31). Indeed, he undertakes to resolve the problem of modernity by moving in the proper direction—through the mediation of language: "Membership in the ideal communicative community is, in Hegelian terms, constitutive of both the I as universal and the I as individual" (Habermas 1984, 97).

In Habermas's alternative paradigm, subjectivity and universality are reconciled through communication, where neither individual subjectivity nor universality is sacrificed:

> A different model for the mediation of the universal and the individual is provided by the *higher-level intersubjectivity of an uncoerced formation of will* within a communication community existing under constraints toward cooperation in the universality of an uncoerced consensus arrived at among free and equal persons, individuals retain a court of appeal that can be called upon even against particular forms of institutional concretization of the common will. (Habermas 1987, 40; emphasis original)

The importance of language as the medium through which subjectivity and universality are reconciled cannot be overemphasized: "The human interest in autonomy and responsibility . . . can be apprehended a priori. What raises us out of nature is the only thing whose nature we can know: language. Through its structure, autonomy and responsibility are posited for us. Our first sentence expresses unequivocally the intention of a universal and unconstrained consensus" (Habermas 1971, 314). Habermas demonstrates the peculiar capacity of language both to manifest the freedom of individual subjectivity in uttering completely idiosyncratic sentences and, at the same time, to be universally understandable within the membership of the language group.

This reconciliation between subjective freedom and universality can take place only in the modern era, however: in premodern (traditional or religious-metaphysical) society, with its "sacred" and "profane" spheres, the sacred sphere was immune to communicative action orientation (Habermas 1984, 189–90). Only with modernity are the functions of social integration and expressivity, originally performed through ritual, gradually taken over by communicative action, and the authority vested in the sacred replaced by the authority of the achieved consensus (Habermas 1984, 77).

In recent years, Habermas has engaged in sometimes polemical debate with the poststructuralist critics of modernity, accusing the proponents of "negative dialectic," genealogy, and deconstruction, and Weberian iron-cage rationalization of wishing to do away with subjectivity altogether. Habermas contends that they and their theories, by viewing the subjectivity of modern times as the culprit in the phenomenon of domination, are throwing out the baby with the bathwater; indeed, that they are involved in

> undialectical rejection of subjectivity. [They condemn] not only the devastating consequences of an objectifying relation-to-self . . . along with this principle of modernity, but also the *other* connotations once associated with subjectivity as an unredeemed promise: the prospect of a self-conscious practice, in which the . . . self-determination of all was to be joined with the self-realization of each. (Habermas 1987, 337–38; emphasis original)

The poststructuralist critics of modernity thus discard the very normative content of modernity—the autonomy of subjectivity: "What is thrown out is precisely what a modernity reassuring itself once meant by the concepts of self-consciousness, self-determination, and self-realization" (Habermas 1987, 338).

This error, according to Habermas, is firmly rooted in the work of Max Weber, who, though he distinguished between the objective, social, and subjective spheres and their correlates, instrumental rationality, moral-practical discourse, and aesthetic expressivity, failed to acknowledge that each sphere might develop independently, and who instead equated subjectivity only with domination and its vehicle in the modern world, namely, instrumental rationality, contending that all the spheres were dominated and pervaded by instrumental rationality. To be sure, admits Habermas, there is a strong tendency for the "system imperatives" of the "steering media" of money and power to colonize the three spheres of the lifeworld (see, for example, Habermas 1984, 354–55). But this colonization is neither total nor irreversible. Indeed, it is "the project of modernity formulated in the eighteenth century by the philosophers of the Enlightenment," which Habermas has undertaken, to separate the spheres, allowing "objective science, universal morality and law, and autonomous art" to develop "according to their inner logic," and, in so doing, to "decolonize" them (1981b, 22).

In the face of the recent resurgence of nihilism, expressed in certain strands of genealogy and poststructuralism, Habermas's efforts to redeem the project of modernity are nothing less than heroic. There are, however, two criticisms of Habermas's model, and of his discourse ethics and general will formation in particular, that have important bearing on the theoretical constructs we are concerned with here. The first is that, because of its logocentric nature, it lends itself to the "colonization" of the relationship between subject and inner and outer nature. Thus, as Rainer Nagele (1981, 55) notes in his psychoanalytic critique,

> the backbone of [Habermas's] model is the concept of the self-identical subject that has full control over all of its discourse. Habermas appoints as absolute ruler what in Freud is presented as an extremely precarious and

constantly shifting position of authority, which, on the one hand, attains at best to the limited role of "constitutional monarch," and, on the other, courts as a "slave" his "master's love" of it.

Although Habermas does not seem to have addressed this issue in any great detail, he has tried to distance himself from the Kantian radical opposition between reason and inclination: "Discourse ethics gives up Kant's dichotomy between an intelligible realm comprising duty and free will and a phenomenal realm comprising inclinations [and] subjective motives "(Habermas 1993, 326).

The second criticism, and one that can be leveled at any theory of universalization, is that Habermas's model leaves little, if any, space for difference and pluralism.[11] Habermas has rejected this charge, but done so at the risk of trivializing the problem of totalization central to universality:

> Neither Kantian ethics nor discourse ethics lays itself open to the objection that a moral point of view based on the generalizability of norms necessarily leads to the neglect, if not the repression, of existing conditions and interests in a pluralist society. As interests and value orientation become more differentiated in modern societies, the morally justified norms that control the individual's scope of action in the interest of the whole become even more general and abstract. Modern societies are also characterized by the need for regulation that impinge only on particular interests. While these matters do require regulation, a discursive consensus is not needed; compromise is quite sufficient in this area. (1993, 328)

As a way out of this dilemma, Seyla Benhabib (1986, 341) has proposed a form of universalization that takes into account difference and plurality and our desire for both:

> Our relation to the other is governed by the norm of complementary reciprocity: each is entitled to expect and to assume from the other forms of be-

11. Here we should note the correspondence between the ideas of universal subjectivity or the ethics of general will and the emergence of "the people" (later, "the masses"), in the aftermath of the French Revolution. The emergence of "the people" has been interpreted, on the one hand, to have generated excitement about and widespread enthusiasm for the universalization of subjectivity (Hegel), and, on the other, to have struck a mortal blow to the notions of subjectivity and human emancipation (Le Bon and other early analysts of mass psychology). It seems to me that these two contrary interpretations reflect the antithetical dimension of the relationship between subjectivity and universality, a dimension most evident in populist and totalitarian regimes, whose elites manipulate the masses by using the principle of universality to negate individual subjectivity.

havior through which the other feels recognized and confirmed as a concrete, individual being with specific needs, talents, and capacities. Our differences in this case complement rather than exclude one another.

Whether "complementary reciprocity" will indeed prove to be a way out of the dilemma of the totalizing tendency of universality remains to be seen. But what it serves to point out is our continuing need for a workable synthesis in which subjectivity and universality can coexist without each cancelling out the other.

Works Cited

Abrahamian, Ervand. 1980. "Kasravi: The Integrative Nationalist of Iran." In Elie Kedourie and Sylvia Haim, eds., *Towards a Modern Iran: Studies in Thought, Politics and Society*. London: Frank Cass.

——. 1982. *Iran Between Two Revolutions*. Princeton, N.J.: Princeton Univ. Press.

——. 1993. *Khomeinism: Essays on the Islamic Republic*. Berkeley: Univ. of California Press.

——. 1999. *Tortured Confessions: Prisons and Public Recantations in Modern Iran*. Berkeley: Univ. of California Press.

Adamiyat, Fereydun. 1961. *Fekr Azadi va Moqadameh Nehzat Mashrutiyat* (The idea of freedom and the beginning of the Constitutional movement). Tehran: Sokhan.

——. 1970. *Andisheha-ye Mirza Fathali Akhundzadeh* (The ideas of Mirza Fathali Akhundzadeh). Tehran: Kharazmi.

——. 1975. *Fekr Demokrasi Ejtema'i dar Nehzat Mashrutiyat Iran* (The idea of Social Democracy in the Constitutional movement of Iran). Tehran: Payam.

——. 1976. *Idiologi Nehzat Mashrutiyat Iran* (The ideology of the Constitutional movement of Iran). Tehran: Payam.

——. 1977. *Andishe Taraqi va Hukumat Qanun: Asr Sepahsalar* (The idea of progress and the rule of law: The era of Sepahsalar). Tehran: Kharazmi

——. 1978. *Andisheha-ye Mirza Aqa Khan Kermani* (The ideas of Mirza Aqa Khan Kermani). Tehran: Payam.

——. 1983. *Amir Kabir va Iran* (Amir Kabir and Iran). Tehran: Kharazmi.

——. 1984. *Andisheha-ye Talibuf Tabrizi* (The ideas of Talibuf Tabrizi). Tehran: Damavand.

——. 1985. "Ashuftegi Fekr-e Tarikhi" (Confusion of historical thought). In Ali Dehbashi, ed., *Yadnameh-ye Jalal Al-e Ahmad* (Memorial book of Jalal Al-e Ahmad). Tehran: Pasargad.

Adorno, Theodor. 1974. *The Jargon of Authenticity*. Evanston, Ill.: Northwestern Univ. Press.

——. 1978. "Freudian Theory and the Pattern of Fascist Propaganda." In A. Arato and E. Gebhart, eds., *The Essential Frankfurt School Reader*. New York: Urizen.

Adorno, Theodor, and Max Horkheimer. 1972. *Dialectic of Enlightenment*. New York: Herder and Herder.

Afghani, Seyyed Jamal al-Din. 1958. *Ara' va Mu'taqedat Seyyed Jamal al-Din Afghani* (The opinions and beliefs of Seyyed Jamal al-Din Afghani). Edited by Morteza Modaresi. Tehran: Eqbal.

———. 1968a. "Lecture on Teaching and Learning." In *An Islamic Response to Imperialism: Political and Religious Writings of Sayyid Jamal ad-Din "al-Afghani,"* translated by Nikki Keddie. Los Angeles: Univ. of California Press.

———. 1968b. "The Benefits of Philosophy." In *An Islamic Response to Imperialism: Political and Religious Writings of Sayyid Jamal ad-Din "al-Afghani,"* translated by Nikki Keddie. Los Angeles: Univ. of California Press.

———. 1968c. "Answer of Jamal ad-Din to Renan, *Journal des Débats*, May 18, 1883." In *An Islamic Response to Imperialism: Political and Religious Writings of Sayyid Jamal ad-Din "al-Afghani,"* translated by Nikki Keddie. Los Angeles: Univ. of California Press.

———. 1968d. "The Truth about the Neicheri Sect and an Explanation of the Neicheris." In *An Islamic Response to Imperialism: Political and Religious Writings of Sayyid Jamal ad-Din "al-Afghani,"* translated by Nikki Keddie. Los Angeles: Univ. of California Press.

———. 1969. *Eslam va Elm, be Zamime Resaleh Qaza va Qadar* (Islam and science, with the treatise on fatalism). Edited by Hadi Khosroshahi. Tabriz: Saidi.

Afshar, Aljai. 1923. "Ma'aref dar Iran" (Culture in Iran). *Iranshahr* 2, no. 3 (Nov).

Afshar, Iraj. 1978. *Abd al-Rahim Talibuf Tabrizi: Azadi va Siasat* (Abd al-Rahim Talibuf Tabrizi: Freedom and politics). Tehran: Sahar.

Afshar, Mahmud. 1925. "Matlub Ma: Vahdat Melli Iran" (Our ideal: The national unity of Iran). *Ayandeh* 1, no. 1.

———. 1926. "Masaleh Meliyat va Vahdat Melli Iran" (The question of nationalism and national unity). *Ayandeh* 2, no. 11.

Agahi, Abdulhussein. 1964. "Be Monasebat Bist o Panjomin Sal-e Dargozasht Doktor Arani" (On the twenty-fifth anniversary of Doctor Arani's death). *Donya*, 2d ser., vol. 5, no. 3 (Fall).

Ahmadzadeh, Mas'ud. 1978. *Mobarezeh Mosalahaneh: Ham Esterategi, ham Taktiki* (Armed struggle: Both a strategy and a tactic). N.p.: Setigh.

Akhundzadeh, Mirza Fathali. 1972. *Maqalat* (Articles). Edited by Baqer Mu'meni. Tehran: Ara.

———. 1978. *Maktubat va Alefba-ye Jadid* (Letters and the new alphabet). Edited by Hamid Mohammadzadeh. Tabriz: Ehya.

———. 1985. *Maktuba* (Letters). N.p.

Al-e Ahmad, Jalal. 1977. *Gharbzadegi* (Westoxication). Tehran: Ravaq.

———. 1980. *Dar Khedmat va Khianat Rushanfekran* (On the services and treasons of intellectuals). Tehran: Ravaq.

————. 1981. *Sangi Bar Guri* (A stone on a grave). Tehran: Ravaq.

Algar, Hamid. 1973. *Mirza Malkum Khan: A Study in the History of Iranian Modernism.* Berkeley: Univ. of California Press.

Althusser, Louis. 1971. *Lenin and Philosophy and Other Essays.* New York: Monthly Review Press.

Amir-Arjomand, Said. 1984. *The Shadow of God and the Hidden Imam: Religion, Political Order and Social Change in Shi'ite Iran from the Beginning to 1890.* Chicago: Univ. of Chicago Press.

————. 1986. *Authority and Political Culture in Shi'ism.* Albany: State Univ. of New York Press.

————. 1988. *The Turban for the Crown: The Islamic Revolution in Iran.* New York: Oxford Univ. Press.

Arani, Taqi. 1963. "Matn Defa' Doktor Arani dar Dadgah Panjah o Se Nafar" (Text of Doctor Arani's defense in the trial of the Fifty-three). *Donya,* 2d ser., vol. 2, nos. 1–2. (Spring–Summer).

————. [1970?]. *Erfan va Usul Madi* (Mysticism and principles of materialism). Tehran: Karang.

————. [1983]. *Honar dar Iran Jadid* (Art in modern Iran). Reprinted in Cosroe Chaqueri, ed., *Asar Taqi Arani* (The works of Taqi Arani). Vol. 2. Tehran: Mazdak.

Ashraf, Ahmad. 1981. "The Roots of the Emerging Dual Class Structure in Twentieth Century Iran." *Iranian Studies* 14 (Winter–Spring).

Ashuri, Daryush. 1991. "Ba Khalil Maleki dar Vapasin Salha-ye Zendegi" (With Khalil Maleki in the last years of life). In Amir Pishdad and Homayun Katouzian, eds., *Yadnameh Khalil Maleki* (Memorial book of Khalil Maleki). Tehran: Enteshar.

————. 1995. "Jalal Al-e Ahmad." In Ali Dehbashi, ed., *Yadnameh Jalal Al-e Ahmad* (Memorial book of Jalal Al-e Ahmad). Tehran: Pasargad.

Banani, Amin. 1961. *The Modernization of Iran: 1921–1941.* Stanford, Calif.: Stanford Univ. Press.

Banuazizi, Ali. 1993. "Ravanparishi Farhangi va Mujadeleh Sad Saleh ba Gharb" (Cultural schizophrenia and the hundred years' debate with the West). *Iran Nameh* 11, no. 4 (Fall).

————. 1995. "Faltering Legitimacy: The Ruling Clerics and Civil Society in Contemporary Iran." *International Journal of Politics, Culture and Society* 8, no. 4.

Bayat, Mangol. 1974. "Mirza Aqa Khan Kirmani: A Nineteenth-Century Persian Nationalist." *Middle Eastern Studies* 10, no. 1 (Jan.).

————. 1981. "Tradition and Change in Iranian Socio-Religious Thought." In Michael E. Bonine and Nikki Keddie, eds., *Continuity and Change in Modern Iran.* Albany: State Univ. of New York Press.

Beck, Lewis W. 1988. "Introduction." In Beck, ed., *Kant: Selections.* New York: Macmillan.

Bell, Daniel. 1978. *The Cultural Contradictions of Capitalism.* New York: Basic Books.

Benhabib, Seyla. 1986. *Critique, Norm and Utopia: A Study on the Foundations of Critical Theory.* New York: Columbia Univ. Press.

Berger, Peter. 1977. *Facing up to Modernity: Excursions in Society, Politics, and Religion.* New York: Basic Books.

Berman, Marshal. 1988. *All That Is Solid Melts into Air: The Experience of Modernity.* New York: Penguin.

Bina, Ali Akbar. 1954. *Tarikh Siasi va Diplomasi Iran* (The political and diplomatic history of Iran). Vol. 1. Tehran: Tehran Univ. Press.

Boroujerdi, Mehrzad. 1994. "The Encounter of Post-Revolutionary Thought in Iran with Hegel, Heidegger and Popper." In Serif Mardin, ed., *Cultural Transitions in the Middle East.* Leiden: Brill.

———. 1996. *Iranian Intellectuals and the West: The Tormented Triumph of Nativisim.* Syracuse, N.Y.: Syracuse Univ. Press.

Browne, Edward. 1910. *The Persian Revolution of 1905–1909.* London: Cambridge Univ. Press.

Cahoone, Lawrence E. 1987. *The Dilemma of Modernity: Philosophy, and Anti-Culture.* Albany: State Univ. of New York Press.

Cascardi, Anthony J. 1992. *The Subject of Modernity.* Cambridge: Cambridge Univ. Press.

Chaqueri, Cosroe. 1983. *Asar Taqi Arani* (The works of Taqi Arani). Vol. 2. Tehran: Mazdak

———. 1993. *Asnad Tarikhi Jonbesh Kargari, Sosial Demokrasi va Komonisti Iran* (The historical documents of the workers', the Social Democratic, and the Communist movements in Iran). Vol. 22. N.p.: Antidote.

Chehabi, H. E. 1990. *Iranian Politics and Religious Modernism: The Liberation Movement of Iran under the Shah and Khomeini.* Ithaca, N.Y.: Cornell Univ. Press.

Dabashi, Hamid. 1989. *Authority in Islam: From the Rise of Muhammad to the Establishment of Umayyads.* New Brunswick, N.J.: Transaction.

———. 1993. *Theology of Discontent: The Ideological Foundation of the Islamic Revolution in Iran.* New York: New York Univ. Press.

Daftary, Farhad. 1992. *The Isma'ilis: Their History and Doctrines.* New York: Cambridge Univ. Press.

———. 1995. *The Assassin Legends: Myths of the Isma'ilis.* New York: Tauris.

Dallmayr, Fred. 1989. "Life-World: Variations on a Theme." In Stephen K. White, ed., *Life-World and Politics: Between Modernity and Postmodernity.* Notre Dame, Ind.: Univ. of Notre Dame Press.

———. 1993. *G. W. F. Hegel: Modernity and Politics.* Newbury Park, Calif.: Sage.

Davar, Ali Akbar. 1926. "Bohran" (Crisis). *Ayandeh* 2, no. 1 (Dec.).

Davari-Ardakani, Reza. 1980. *Falsafe Chist?* (What is philosophy?). Tehran: Iranian Academy of Philosophy.

————. 1982. *Enqelab-e Islami va Vaz'-e Kununi 'Alam* (The Islamic Revolution and the current conditions of the world). Tehran: 'Alame Tabatabai Center for Culture.

————. 1985. *Nasionalism, Hakemiyat-e Melli va Esteqlal* (Nationalism, national sovereignty and independence). Esfahan: Porsesh.

————. 1994. *Falsafe dar Bohran* (Philosophy in crisis). Tehran: Amir Kabir.

————. 1995. "Rahbordha-ye Jadid-e Falsafe: Goftegu ba Doktor Reza Davari-Ardakani" (New paths to philosophy: Interview with Doctor Reza Davari-Arkadani). *Kayhan Farhangi* 12, no. 124 (Dec.–Jan.).

Dehbashi, Ali. 1985. *Yadnameh Jalal Al-e Ahmad* (Memorial book of Jalal Al-e Ahmad). Tehran: Pasargad.

Descartes, René. 1927. *Selections*. Edited by Ralph Eaton. London: Scribner's.

Dowlatabadi, Yahya. 1982. *Hayat Yahya* (Life of Yahya). Tehran: Attar.

Dupré, Louis. 1982. "Spiritual Life in a Secular Age." *Daedalus* 111, no. 1 (Winter).

————. 1993. *Passage to Modernity: An Essay in the Hermeneutics of Nature and Culture*. New Haven, Conn.: Yale Univ. Press.

Ehsani, Kaveh. 1995. "Islam, Modernity, and National Identity." *Middle East Insight* 11, no. 5.

Entekhabi, Nader. 1993. "Nasionalism va Tajadud dar Farhang Siasi Iran" (Nationalism and modernization in Iran's political culture). *Iran Nameh* 11, no. 2 (Spring).

Farman Farmayan, Hafez. 1966. "The Forces of Modernization in Nineteenth-Century Iran: A Historical Survey." In W. Polk and R. Chamber, eds., *Beginnings of Modernization in the Middle East*. Chicago: Univ. of Chicago Press.

Foucault, Michel. 1979. *Discipline and Punish: The Birth of the Prison*. New York: Vintage.

————. 1980. *The History of Sexuality*. Vol. 1, *An Introduction*. New York: Vintage.

Freud, Sigmund. 1965. *Group Psychology and the Analysis of the Ego*. New York: Bantam.

Gheissari, Ali. 1989. "The Ideological Formation of the Iranian Intelligentsia: From the Constitutional Movement to the Fall of the Monarchy." Ph.D. diss., Univ. of Oxford.

————. 1998. *Iranian Intellectuals in the Twentieth Century*. Austin: Univ. of Texas Press.

Ghods, Reza. 1989. *Iran in the Twentieth Century: A Political History*. Boulder, Colo.: Reinner.

Guyer, Paul. 1992. "The Starry Heavens and the Moral Law." In Paul Guyer, ed., *The Cambridge Companion to Kant*. New York: Cambridge Univ. Press.

Habermas, Jürgen. 1971. *Knowledge and Human Interest*. Boston: Beacon.

————. 1981a. *The Theory of Communicative Action*. Vol. 1, *Reason and the Rationalization of the Society*. Boston: Beacon.

————. 1981b. "Modernity versus Postmodernity." *New German Critique* 22 (Winter).

————. 1983. "Newconservative Cultural Criticism in the United States and West Germany." *Telos* 56.

————. 1984. *The Theory of Communicative Action*. Vol. 2, *Lifeworld and System: A Critique of Functionalist Reason*. Boston: Beacon.

————. 1987. *The Philosophical Discourse of Modernity—Twelve Lectures*. Cambridge, Mass.: MIT Press.

————. 1993. "Morality and Ethical Life: Does Hegel's Critique of Kant Apply to Discourse Ethics?" In Ronald Beiner and William Booth, eds., *Kant and Political Philosophy: The Contemporary Legacy*. New Haven, Conn.: Yale Univ. Press.

Hairi, Abdul-Hadi. 1977. *Shi'ism and Constitutionalism in Iran: A Study of the Role Played by the Persian Residents of Iraq in Iranian Politics*. Leiden: Brill

Held, David. 1980. *Introduction to Critical Theory: Horkheimer to Habermas*. Berkeley: Univ. of California Press.

Hegel, Georg Wilhelm Friedrich. 1967. *Hegel's Philosophy of Right*. Edited by T. M. Knox. Oxford: Oxford Univ. Press.

————. 1975. *Hegel: Lectures on the Philosophy of World History. Introduction: Reason in History*. Edited by Johannes Hoffmeister. Cambridge: Cambridge Univ. Press.

————. 1991. *Elements of the Philosophy of Right*. Edited by Allen W. Wood. Cambridge: Cambridge Univ. Press.

Hyppolite, Jean. 1974. *Genesis and Structure of Hegel's Phenomenology of Spirit*. Evanston, Ill.: Northwestern Univ. Press.

Inwood, M. J. 1984. "Hegel, Plato and Greek 'Sittlichkeit.' " In Z. A. Pelczynski, ed., *The State and Civil Society: Studies in Hegel's Political Philosophy*. Cambridge: Cambridge Univ. Press.

Iranshar, Hussein Kazemzadeh. 1923. "Ma'aref va Ma'arefparvaran Iran" (Culture and the culturists of Iran). *Iranshar* 2, no. 2 (Oct.).

————. 1924. "Ma'aref va Arkan Se Ganeh an" (Culture and its three pillars). *Iranshar* 2, no. 8 (Apr.).

————. 1926. "Ayandeh Bashar" (The future of man). *Iranshahr* 4, no. 4 (June).

————. 1956. *Rahbar Nezhad Nu* (The leader of the new nation). Tehran: Eqbal.

Iranshahr, Kazem Kazemzadeh. 1984. *Asar va Ahval Iranshahr* (The works and biography of Iranshahr). Tehran: Eqbal.

Jameson, Fredric. 1981. *The Political Unconscious: Narrative as a Socially Symbolic Act*. Ithaca, N.Y.: Cornell Univ. Press.

————. 1984. "Post Modernism, or The Cultural Logic of Late Capitalism." *New Left Review* 146 (July-Aug.).

————. 1991. *Post Modernism, or The Cultural Logic of Late Capitalism*. Durham, N.C.: Duke Univ. Press.

Jazani, Bijan. 1976. *Pishahang va Tudeh* (The vanguard and the mass). N.p.: Nashrieh Nuzdah Bahman.

————. 1978a. "Marksism Enqelabi va Marksism Borzhuazi" (Revolutionary Marxism and bourgeois Marxism). In *Chand Maqaleh va Cheguneh Mubarezeh Enqelabi Mishavad* (Some articles and how the struggle becomes revolutionary). N.p.

———. 1978b. "Rabeteh Junbeshe Enqelabi Musalahaneh ba Khalq" (The relation of the armed revolutionary struggle with the people). In *Chand Maqaleh va Cheguneh Mubarezeh Enqelabi Mishavad* (Some articles and how the struggle becomes revolutionary). N.p.

———. 1978c. "Ravanshenasi Ejtema'i" (Social psychology). In *Chand Maqaleh va Cheguneh Mubarezeh Enqelabi Mishavad* (Some articles and how the struggle becomes revolutionary). N.p.

Kant, Immanuel. 1930. *Lecture on Ethics*. London: Century.

———. 1949. "What Is Enlightenment?" In Carl Friedrich, ed., *The Philosophy of Kant: Immanuel Kant's Moral and Political Writings*. New York: Harper and Row.

———. 1960. *Religion Within the Limits of Reason Alone*. Translated and edited by Theodore M. Green and H. Hudson. New York: Harper and Row.

———. 1970. *Kant's Political Writings*. Edited by Hans Reiss. Cambridge: Cambridge Univ. Press.

Karimi, Ataollah. 1990. *Faqr-e Tarikhnegari: Barasi-ye Enteqadi Maqalat Qabz va Bast Shari'at az Doktor Sorush* (Poverty of historicism: A critical review of the essays of contraction and expansion by Doctor Sorush). Tehran: 'Alame Tabatabai.

Kasravi, Ahmad. [1944]. *Shi'ehgar* (Shiism). N.p.: Tooka.

———. [1945]. "Emroz Chareh Chist" (What is the solution now)? N.p.: Tooka.

———. 1951. *Tarikh Mashruteh Iran* (The history of the Iranian constitution). Tehran: Amir Kabir.

———. 1961. *Varjavand Bonyad* (The sacred foundation). Tehran: Elmi.

———. 1962. *Zendegani Man* (My life). N.p.

Katouzian, Homa[yun]. 1981. *The Political Economy of Modern Iran: Despotism and Pseudo-Modernism, 1926–1979*. New York: New York Univ. Press.

———. 1983. *Khalil Maleki: Khaterat Siasi* (Khalil Maleki: Political memoir). N.p.: Jebheh.

Kazemzadeh, Firuz. 1991. "Iranian Relations with Russia and the Soviet Union, to 1921." In Peter Avery, Gavin Hambley, and C. P. Melville, eds., *Cambridge History of Iran*. Vol. 7. Cambridge: Cambridge Univ. Press.

Keddie, Nikki. 1968. *An Islamic Response to Imperialism: Political and Religious Writings of Sayyid Jamal ad-Din "al-Afghani."* Los Angeles: Univ. of California Press.

———. 1972. *Sayyid Jamal ad-Din "al-Afghani": A Political Biography*. Los Angeles: Univ. of California Press.

———. 1981. *Roots of Revolution: An Interpretive History of Modern Iran*. New Haven, Conn.: Yale Univ. Press.

Keddie, Nikki, and Eric Hoogland, eds. 1986. *The Iranian Revolution and the Islamic Republic*. Syracuse, N.Y.: Syracuse Univ. Press.

Kellner, Douglas. 1989. *Critical Theory, Marxism, and Modernity*. Baltimore: Johns Hopkins Univ. Press.

Kermani, Mriza Aqa Khan. 1906. *Ayeneh Sekandari* (Alexandrian mirror). N.p.

————. 1983. *Haftad Du Mellat* (Seventy-two peoples). Tehran: Attaii.

Kermani, Nazem al-Islam. 1967. *Tarikh Bidari Iranian* (The history of the awakening of Iranians). Tehran: Farhang.

Kersting, Wolfgang. 1992. "Politics, Freedom and Order: Kant's Political Philosophy." In Paul Guyer, ed., *The Cambridge Companion to Kant*. New York: Cambridge Univ. Press.

Khomeini, Ruhollah. [1944?]. *Kashf al-Asrar* (Secrets unveiled). N.p.

————. 1973. *Mobarezeh Ba Nafs, ya Jahad-e Akbar* (The struggle against the self, or the greatest jihad). Najaf, Iraq: al Adab.

————. 1978. *Velyat-e Faqih* (Governance of the jurist). Tehran: Sepehr.

————. 1981a. *Masael Siasi va Huquqi* (Political and legal problems). Edited by Abdulkarim Biazar Shirazi. Tehran: Anjam Ketab.

————. 1981b. *Islam and Revolution: Writings and Declarations of Imam Khomeini*. Translated by Hamid Algar. Berkeley, Calif.: Mizan.

————. 1982. *Shahid va Shahadat* (The martyr and martyrdom). Tehran: Sepehr.

————. 1983a. *Talab va Eradeh* (Desire and will). Edited by Ahmad Fahri. Tehran: Center for Scientific and Cultural Publications.

————. 1983b. *Mellat, Ommat* (Nation, community). Tehran: Amir Kabir.

————. 1985. *Simay-e Zan Dar Kalam-e Imam Khomeini* (The image of woman in the discourse of Imam Khomeini). Tehran: Ministry of Islamic Guidance.

Khorasani, Badi' al-Zaman. 1925. "Rah Ahan" (Railroad). *Ayandeh* 1, no. 1 (June–July).

Kojeve, Alexandre. 1980. *Introduction to the Reading of Hegel*. Ithaca, N.Y.: Cornell Univ. Press.

Kolb, David. 1986. *The Critique of Pure Modernity: Hegel, Heidegger and After*. Chicago: Univ. of Chicago Press.

Larijani, Sadeq. 1993. *Qabz va Bast dar Qabz va Basti Digar* (Contraction and expansion in another contraction and expansion). Tehran: Markaz-e Tarjome va Nashr-e Ketab.

Lee, Robert D. 1997. *Overcoming Tradition and Modernity: The Search for Islamic Authenticity*. Boulder, Colo.: Westview.

Lewis, Bernard. 1985. *The Assassins: A Radical Sect in Islam*. London: Al Saqi.

Lyotard, Jean-François. 1984. *The Postmodern Condition: A Report on Knowledge*. Minneapolis: Univ. of Minnesota Press.

Maleki, Khalil. 1983. *Khalil Maleki: Khaterat Siasi* (Khalil Maleki: Political memoir). Edited by Homayun Katouzian. N.p.: Jebheh.

————. 1995. *Khalil Maleki: Barkhord 'Aqayed va Ara* (Khalil Maleki: The interplay of beliefs and views). Edited by Amir Pishdad and Homayun Katouzian. Tehran: Markaz.

Malekzadeh, Mehdi. 1949. *Tarikh Enqelab Mashrutiyat Iran* (The history of the Constitutional Revolution in Iran). Tehran: Soqrat.

Malkum Khan, Mirza. 1890. *Qanun*, Apr. 20.

———. 1948a. *Ketabcheh Gheibi* (The occult booklet). In Mohammad Mohit Tabatabi, ed., *Majmu'e Asar Mirza Malkum Khan* (The collected works of Mirza Malkum Khan). Tehran: Danesh.

———. 1948b. *Dastgah Divan* (The bureaucracy). In Mohammad Mohit Tabatabi, ed., *Majmu'e Asar Mirza Malkum Khan* (The collected works of Mirza Malkum Khan). Tehran: Danesh.

———. 1948c. *Daftar Qanun* (The book of law). In Mohammad Mohit Tabatabi, ed., *Majmu'e Asar Mirza Malkum Khan* (The collected works of Mirza Malkum Khan). Tehran: Danesh.

———. 1948d. *Neday Edalat* (The voice of justice). In Mohammad Mohit Tabatabi, ed., *Majmu'e Asar Mirza Malkum Khan* (The collected works of Mirza Malkum Khan). Tehran: Danesh.

Maraghei, Haj Zein al-Abedin. 1965. *Siahatnameh Ebrahim Beg* (The travelogue of Ebrahim Beg). Tehran: Sadaf.

Martin, Vanessa. 1989. *Islam and Modernism: The Iranian Revolution of 1906.* Syracuse, N.Y.: Syracuse Univ. Press.

Marx, Karl, and Friedrich Engels. 1872. *The Communist Manifesto.* In R. Tucker, ed., *The Marx-Engels Reader.* New York: Norton, 1978.

Mojtahed-Shabestari, Mohammad. 1996. *Hermenutik, Ketab va Sonnat* (Hermeneutics, the Book, and tradition). Tehran: Tarh-e Nu.

Morris, James Winston. 1981. *The Wisdom of the Throne: An Introduction to the Philosophy of Mulla Sadra.* Princeton, N.J.: Princeton Univ. Press.

Moscovici, Serge. 1985. *The Age of the Crowd: A Historical Treatise on Mass Psychology.* Cambridge: Cambridge Univ. Press.

Mossadeq, Mohammad. 1925. "Nutq Aqa-ye Doktor Mussadeq" (Mr. Mussadeq's speech). *Ayandeh* 1, no. 4 (Oct.–Nov.).

Motahhari, Morteza. 1974. *Adl-e Ellahi* (Divine justice). Tehran: Entesharat-e Islami

———. [1978?]a. "Ensan va Iman" (Man and faith). In *Moqadameh-i bar Jahanbini Islami* (A prologue to the Islamic worldview). Qom: Sadra.

———. [1978?]b. "Jame'e va Tarikh" (Society and history). In *Moqadameh-i bar Jahanbini Islami* (A prologue to the Islamic worldview). Qom: Sadra.

———. [1979?]a. *Ensan dar Quran* (Man in the Quran). Qom: Sadra.

———. 1979b. *Jahanbini Tohidi* (The monotheistic worldview). Qom: Sadra.

———. 1979c. *Ensan va Sarnevesht* (Man and destiny). Qom: Sadra.

———. 1979d. *Bist Goftar* (Twenty lectures). Qom: Sadra.

———. 1980. *Qiyam va Enqelab-e Mahdi az Didgah-e Tarikh* (The uprising and revolution of the Mahdi from the perspective of philosophy of history). Qom: Sadra.

———. 1985a. *Fundamentals of Islamic Thought: God, Man and the Universe.* Translated by R. Campbell. Berkeley, Calif.: Mizan.

———. 1985b. *Piramun-e Jomhuri Islami* (Regarding the Islamic Republic). Qom: Sadra.

————. 1987. *Falsafe-ye Akhlaq* (The philosophy of ethics). Tehran: Sadra.

————. 1991. *Masal-e Hejab* (The question of the veil). Tehran: Sadra.

Motahhari, Morteza, and Mohammad Hussein Tabatabai. [1978?]. *Usul-e Falsafe va Ravesh-e Realism* (The principles of philosophy and the methodology of realism). Vol. 1. Qom: Sadra.

Mothersilk, Mary. 1967. "Duty." In Paul Edwards, ed., *The Encyclopedia of Philosophy*. Vol. 2. Reprint, New York: Collier Macmillan, 1972.

Mottahedeh, Roy. 1985. *The Mantle of the Prophet: Religion and Politics in Iran*. New York: Simson and Schuster.

Moussavi, Kazem. 1992. "A New Interpretation of the Theory of Vilayati Faqih." *Middle Eastern Studies* 28, no. 1.(Jan.).

Mustashar al-Duleh, Mirza Yusef Khan. 1985. *Yek Kalameh* (One word). Tehran: Nashr Tarikh Iran.

Nagele, Rainer. 1981. "Freud, Habermas and the Dialectic of Enlightenment: On Real and Ideal Discourse." *New German Critique* 22 (Winter).

Naini, Mohammad Hussein. 1955. *Tanbih al-Ummah va Tanzih al-Millah* (The awakening of the community and the refinement of the nation). N.p.

Najmabadi, Afsaneh. 1987. "Iran's Turn to Islam: From Modernism to Moral Order." *Middle East Journal* 41, no. 2 (Spring).

Naraqi, Ehsan. 1974. *Ghorbat Gharb* (The alienation of the West). Amir Kabir: Tehran.

————. 1976. *Ancheh Khud Dasht* (What the self had). Amir Kabir: Tehran.

Nateq, Homa. 1988. *Iran dar Rahyabi Farhangi* (Iran in cultural exploration). London: Payam.

Nietzsche, Friedrich. 1967. *On the Genealogy of Morals*. Translated and edited by Walter Kaufman. New York: Vintage.

————. 1968. *The Will to Power*. Translated and edited by Walter Kaufman. New York: Vintage.

Nuri, Sheikh Fazlollah. 1983. *Majmu'eh-i az Rasael, E'lamie-ha, Maktubat va Ruznameh Sheikh Fazlollah Nuri* (A collection of the treatises, pronouncements, letters, and the journal of Sheikh Fazlollah Nuri). Edited by Mohammad Turkaman. Tehran: Rasa.

Parsons, Talcot. 1963. *The Social System*. Glencoe, Ill.: Free Press of Glencoe.

Pelczynski, Z. A. 1984. "The Significance of Hegel's Separation of the State and Civil Society." In Pelczynski, ed., *The State and Civil Society: Studies in Hegel's Political Philosophy*. Cambridge: Cambridge Univ. Press.

Rahman, Fazlur. 1975. *The Philosophy of Mulla Sadra*. Albany: State Univ. of New York Press.

Rahnema, Ali. 1998. *An Islamic Utopian: A Political Biography of Ali Shariati*. New York: Tauris.

Reiss, Hans. 1970. "Introduction." In Reiss, ed., *Kant's Political Writings*. Cambridge: Cambridge Univ. Press.

Rundell, John F. 1987. *Origins of Modernity: The Origins of Modern Social Theory from Kant to Hegel to Marx.* Madison: Univ. of Wisconsin Press.

Salehi-Najafabadi, Ne'matollah. 1984. *Velayat-e Faqih: Hukumat-e Salehan* (Governance of the jurist: The government of the righteous). Tehran: Rasa.

Sanjabi, Maryam. 1995. "Reading the Enlightenment: Akhundzada and His Voltaire." *Iranian Studies* 28, nos. 1–2 (Winter–Spring).

Schneewind, J. B. 1992. "Autonomy, Obligation and Virtue: An Overview of Kant's Moral Philosophy." In Paul Guyer, ed., *The Cambridge Companion to Kant.* New York: Cambridge Univ. Press.

Shariati, Ali. 1968. *Ravesh-e Shenakht-e Islam* (The methodology for studying Islam). Tehran: Husseinieh Ershad.

———. 1971a. *Fatemeh Fatemeh Ast* (Fatima is Fatima). Tehran: Husseinieh Ershad.

———. 1971b. *Tashayo'-e Alavi va Tashayo' e Safavi* (Alavid Shiism and Safavid Shiism). N.p.

———. [1972?]a. *Islamshenasi* (Islamology). N.p.

———. 1972b. *Rushanfekr va Masuliyat-e Ou dar Jame'-e* (The intellectual and his responsibility in society). Tehran: Husseinieh Ershad.

———. 1975. *Az Koja Aghaz Konim?* (Whence do we begin?). N.p.: Muslim Students Association.

———. 1976a. "Bazgasht be Khish" (Return to the self) N.p.

———. 1976b. *Entezar, Mazhab-e E'teraz* (Awaiting, the creed of protest). N.p.

———. 1977a. *Bazgasht be Khish* (Return to the self) N.p.

———. 1977b. *Haft Nameh* (Seven letters). Tehran: Abuzar.

———. 1977c. *Mashin dar Esarat-e Mashinizm* (Machine enslaved by machinism). N.p.

———. 1979a. *Tamadon va Tajadod* (Civilization and modernity). Solon, Ohio: Muslim Students Association.

———. 1979b. *Ommat va Imamat* (Community and leadership). Tehran: Qalam.

———. [1980?]. *Ensan va Islam: Majmu'e-ye Shesh Sokhanrani va Yek Mosahebeh* (Man and Islam: Collection of six lectures and one interview). N.p.

———. [1981?]. *Tarikh va Shenakthe Adyan* (History and the knowledge of religions). Tehran: Alborz.

———. 1983a. *Kavir* (The desert). [Collected Works, vol. 13]. Tehran: Chapakhsh.

———. 1983b. *Hubut* (The Fall). [Collected Works, vol. 13]. Tehran: Chapakhsh.

———. 1983c. *Ma'bad* (The temple). [Collected Works, vol. 13]. Tehran: Chapakhsh.

———. 1994. *Abuzar* [Collected Works, vol. 3]. Tehran: Elham.

Shayegan, Daryush. 1992a. *Asia Dar Barabar-e Gharb* (Asia confronting the West). Tehran: Bagh Ayneh.

———. 1992b. *Cultural Schizophrenia: Islamic Societies Confronting the West.* London: Saqi.

———. 1995. *Zir Asmanha-ye Jahan* (Under the skies of the world). Tehran: Farzan Ruz.

Siasi, Ail Akbar. 1988. *Gozaresh Yek Zendegi* (Report of a life). London: Paka.

Skocpol, Theda. 1982. "Rentier State and Shi'a Islam in the Iranian Revolution." *Theory and Society* 11, no. 3 (May).

Sorush, Abdolkarim. 1978. *Naqdi va Daramadi bar Tazad-e Dialiktik* (A critique and introduction to dialectical contradiction). Reprint, Tehran: Sera, 1994.

———. 1982. *Ideologi-e Sheytani: Dogmatizm-e Neqabdar* (Satanic ideology: Masked dogmatism). Tehran: Yaran.

———. 1984. *Hekmat va Ma'ishat* (Philosophy and Life). Tehran: Serat.

———. 1987. *Tafarroj-e Son'* (Promenading Creation). Tehran: Sorush.

———. 1988. *Rushanfekri va Dindari* (Modern enlightenment and religion). Tehran: Nashr-e Puyeh.

———. 1991. *Qabz va Bast-e Teoriki-e Shariat* (The theoretical contraction and expansion of the Sharia). Tehran: Serat.

———. 1992. "Paradoks-e Modernizm" (The paradox of modernism). *Kayhan Havai* 12, no. 275 (Apr. 1).

———. 1994a. "Akhlaq-e Khodayan" (Ethics of the gods). *Kiyan* 4, no. 18 (Apr.–May).

———. 1994b. "Modara va Modiriyat-e Mo'menan: Sokhani dar Nesbat-e Din va Demokrasi" (Conciliation and administration of the faithful: A discourse on the relation between religion and democracy). *Kiyan* 4, no. 21 (Sept.–Oct.).

———. 1995. "Danesh va Dadgari" (Knowledge and justice). *Kiyan* 4, no. 22 (Nov.–Jan.).

———. 1996a. "Gozaresh-e Safar-e Doktor Sorush be Landan" (Report of Doctor Sorush's trip to London). *Kiyan* 6, no. 33 (Nov.–Dec.).

———. 1996b. "Tahlil-e Mafhum-e Hukumat-e Dini" (An analysis of the concept of religious government). *Kiyan* 6, no. 32 (Sept.–Oct.).

———. 1996c. "Aql va Azadi" (Reason and freedom). In *Farbeh Tar az Ideologi* (Richer than ideology). Tehran: Serat.

———. 1996d. "Hukumat-e Demokratik-e Dini" (The democratic religious government). In *Farbeh Tar az Ideologi* (Richer than ideology). Tehran: Serat.

———. 2000. *Reason, Freedom, and Democracy in Islam: Essential Writings of Abdolkarim Sorush.* New York: Oxford Univ. Press.

Tabari, Ehsan. 1961. "Jonbesh Enqelabi Daravish Irani dar Qarn Hashtum Hejri" (The revolutionary movement of Iranian Dervishes in the eighth-century hegira). *Donya,* 2d ser., vol. 2, no. 2 (Summer).

———. 1963. "Dar Bareh Seresht va Sarnevesht Ensan" (On human nature and destiny). *Donya,* 2d ser., vol. 4, no. 4 (Winter).

———. 1964. "Marksism va Umanism" (Marxism and humanism). *Donya,* 2d ser., vol. 5, no. 1 (Spring).

———. 1975. *Forupashi Nezam Sunati va Zayesh Sarmayedari dar Iran* (The disintegration of traditional system and the birth of capitalism in Iran). Stockholm: Tudeh.

———. [1977?]a. "Barkhi Andishe-ha va Daryaft-ha dar Bareh Adami va Marg" (Some thoughts and perception on man and death). In *Neveshteha-ye Falsafi va Ejtema'i* (Philosophical and social writings). N.p.

———. [1977?]b. "Mokhtasat Jahan va Duran Ma: Chashmandazi az 'Omdehtarin Masael" (The characteristics of our world and time: A perspective on the most important issues). In *Neveshteha-ye Falsafi va Ejtema'i* (Philosophical and social writings). N.p.

———. [1977?]c. "Shahr Khorshid: Bahsi Falsafi va Ejtema'i dar bare Ayandeh Ensan" (The city of the sun: A philosophical and social discussion about man's future). In *Neveshteha-ye Falsafi va Ejtema'i* (Philosophical and social writings). N.p.

Talebuf, Abd al-Rahim. 1893. *Ketab Ahmad* (The book of Ahmad). Vol. 1. Istanbul: Akhtar.

———. 1894. *Ketab Ahmad* (The book of Ahmad). Vol. 2. Istanbul: Khorshid.

———. 1906. *Masael al-Hayat* (Questions of life). Tbilisi: Gheyrat.

———. 1968. *Masalik al-Muhsinin* (The paths of the blessed). Tehran: Jibi.

Taqizadeh, Hasan. 1972. *Maqalat Taqizadeh: Zaban va Farhang, Ta'lim va Tarbiyat* (Articles of Taqizadeh: Language and culture; education and development). Vol. 3. Edited by Iraj Afshar. Tehran: Bist o Panj Shahrivar.

———. 1974. *Maqalat Taqizadeh: Juhar Tarikh va Mabahes Ejtemai va Madani* (Articles of Taqizadeh: The essence of history; social and civil issues). Vol. 4. Edited by Iraj Afshar. Tehran: Shukufan.

Taylor, Charles. 1975. *Hegel.* Cambridge: Cambridge Univ. Press.

———. 1979. *Hegel and Modern Society.* Cambridge: Cambridge Univ. Press.

Tönnies, Ferdinand. 1963. *Community and Society: Gemeinschaft und Gesellschaft.* New York: Harper and Row.

Weber, Max. 1958. *The Protestant Ethic and the Spirit of Capitalism.* New York: Scribner's.

———. 1964. *The Sociology of Religion.* Boston: Beacon.

Williams, Raymond. 1966. *Culture and Society: 1780–1950.* New York: Harper and Row.

Zabih, Sepehr. 1966. *The Communist Movement in Iran.* Berkeley: Univ. of California Press.

———. 1986. *The Left in Contemporary Iran: Ideology, Organization and the Soviet Connection.* Stanford, Calif.: Hoover Institution Press.

Zarshenas, Shahriar. 1992. *Jam'e-ye Baz, Akharin Otopi Tamadon-e Gharb* (Open society, the final utopia of the Western civilization). Tehran: Islamic Propaganda Organization, Artistic Division.

Index